# THE CAREER OF
## LUJO BRENTANO

# THE CAREER OF
# LUJO BRENTANO

*A Study of Liberalism and Social Reform in Imperial Germany*

JAMES J. SHEEHAN

THE UNIVERSITY OF CHICAGO PRESS

CHICAGO AND LONDON

*Library of Congress Catalog Card Number: 66–20574*
THE UNIVERSITY OF CHICAGO PRESS, CHICAGO & LONDON
The University of Toronto Press, Toronto 5, Canada
© *1966 by The University of Chicago*
*All rights reserved*
*Published 1966*
*Printed in the United States of America*

*To my parents*

# Acknowledgments

I would like to express my gratitude to the Woodrow Wilson Foundation for supporting the initial research for this study and to the Office of Research Co-ordination at Northwestern University for financial aid in the final preparation of the manuscript. It is a pleasure to be able to thank those who have so graciously given me their time and knowledge and thus made this work possible: J. C. M. Brentano, Hugh Clegg, Richard Comfort, the late Theodor Heuss, Richard Kuisel, Franziska Mayer-Hillebrand, Henryk Skrzypczak, Miss Josefa Ruess, and the staff of the Bundesarchiv in Koblenz. Professor Hans Rosenberg was kind enough to read an earlier version of the study and to offer relevant and stimulating advice. Miss Jacqueline Strain deserves special mention for her patient assistance. Hans Ulrich Wehler has helped me to think more clearly about German history, and about the enterprise of historical writing as well. It was my good fortune to have been introduced to the problems of intellectual history by Professor Carl E. Schorske. His comments on historical method and his specific criticisms of the present work have been invaluable. I am grateful to Professor Raymond Sontag for his encouragement and friendship. Finally, I wish to acknowledge publicly a very private debt to my wife, Elena.

Evanston, Illinois

# Contents

# Introduction

## 1 —

The most active years of Lujo Brentano's long life (1844–1931) coincided with the half-century of the German Empire. During the period from the Austro-Prussian War of 1866 to the German collapse of 1918, he was an alert observer of German politics and society. The extensive collection of Brentano's papers in the German Federal Archives at Koblenz and his voluminous publications provide the historian with an ever-changing vantage point from which the course of the Empire may be studied. Brentano, however, sought to be more than an observer of the German scene. At several points in his career he searched for a means of transforming the realities of German life. An examination of his program for reform and of his attempts to realize this program illuminates some important themes of modern German history.

In the following study I have emphasized three major aspects of Brentano's career: his activities as a liberal social reformer, his role as a German academician, and his relationship to the German nation.

Liberalism was the foundation for Brentano's thought and action. The origin of his liberal outlook during the late 1860's is the first problem in his intellectual biography. After 1871, the development of Brentano's liberal ideals within the context of imperial Germany suggests some of the problems of the German liberal movement. Moreover, his efforts to reconcile liberalism and the need for social reform illustrate a basic problem confronting liberals all over Europe in the last third of the nineteenth century.

Brentano's position as a university professor provided the framework within which he sought to find answers for the problems of imperial Germany. A study of his academic career sheds light on this important group in German society. Moreover, by examining his political attitudes, which were shaped to a large extent by his role in the academic community, we can deepen our understanding of the relationship between German intellectuals and politics in the years 1871–1918.

The development of Brentano's attitude toward the German nation is an example of the evolution from "cosmopolitanism to nationalism" that is so typical of the nineteenth century. During the 1860's he retained his family's European orientation and anti-Prussian bias. After 1871, his attachment to the newly-formed Germany steadily increased and, despite traces of anti-Prussianism, he remained a German patriot until his death. At the same time, however, he had interests and experiences which transcended national boundaries. His intense and lasting admiration for Great Britain makes him an interesting case study of the rich and complex cultural relationship between Germany and England.

Let me make clear the limits which I have imposed on this study of Brentano's career. In the first place, after a discussion of the formation of his ideas I have concentrated on Brentano's activity during the imperial period. Although he lived for more than a decade after the founding of the German Republic, I believe that his signficance for the historian ends with the Empire in 1918. Secondly, I have not set out to write a full scale biography which would analyze Brentano's personal as well as his public life. Such an undertaking is precluded by the nature of evidence available. Finally, I am not concerned with an exposition of the full range of Brentano's ideas. I have considered his scholarly activity, his methodology, and his ideas on economic theory only in so far as these are relevant to his relationship to German social, economic, or political developments.

My method has been to consider Brentano's ideas in the historical context within which they developed. This approach does not reflect a belief that ideas are simply the products of economic, social, or political realities. Instead, the method rests on the conviction that ideas can be fully understood only in the light of the historical situation which the thinker confronts, that there is, in other words, a significant relationship between thought and the economic, social, and political circumstances of the thinker. This relationship between Lujo Brentano's intellectual development and the history of Germany between 1866 and 1918 is the main theme of my study.

2 –

The most vivid descriptions of Brentano have come from those who sat in his crowded lecture hall and listened to his courses on economics. Brentano's success as a teacher came early in his career and by the 1890's his fame had spread throughout Europe. His correspondence is filled with letters written by admiring students from England, France, the United States, Japan, Russia, and eastern Europe. When he lectured each afternoon at four, the University of Munich's largest hall was filled to capacity with students and townspeople. As he entered the room, to be greeted by the applause traditionally given the German professor, his step was quick and confident, his head held high. Broad-shouldered and robust, he had a forceful presence which dominated the room. Many of his students were reminded of an Old Testament prophet by his full-bearded, handsome face with its prominent nose. His voice was rather high pitched, even squeaky, but it filled the hall to the last seat. Slowly, effortlessly, he began to speak, giving his ideas an artistic, memorable formulation. As he grew more involved in his lecture, his dark eyes flashed beneath gold-rimmed spectacles. For his admirers, Brentano's course was most exciting when he was engaged in some scholarly or political polemic. He might then use the subject of his lecture as a springboard from which he would launch a biting and sarcastic attack upon his opponents, to which his loyal following would respond with cheers of approval.[1]

This picture of the fighter for justice surrounded by his

[1] For a description of Brentano as a lecturer, see L. Curtius, *Deutsche und antike Welt: Lebenserinnerungen* (Stuttgart, 1951), pp. 123–27; K. A. von Müller, *Aus Gärten der Vergangenheit: Erinnerungen 1882–1914* (Stuttgart, 1958), pp. 228–29; M. Bonn, *So macht man die Geschichte* (Munich, 1953), pp. 58 ff.; Erich Eyck, *Auf Deutschlands politischem Forum* (Erlenbach-Zürich, 1963), pp. 162–67.

cheering followers is the self-image Brentano cherished. He saw himself as a man with a mission. "My entire life," he wrote at the beginning of his autobiography, "consisted of a series of struggles, one following right after the other."[2] The confidence and conviction with which Brentano spoke to his classes reflected his belief in himself and in his ideas. He seemed always prepared to do battle for the causes he considered just, convinced that he fought for the good of society as a whole against the influence of selfish interests. The passion he poured into his lectures, the slander trials in which he was involved, his unending public polemics, are all indications of his devotion to his ideals and his willingness to struggle to see these ideals transformed into reality.

It would, however, be an error to picture Brentano as an inflexible polemicist or a self-righteous pedagogue. His confidence in the lecture hall and his vigor in public debate masked a personality that was neither as consistent nor as harmonious as it appeared. Those closest to him noted that although at times he would go to any length to defend his ideals, he could also tailor his views to fit the demands of a situation. His reconciliation with a Prussian-led Germany, his eventual acceptance of state-directed social reform, his co-operation with the government during World War I, all suggest a man who was far more flexible than is immediately apparent. Moreover, Brentano was not as comfortable in his role as professor-polemicist as it sometimes seemed. Throughout his career he combined a love of debate with a desire to retreat to the quiet of his study and to engage, undisturbed, in the scholarly search for truth.

Similarly, the self-confident attitude Brentano presented to the world may be questioned. As he grew older his confidence in the future of liberalism waned. He died in a world he didn't understand, a world far from those days of the 1870's when the future looked bright with possibilities and the chances for social harmony seemed great. Even Brentano's personal success was not without shadows. His academic career was a consistent rise to fame and wealth, but it was a triumph always clouded by the

---

[2] *Mein Leben im Kampfe um die soziale Entwicklung Deutschlands* (Jena, 1931), p. 1.

failure of his efforts to mold the history of his nation in accord with his vision of social progress.[3]

[3] On Brentano's personality see the works cited in n. 1, and M. Bonn, "Lujo Brentano," *Frankfurter Zeitung*, September 12, 1931; M. Freund-Hoppe, "Kleine Erinnerungen an Lujo Brentano," *Dresdener Volkszeitung*, September 15, 1931; H. Herkner, "Lujo Brentano," *Der deutsche Volkswirt*, September 18, 1931; J. von Eckardt, *Lebenserinnerungen* (2 vols.; Leipzig, 1910), I, 272–73; G. von Schmoller, "Lujo Brentano zum 70. Geburtstag," *Schmollers Jahrbuch*, XXXIX, No. 1 (1915), 365–70. I am grateful to Professor J. C. M. Brentano, Lujo's nephew, Fräulein Josepha Ruess, his housekeeper, and Professor Theodor Heuss for their personal recollections of Brentano.

# CHAPTER I

# The Making of a Liberal
## 1844-1868

### 1 —

Lujo Brentano's ancestors were Italian aristocrats who settled in Frankfurt and built up a brisk trade in fruits and other commodities from their north Italian homeland. The Brentanos' loyalties remained centered in Italy until the time of Lujo's grandfather, Peter Anton Brentano (1735–97). After Peter Anton was granted full Frankfurt citizenship in 1762, he gave up his Italian lands and, contrary to the family tradition of marrying Italian women, selected the last two of his three wives from among the German lower nobility.[1] Peter Anton's second wife was Maximiliane von la Roche (1756–93), the daughter of a Privy Counselor to the Elector of Trier. Among their children were the famous poets Clemens (1778–1842) and Bettina (1785–1859), and Lujo Brentano's father, Christian (1784–1851).[2]

Christian Brentano was a gifted young man who seems to have spent most of his life searching for a proper outlet for his talents. By the time he was fourteen both his mother and father were dead. He wasted his early manhood wandering from one occupation to another, protected from disaster by the family fortune, but without accomplishments or prospects. Christian's life

---

[1] A good short account of the Brentano family may be found in the *Neue deutsche Biographie* (Berlin, 1955), II, 588 ff. On the Brentanos in Frankfurt, see A. Dietz, *Frankfurter Handelsgeschichte* (Frankfurt, 1925), IV, 238–50.

[2] A brief but helpful summary of the life and works of Clemens and Bettina Brentano is I. Seidel, *Drei Dichter der Romantik: Clemens Brentano, Bettina von Arnim, Achim von Arnim* (Stuttgart, 1956).

changed after 1818 when he began a gradual return to the Catholicism he had lost in his youth. Religion gave him a new sense of purpose and stability. In 1835 he finally settled down and married a young girl named Emily Genger (1810–81), the daughter of a *Landrat* from Nassau.

Christian and his wife made their home in a cloister near Boppard, a town on the Rhine a few miles from Koblenz. Although the area had been under Prussian rule since 1815, many Rhinelanders continued to regard the Prussians as foreign conquerors. The continual friction between the Prussian administrators and the citizens reflected the deep social, economic, and religious differences between the Rhine and the rest of Prussia.[3] Christian Brentano's militant Catholicism and his allegiance to the Austrian emperor led him to share the anti-Prussian sentiments prevalent along the Rhine. His dislike of Prussia increased during the late thirties because of the conflict between the Prussian authorities and the Rhenish Catholic hierarchy. This conflict reached a head in November, 1837, when the Archbishop of Cologne was arrested by Prussian troops and interned in a fortress. These so-called *Kölner Wirren* evoked a sharp response from German Catholics: troops had to be called out to put down a demonstration in Cologne, and individual Catholics like Wilhelm Freiherr von Ketteler and Count Galen, then Minister to Brussels, left the Prussian state service. Christian Brentano was forced to sell his property at a financial loss and leave Prussia because of his outspoken criticism of the Prussian action.[4]

For their new home, the family chose Aschaffenburg, a lovely little town on the Main River in Bavaria. The Brentanos purchased a vine-covered villa on a bluff overlooking the river, and

---

3 See F. Schnabel, *Deutsche Geschichte im neunzehnten Jahrhundert* (Freiburg, 1955), IV, 106 ff. Jacques Droz, *Le libéralisme rhénan 1815–1848: Contribution à l'histoire du libéralisme allemand* (Paris, 1940), pp. 42–43, and H. Heffter, *Die deutsche Selbstverwaltung im 19. Jahrhundert* (Stuttgart, 1950), pp. 224 ff.

4 On the *Kölner Wirren*, see Schnabel, *Deutsche Geschichte*, IV, 137 ff., and Heinrich von Treitschke, *History of Germany in the Nineteenth Century* (London, 1919), IV, 243 ff. On Ketteler's reaction, see Fritz Vigener, *Ketteler: Ein deutsches Bischofsleben des 19. Jahrhunderts* (Munich and Berlin, 1924), pp. 12–18. For the Brentanos' reaction, see *Christian Brentano's Nachgelassene religiöse Schriften* (Munich, 1854), I, xlii.

it was here, on December 18, 1844, that Lujo Brentano was born, the youngest of five children.[5]

When Christian Brentano died in 1851, his widow sought to raise their children in the light of his ideals.[6] Lujo, therefore, grew up in an atmosphere marked by fervent religious devotion and intense cultural activity. The Brentano children were encouraged to be creative and to emulate the artistic achievements of their Aunt Bettina and Uncle Clemens, although Emily Brentano made sure that their activities remained within the limits imposed by a strict religious orthodoxy. Religion and art seem to have been the major concerns at the *Brentanohaus*.[7] Politically, the Brentanos were conservatives, who condemned the development of the modern state as a dictatorship either of mass democracy or centralized bureaucracy. Their dislike of the bureaucracy was reinforced by their dislike of Prussia and by their unhappy experience with the excesses of the Prussian administration in the Rhineland.

There is no indication that the Brentanos were concerned with the immense social and economic changes taking place in Germany in the mid-nineteenth century. Aschaffenburg remained a quiet, peaceful town, far removed from the forces that were transforming German life.[8] Although they were sensitive to the problems of the lower classes, the Brentanos viewed these problems as the suffering of impoverished individuals. As such, pov-

---

[5] The best source for Lujo's childhood is his autobiography, *Mein Leben im Kampfe um die soziale Entwicklung Deutschlands* (Jena, 1931), pp. 18 ff. Hereafter cited as *Mein Leben*. In an article on her brother Franz, Lujo's sister Claudine has given a pleasant picture of the family, "Jugenderinnerungen an meinen Bruder," *Monatshefte für pädagogische Reform, Sonderheft* (1918). See also Ewald Reinhard, *Die Brentanos in Aschaffenburg* (Aschaffenburg, 1928), and Georg von Hertling, *Erinnerungen aus meinem Leben* (Kempten and Munich, 1919), I, 3.

[6] On Christian's religious orientation, see his *Nachgelassene religiöse Schriften*. Brentano's religious ideas were influenced by Johann Michael Sailer and Cardinal von Diepenbrock; for a brief summary of their views see Franz Schnabel, *Deutsche Geschichte im neunzehnten Jahrhundert*, IV, 50–55.

[7] *Mein Leben*, pp. 18 ff.

[8] In 1855 the population of Aschaffenburg was only 9,412, just a thousand more than it had been in 1812. Erich Keyser, *Bevölkerungsgeschichte Deutschlands* (Leipzig, 1938), p. 328.

erty was to be combated by acts of Christian charity, not by social reform.[9]

Surrounded by these traditions of religious orthodoxy and political conservatism, Lujo Brentano grew to manhood. As a child, he seems to have been in the shadow of his brother Franz, an enormously gifted young man who was the center of attention in the *Brentanohaus*. Perhaps this is one reason for the restlessness which one can detect in Lujo's youth.[10] In any case, his mother came to feel that her youngest son needed the discipline of a boarding school and sent him to the famous Benedictine school at Augsburg, where she could be sure that the religious and political principles of the family would be strictly upheld.[11]

Brentano began to react against the limitations of his education as early as his return home from the Benedictines in 1860. It was at this time that he read Michelet and began to look at some newspapers other than the conservative journals he had read at Augsburg. In these papers he read news of the Italian unification and became enthusiastic over the *Risorgimento,* despite its obvious opposition to his family's sympathies for Austria and for the sovereignty of the papal states. Perhaps in an effort to distract Lujo from these new ideas, in 1861 his mother decided to send him away again, this time to stay with his sister and brother-in-law in Dublin.

Brentano's older sister Sophie was married to Peter Le Page Renouf (1822–97), who taught at the Catholic college in Dublin founded by John Henry Newman. Renouf was, in Lord Acton's

[9] As Fritz Vigener has remarked, one of the reasons for the slow development of Catholic social thought was the Catholics' belief that they already had an answer to the social problem in *Caritas,* Christian charity (*Ketteler,* p. 420). Other members of the Brentano family published works which are clearly in the *Caritas* tradition: see Clemens Brentano's *Die Barmherzigen Schwestern in Bezug auf Armen- und Krankenflege* (1831) and Bettina von Arnim, *Dies Buch gehört dem König* (1843). On Emily Brentano's charitable activity, see Reinhard, *Die Brentanos,* p. 26.

[10] This idea has been suggested by Professor Franziska Mayer-Hillebrand, who is presently at work on a biography of Franz Brentano. I am grateful for the opportunity of discussing the Brentano family with her. For a suggestion of this feeling, see Lujo Brentano to Gustav Schmoller, January 14, 1873, Franz Brentano Papers.

[11] Ludwig Curtius, *Deutsche und antike Welt: Lebenserinnerungen* (Stuttgart, 1951), contains an account of the school at Augsburg, pp. 87–88.

opinion, "the most learned Catholic" in Great Britain.[12] He evidently exercised a powerful influence on his young guest who, almost seventy years later, recalled that his stay in Dublin had been "of the greatest significance for my entire life."[13] During Brentano's year with the Renoufs he mastered the English language and began his long-lasting enthusiasm for things English. More important, it was through Renouf that he first came into contact with liberalism. Renouf was both a liberal and a Catholic. He was part of the movement within English Catholicism that sought to reconcile the new learning of the nineteenth century with the doctrines of the church.[14] The early 1860's were a crucial period in this struggle and Brentano could not but have been impressed by the efforts of Renouf and his associates to find a synthesis of faith and reason.[15] In the tolerant atmosphere of Renouf's home Brentano explored for the first time a world of ideas hitherto closed to him. Under the impact of the "purely objective, scientific nature of Renouf's mind"[16] he turned away from the restrictions of the *Brentanohaus* and the Benedictines at Augsburg. As Brentano put it, it was in Dublin that "I developed from a conservative into a liberal. . . ."[17]

In one sense, Brentano doubtlessly overestimated the maturity of his political beliefs when he described himself as a liberal in 1862. His conservative religious and political convictions dissolved gradually during the sixties, and there is no evidence that his liberalism had any philosophical basis until after 1866. Yet in 1861 Brentano acquired something more significant than the specific concepts of a liberal ideology. His relationship with Renouf provided him with a model of a man willing to risk everything—perhaps even his salvation—in the search for truth.

[12] J. L. Altholz, *The Liberal Catholic Movement in England: The Rambler and its Contributors, 1848–1864* (London, 1960), p. 202.

[13] *Mein Leben,* p. 26.

[14] In 1864 Renouf wrote: "The interests of the most conservative theology are . . . identical with those of critical science" (Altholz, *Liberal Catholic Movement,* p. 205). On this group see also the recent study by Hugh A. MacDougall, *The Acton-Newman Relations: The Dilemma of Christian Liberalism* (New York, 1962).

[15] Altholz, *Liberal Catholic Movement,* pp. 152 ff., describes the situation in the early 1860's.

[16] The phrase is Lord Acton's, quoted in *ibid.,* p. 203.

[17] *Mein Leben,* p. 26.

Moreover, in the Renouf household Brentano found a tolerance for new ideas and a devotion to free inquiry notably lacking in his family environment. These habits of mind were the prerequisites for his eventual rejection of the most cherished elements in the Brentanos' religious and political legacy.

2 —

In 1862 Brentano left Dublin and returned to Aschaffenburg to pass his *Abitur*. That fall, a few months before his eighteenth birthday, he enrolled at the University of Münster. He found little there to interest him and after a short time moved to Munich. At Munich the lectures of the great scholar Windscheid inspired him to study jurisprudence. He attended lectures on legal history and theory at the universities of Heidelberg and Würzburg. In February, 1866, he was given his Doctor of Laws degree at Heidelberg.[18]

Four months after Brentano received his doctorate, the war between Prussia and Austria began. When it became clear that Prussia would win, a mood of shock and despair spread among German Catholics because the defeat of Austria represented a destruction of the center of their political hopes and allegiances.[19] Considering the Brentanos' political views, they could not but share in this mood. As pro-Austrians, they saw the war as the final extrusion of the Habsburgs from German affairs. As Catholics, they knew that this made them a minority within a Germany unified under Prussian leadership. Family feelings against Prussia were further aroused by the news of the harsh treatment given to Frankfurt, and the report that an elderly relative had been forced to quarter a large number of Prussian troops in her house.[20]

Lujo Brentano was in Munich when the war began. When he heard that the opposing armies would meet near Aschaffenburg he rushed home to be with his mother. The town had already been captured when he arrived, and he was forced by the

18 *Mein Leben*, pp. 24–31.
19 For the impact of the war on German Catholics, see George C. Windell, *The Catholics and German Unity 1866–1871* (Minneapolis, 1954), pp. 3 ff., and Vigener, *Ketteler*, pp. 471 ff.
20 *Mein Leben*, p. 39.

Prussian troops to remain there for the duration of the war. During this time, it may be imagined, he considered the effects of the war on his future. To judge from the brief account in *Mein Leben*, Brentano had previously decided to join the Bavarian civil service. The defeat of the South German states changed this, because, as he wrote, he had no desire to serve either the victorious Prussians or the defeated Bavarians.[21] His second choice was an academic career, and with this in mind Brentano went to Göttingen in the fall of 1866 to study economics.

When he arrived in Hanover in October, 1866, the country was still in an uproar over its annexation by Prussia. Tension between the Prussians and the Hanoverians continued throughout his stay. In May, 1867, for example, when the Prussian administration forbade any celebration of the King of Hanover's birthday, each house in Göttingen displayed two candles, and sand colored with the Hanoverian white and yellow was spread on the pavements.[22] Thus, Brentano's year in Göttingen did nothing to counteract the hostility to Prussia he had learned at home.

Considering Brentano's intellectual development, there was another tradition at Göttingen more significant than its anti-Prussianism. The university had been founded in 1732 by George II of England, acting in his capacity as Elector of Hanover. During the late eighteenth and early nineteenth centuries a close relationship had existed between the university and English intellectual life.[23] It was during this period that Adam Smith's *Wealth of Nations* first became known in Germany, through the efforts of Göttingen professors who taught Smith's ideas to an

---

21 *Mein Leben*, p. 38. In 1914 Brentano remarked that before 1866 he was planning to become an *Anwalt* in Frankfurt. Since there is no evidence to verify either of these accounts, I have taken the version in *Mein Leben* as the later and more permanent one. In any case, this discrepancy does not obscure the fact that 1866 marked a turning point in Brentano's career both personally and politically. See Münchener volkswirtschaftliche Gesellschaft, *Lujo Brentano. Kundgebungen zu seinem 70. Geburtstag (18. Dezember 1914)* (Munich and Leipzig, 1915), pp. 21–22.

22 *Mein Leben*, pp. 38–39.

23 On the University of Göttingen, see Goetz von Selle, *Die Georg August Universität zu Göttingen 1837–1937* (Göttingen, 1937). For the relationship between the university and England, see pp. 183 ff.

important generation of German leaders like Stein and Hardenberg.[24]

After his arrival at Göttingen, Brentano quickly came under the influence of J. A. R. von Helferich (1819–92), who taught economics very much within the tradition of those professors who had first brought Adam Smith to Germany. Although Helferich was a persuasive lecturer and an enthusiastic, skillful teacher, he was not a particularly original economic theorist. Most of his ideas were derived from F. B. W. von Hermann (1795–1868), one of the foremost advocates of British classical economics in Germany.[25] Hermann's thought was based on the work of Smith and Ricardo. His early training as a mathematician led him to emphasize the abstract approach of some of the classical economists. Thus, both Hermann and Helferich were committed to the method and the ideals of economic freedom and individualism characteristic of British liberal economics in the first half of the nineteenth century.[26]

Helferich was also interested in the writings of the German economist Johann von Thünen (1783–1850). As a dissertation topic, Helferich suggested to Brentano that he analyze von Thünen's attempt to derive a mathematical formula for the level which wages and interest could not exceed.[27] In his dissertation, Brentano was confronted for the first time with the question of wages, and he was forced to consider carefully the ideas of the classical economists on this problem. However, the dissertation's chief significance is as an indication of the extent to

24 Wilhelm Treue, "Adam Smith in Deutschland. Zum Problem des 'politischen Professors' zwischen 1776 und 1810," *Deutschland und Europa. Historische Studien zur Volks- und Staatenordnung des Abendlandes,* ed. Werner Conze (Düsseldorf, 1951). See especially pp. 102–7.

25 See Georg Friedrich Knapp, "Hermann und Helferich aus den Jahren 1861 und 1864," in *Grundherrschaft und Rittergut* (Leipzig, 1897), pp. 131–36.

26 See W. Braeuer, "Johann von Helferich," *Zeitschrift für die gesamte Staatswissenschaft,* CVIII, No. 1 (1952), 137.

27 A few years before Brentano came to Göttingen, Helferich had assigned Thünen's work to Georg Knapp, who sought to disprove Thünen's thesis. Knapp claimed that Helferich gave a similar assignment to Brentano in order to restore Thünen to his proper place in economics. See Knapp, "Hermann und Helferich," p. 140, and Knapp's autobiography, *Eine Jugend,* ed. Elly Heuss-Knapp (Stuttgart, 1947), p. 184.

which Brentano accepted the abstract method of Helferich and von Thünen. Von Thünen had constructed an "isolated state" in which there were no variables to be considered except the economic data in the formula he was seeking to derive. Brentano felt that such a method was entirely justified and that it was analogous to the use of a vacuum to demonstrate physical laws.[28] He summed up the view of economics he had learned at Göttingen in the following words:

> At that time I believed that the claims of economics to be a science could only be supported if economic doctrines were derived from a single principle, and I subscribed to the opinion represented by John Stuart Mill in his *Unsettled Questions of Political Economy* that economics was an exact, theoretical science.[29]

Considering Brentano's youth and Helferich's great effectiveness as a teacher, it is not difficult to understand why the student adopted his master's liberal economics. Furthermore, Brentano had been attracted to British thought since his trip to Dublin in 1861. However, to explain fully why he was so taken with classical economics we must also examine the biographical context within which he confronted it. Brentano turned to the study of economics after a career in state service had forcibly been closed to him. Furthermore, on the battlefield of Königgrätz, Brentano, like most German Catholics, had lost the framework within which he had been accustomed to view politics. Now as it has been described here, the form of economic liberalism taught at Göttingen was deductive in method, rather mathematical in orientation, and laissez faire in its attitude toward the state. Equally important, this kind of economics tended to look at events in purely economic terms; there was, after all, no need for politics or history in Thünen's "isolated state." The attraction of this way of looking at the world for a young man whose political framework had been suddenly shattered is clear. In its abstraction, classical liberalism provided a way of studying re-

---

28 Lujo Brentano, *Über J. H. von Thünens naturgemässen Lohn- und Zinsfluss im isolierten Staate* (Göttingen, 1867), p. 5. See also *Mein Leben*, p. 40. On von Thünen, see Wilhelm Seedorf and H. Seraphim, *Johann Heinrich von Thünen zum 150. Geburtstag* (Rostock, 1933).

29 *Mein Leben*, p. 40. See also Brentano's *Arbeitergilden der Gegenwart* (Leipzig, 1871), I, ix.

ality which could exclude the disagreeable present; in its opposition to state intervention it could be construed as a protest from a man virtually without a state; and in its implicit denial of politics it had an obvious appeal for someone for whom political action seemed to have become impossible.

Soon after Brentano left Göttingen in 1867, he came to feel that he had outgrown the kind of economics he had learned from Helferich.[30] Helferich, however, had played a vital role in his development. At Göttingen, Brentano accepted a view of economics based on the study of Smith, Ricardo, and John Stuart Mill that he had made under Helferich's direction.[31] For the first time, the vague liberal sentiments he had acquired in Dublin began to crystallize into a coherent set of principles. Much of the remainder of this study will be concerned with the extension and modifications Brentano was forced to make in order to preserve the liberal view of the world he acquired at Göttingen.

3 —

In October, 1867, Brentano left Göttingen for Berlin, in order to enroll in a program of studies offered at the Prussian Statistical Bureau. Although by the 1860's the Bureau had become an important training ground for German economists, Brentano was initially dissatisfied with the quality of instruction.[32] During his first months in Berlin, therefore, he drifted away from his books and spent the greater part of his time getting to know the North German branch of his family. His father's sister Bettina had married Achim von Arnim, a Prussian nobleman, and their children were living in Berlin. When he first arrived in the Prussian capital, Brentano stayed with his cousin Claudine von Arnim and frequented the salon of another cousin, the Countess Oriola. In this circle he met some of the leading members of Berlin society, including, on one occasion, Bismarck himself. In

---

[30] In 1871 Brentano wrote to his brother that although Helferich was the most popular teacher in Germany, his ideas were already anachronistic. Lujo to Franz Brentano, June 26, 1871, Franz Brentano Papers.

[31] Lujo Brentano's papers contain the extensive reading notes which he took from the *Wealth of Nations* in November and December, 1866, and from Ricardo's *Principles of Political Economy* in January and February, 1867.

[32] *Mein Leben*, pp. 41–42.

*Mein Leben,* Brentano gave an affectionate picture of these relatives, but went on to say that "in spite of all the friendship with which I was met there, I remained in my heart an aggrieved Frankfurter."[33] We know that when Brentano left Berlin a year later he was still strongly anti-Prussian,[34] yet it would be difficult to imagine that this friendly acceptance by Berlin society did not have some influence on his later reconciliation with a Prussian-led Germany.

After a few months in Berlin, Brentano withdrew from the social world of his relatives in order to devote himself full time to a new and more pressing concern. Sometime in the fall of 1867 he developed the interest in social problems that was to form a main theme for his life's work. We have very little evidence to explain the origins of Brentano's quest for an answer to the social question. Perhaps one reason for his interest came from the very fact of his being in Berlin. During the 1860's the Prussian capital was a fast-growing, economically dynamic city in which Brentano could observe, possibly for the first time, the problems of industrial society.[35] It might have been a confrontation with the hardships of Berlin's lower classes that convinced him that the isolated acts of Christian charity he had observed at home were insufficient to ease society's ills. Furthermore, Brentano may have been struck by the increasingly active and independent labor movement which was just beginning to articulate the demands of the workers.[36]

There is no doubt that an important impetus for Brentano's interest in social problems was provided by Ernst Engel, the director of the Prussian Statistical Bureau. In March, 1867, Engel had submitted to the Crown Prince of Prussia a plan which he felt would end social tension. Engel's scheme was called the

33 *Mein Leben,* p. 41. See also Johannes Werner, *Maxe von Arnim: Tochter Bettinas, Gräfin Oriola (1818–1894)* (Leipzig, 1937), pp. 39, 255–56.

34 John Malcolm Ludlow referred to Brentano's anti-Prussianism during his stay in England in 1868 in a letter of September 5, 1870.

35 As early as 1854 one observer referred to Berlin as a great *Fabrikstadt.* In the decade from 1860 to 1870 the population increased from 524,000 to 826,000. See Hans Herzfeld, "Berlin als Kaiserstadt und Reichshauptstadt, 1871–1945," in *Ausgewählte Aufsätze* (Berlin, 1962), pp. 300, 308.

36 On the Berlin labor movement in the 1860's, see E. Bernstein, *Die Geschichte der Berliner Arbeiterbewegung,* Vol. I (Berlin, 1907).

"industrial partnership system." It involved a program of profit sharing, through which the workers were supposed to be given a gradually evolving role in the ownership and management of the enterprise in which they were employed. Engel expressed the greatest confidence in this plan and ended his proposal with the words: "Thus the social question is no longer a question, its solution has been discovered and the translation of this solution into practice has already begun."[37] In January, 1868, the partnership system was introduced in a Berlin brass factory on a trial basis.

Sometime early in 1868 Engel succeeded in interesting Brentano in the system and provided him with the material for a series of articles which were first published in an Augsburg newspaper and later reprinted as a brochure.[38] Although Brentano based his articles on Engel's work, he made a number of points which are of interest in the light of his own later career.

In the first place, Engel's "partnership system" directed Brentano's attention to the social reform movement in Great Britain. Engel's plan was based on a similar venture by a British mining company.[39] Thus, Brentano began his pamphlet with a statement on the importance of the British experience as a model for social reform. Britain, he argued, was economically far ahead of Germany and, since the problems of industrialism are of a universal nature, Germans could profit from a study of British attempts to solve the social question.[40]

Brentano's adoption of Engel's plan also led him to make a few tentative revisions in his view of economic liberalism. When first proposed, Engel's partnership idea had been criticized by some of the more extreme representatives of classical economics in Germany, who, during the 1860's, had grouped themselves

---

37 Engel's speech was reprinted in *Der Arbeiterfreund*, V (1867), 129–54. The quote is from p. 154.

38 *Das Industrial Partnership System: Ein Versuch zur Lösung der Arbeiterfrage* (Augsburg, 1868). The brochure was published anonymously in a series called *Katholische Studien*, Vol. II, No. 2, edited by M. Huttler. It will be hereafter cited as *Partnership*.

39 The company was the Henry Briggs and Son Coal Mine in Yorkshire. On the Briggs plan, see H. Frommer, *Die Gewinnbetheilung, Staats- und Sozialwissenschaftliche Forschungen*, VI (Leipzig, 1886), 11–34.

40 *Partnership*, p. 3.

around a naturalized Englishman named John Prince Smith.[41] These men based their critique of Engel on the incompatibility of his partnership idea with the principles of a free economy and economic individualism. Brentano's defense of Engel called into question some of the most basic premises of classical liberalism. First, he argued, Prince Smith's view of economics presupposed that all men were equal in ability. This was obviously false. In the present freely competitive economic order the superior individual prospered, but the average individual remained in want. Second, Brentano maintained that the classical liberals incorrectly argued that because the worker sells a ware (that is, his labor) he is subject to the laws of supply and demand just like the sellers of any other ware. Brentano granted that the worker was the seller of a ware, but pointed out that since this ware was in reality his own person, he was not in an equal position with regard to the other sellers, because the worker had to sell his ware in order to survive and therefore could not wait for the economically favorable moment. How then could the worker be given an equal opportunity within a free economy? Brentano reviewed the possible alternatives: unions had shown themselves to be ineffective, not only because their strikes usually failed, but also because even if the strike succeeded in gaining a raise in money wages, the economic laws of supply and demand precluded a corresponding raise in real wages. Brentano also dismissed government interference as a means of overcoming the workers' problems. The only solution remaining, he argued, was the industrial partnership system, which provided equality by insuring the employee a fair share of the owner's profits.[42]

It is worthwhile to consider for a moment the idea of industrial partnership within the context of German social thought in the 1860's. Like almost every plan for social reform suggested during that decade, the partnership system was a form of cooperative.[43] To men like Engel and Brentano, co-operation

[41] *Partnership*, pp. 34 and 56 ff. For a further treatment of the classical liberals in Germany, see below, chaps. 3 and 4.

[42] *Partnership*, pp. 23 ff.

[43] Co-operation was proposed as a means for social reform by individuals of every political persuasion: Viktor Aimé Huber gave co-operatives a conservative, Christian formulation; Schulze-Delitsch offered them within a

seemed to provide a direct and immediate solution to the social question, which they conceived as a threat to the existing social and economic order by a suffering and rootless mass. They proposed co-operatives both as a means of improving material conditions and as a way of enabling the workers to participate actively in economic life. Co-operation, in other words, seemed to give the worker a share in the status quo, to make him a partner in the preservation of the existing order of things.

The industrial partnership plan represented a particular stage in the development of the co-operative movement. In the 1860's some social reformers came to feel that industrial organization was too complex for the collective leadership implied in co-operative ownership and management.[44] Factories were no longer as simple as Robert Owen's famous mills at New Lanarck, where co-operative management seemed highly possible. Engel's proposal was an attempt to preserve some sort of co-operative production in the face of increasingly complex industrial organization.[45] Engel felt that a co-operative without an entrepreneur would either fail or would be reconverted into a capitalistic organization by the most able workers.[46] He believed that the industrial partnership system offered the advantages of both private enterprise and co-operation. The owner remained in

---

system of liberal "self-help"; Bishop von Ketteler saw them as a way of winning the workers from a materialistic liberalism; and Lassalle advocated them as means for total social reconstruction. See Helmut Faust, *Ursprung und Aufbruch der Genossenschaftsbewegung* (Neuwied-on-the-Rhine, 1958). Faust gives a helpful survey of the movement but does not provide any analysis of the historical origins and role of co-operatives in Germany.

[44] Earlier in the century similar developments had caused the British co-operative movement to shift its emphasis away from co-operative ownership of the means of production to co-operative control of the distribution of goods. See G. D. H. Cole, *A Century of Cooperation* (London, 1944), and Sidney Pollard, "Nineteenth Century Cooperation: From Community Building to Shopkeeping," in *Essays in Labour History*, ed. A. Briggs and John Saville (London, 1960), pp. 74–112.

[45] See Engel's address to the Crown Prince, quoted in *Partnership*, pp. 9–10.

[46] Brentano accepted Engel's view and repeated it in his later works on co-operatives. See, for example, *Die Productivgenossenschaft und ihre Bedeutung für die Lösung der sozialen Frage* (Breslau, 1873).

control and provided the necessary leadership, while at the same time the workers were gradually given a share in ownership as well as training for management.[47]

Perhaps the nature of the social reform proposed by Engel and Brentano can be illuminated further by contrasting their plan to the kind of total social reconstruction one finds in the writing of Karl Marx during the same period. In his relationship to society, a man like Engel was the polar opposite of Marx. The latter spoke from a position outside existing society and thus could speak in terms of complete social reorganization; Engel, on the other hand, was a bureaucrat whose career was directly linked to the preservation of the existing social and political structure. He turned to reform because he felt society was threatened, and he was willing to introduce only enough innovation to remove this threat. Undoubtedly he was also moved by a thirst for social justice, but it was a thirst to be quenched in the most temperate way possible. Indeed, when one considers that in 1868 Engel and Brentano said that their partnership proposals ended the search for an answer to the social question, one is inclined to conclude that if the failure of an alienated intellectual like Marx was a utopian disregard for reality, the failure of reformers like Engel was the inability to look deeply enough into the social problems brought on by industrialism.

Despite the rather superficial nature of the industrial partnership idea as a solution to social problems, Brentano's year in Berlin was of crucial importance for his later career. His interest in the social question, first developed under Engel's direction, called into question not only the classical liberalism he had learned at Göttingen, but also the abstract methods he had previously employed. Like so many other thinkers in the second half of the nineteenth century, Brentano was forced to modify his liberal view of economics in order to find some answer to the social evils of industrialism. At the same time, his concern with social problems made it impossible for him to be satisfied with the "isolated-state" approach he had accepted at Göttingen. Finding a solution to real problems necessitated a contact with empirical realities not to be found in the abstractions of Hel-

---

[47] *Partnership,* p. 10.

ferich or von Thünen.[48] It is important, however, to note the limits of Brentano's rejection of classical economics. First, he remained committed to a belief in a free economy. Industrial partnership, like all of his reform ideas for the next two decades, appealed to him because it seemed to enable the worker to achieve a position of equality within a free economic order. Second, Brentano's attention remained focused on Britain. Engel's teaching did not lead him to abandon the regard he had felt for England since 1862; rather it transformed the esteem he had developed for British economic theory into a realization of the importance of British practical accomplishments in social reform.

[48] Brentano emphasized this aspect of his development in an essay on the classical economists which he wrote in the 1880's: "Die klassische Nationalökonomie," reprinted in *Der wirtschaftende Mensch in der Geschichte* (Leipzig, 1923), pp. 5–6.

# CHAPTER II

# Liberalism Fulfilled:
# The British Trade Unions
# 1868-1869

## 1 —

Brentano finished his course at the Statistical Bureau in the early summer of 1868. Engel, evidently pleased with his student's enthusiasm for the partnership idea, invited Brentano to accompany him on a study trip to England. Brentano eagerly accepted this opportunity to observe firsthand the problems and achievements of British society.

Engel's and Brentano's journey across the channel was one of many undertaken by German economists and businessmen throughout the nineteenth century.[1] Like Engel and Brentano, these men went to study the nation which they regarded as the paradigm of middle-class, capitalist, industrial society. They believed—in Marx's words—that "the original process always occurs in England—it is the demiurge of the bourgeois cosmos."[2]

[1] On the relationship of Britain and Germany, see Raymond J. Sontag, *Germany and England: Background of Conflict 1848–1894* (New York, 1938); Percy E. Schramm, "Deutschlands Verhältnis zur englischen Kultur nach der Begründung des neuen Reiches," *Schicksalswege deutscher Vergangenheit: Beiträge zur geschichtlichen Deutung der letzten hundertfünfzig Jahre,* ed. Walther Hubatsch (Düsseldorf, 1950), 289–319. Schramm's important monograph, *Hamburg, Deutschland und die Welt* (Munich, 1943), emphasized the practical aspects of Anglo-German relations.

[2] From Marx's *Klassenkämpfe in Frankreich,* quoted by George Lichtheim, *Marxism* (New York, 1962), p. 135. See also Marx and Engels, *On Britain* (Moscow, 1953). The influence of England on Germany is found in both economic theory and practice. See, for example: Julius Becker, *Das deutsche Manchestertum* (Karlsruhe, 1907); J. Prince Smith, *Gesammelte Schriften*

Furthermore, German interest in British society was intensified by two aspects of the English situation which could not be found on most of the continent. The first was economic freedom, which, as Brentano once pointed out, allowed the economic forces to develop without state interference and thus made them more interesting to observe.[3] The second was parliamentarism, which facilitated the accumulation and publication of information on economic progress and problems. As F. B. W. von Hermann told a student in 1861: "Over there great things are happening and parliamentary life brings everything out into the open."[4]

As the social problems created by industrialism in their own country became increasingly apparent to German economic thinkers, it was only natural that they should look to England for possible solutions. The reason for this was not only that England had an industrial proletariat far larger than Germany's, but also that England seemed to be having some success in solving her social problems. It did not pass unnoticed, for example, that while the continent was the scene of bloody revolts in 1848, the British Chartist movement proved to be a relatively peaceful and easily dismissed episode. Even Marx was prompted to remark that "England is the only country where the inevitable social revolution might be effected entirely by peaceful and legal means."[5]

Throughout the nineteenth century, therefore, Germans went to England in search of answers to the problems of industrial society. As early as 1835 the Catholic social thinker Franz von Baader had introduced the concept of a proletariat into the German scene, with a study largely based on observations he had made in England.[6] Ten years later, Viktor Aimé Huber publi-

---

(3 vols.; Berlin, 1877–80); D. Rohr, *The Origins of Social Liberalism in Germany* (Chicago and London, 1963), pp. 85–91; and W. O. Henderson, *Britain and Industrial Europe 1750–1870* (Liverpool, 1954), pp. 139–66.

[3] Lujo Brentano, *Die Arbeitergilden der Gegenwart* (Leipzig, 1871), I, vii–viii. Hereafter cited as *Arbeitergilden* with the volume number.

[4] Georg Friedrich Knapp, *Grundherrschaft und Rittergut* (Leipzig, 1897), p. 136.

[5] Quoted by John H. Clapham, *An Economic History of Modern Britain* (Cambridge, 1932), II, 481. Marx's phrase was cited by Engels in the introduction to the first English translation of *Das Kapital* (1886).

[6] Ernst Schraepler, *Quellen zur Geschichte der sozialen Frage in Deutschland 1800–1870* (Berlin and Frankfurt, 1955), I, 14, 39–45.

cized the co-operatives in a series of works also drawn from the British experience.[7] In 1862, German liberals showed a similar sensitivity to the importance of English affairs when the *Nationalverein* financed a trip to England for twelve workers, in order that they might benefit from a study of the British workers' attempts at self-improvement.[8]

We have already seen to what a large degree Brentano shared the German economists' admiration for England. Like most Germans, he admired the great strides British industry had made, was fascinated by the large degree of industrial freedom, and enthusiastically exploited the evidence provided by the *Blue Books*. Even before he arrived there in 1868, Brentano regarded England as "a kind of laboratory" in which Germany's own future might be discovered.[9] His conviction that the British held the key to Germany's future was reinforced by his experiences in England.[10] By 1870 Brentano's affection for England had increased to the point that he considered emigrating, an idea he abandoned only when he saw that his chances for suitable employment were poor.[11]

Brentano's anglophilia is not difficult to explain when one considers that each of the three important influences on his career before 1868 directed him toward Britain. In Dublin, Renouf inspired in him a feeling for British thought; at Göttingen, Helferich taught him British economic theory; and at Berlin, Engel directed him to a consideration of practical British reforms. Furthermore, England's importance for Brentano was considerably increased by the fact that in 1868 he was still an "aggrieved Frankfurter," more or less without a place in Germany. This estrangement from the Germany which was emerging

---

[7] William Shanahan, *German Protestants Face the Social Question. Vol. I: The Conservative Phase 1815–1871* (Notre Dame, 1954), p. 152.

[8] Hermann Oncken, "Der Nationalverein und die Anfänge der deutschen Arbeiterbewegung 1862–1863," *Archiv für die Geschichte des Sozialismus und der Arbeiterbewegung*, II (1912), 120–27.

[9] *Arbeitergilden*, I, vii.

[10] Brentano frequently maintained that his thought was determined by British rather than German experiences. See, for example, Münchener volkswirtschaftliche Gesellschaft, *Lujo Brentano, Kundgebungen zu seinem 70. Geburtstag* (Munich and Leipzig, 1915), p. 24.

[11] John Malcolm Ludlow to Brentano, January 8, 1870. Unless otherwise stated all unpublished letters are from the Lujo Brentano Papers.

under Bismarck's leadership doubtlessly made Brentano more receptive to foreign influences. Thus in 1868 he discovered in England the archetype of nineteenth-century industrialism, the homeland of liberal economics, a model for social reform, and a center for his affections and loyalties—a center conspicuously absent from the fluid German situation before 1870.

2 –

Brentano and Engel arrived in London at a particularly significant moment in the social history of modern Britain. During the late 1860's the problem of the industrial worker had become increasingly important in British politics. The Reform Bill of 1867 reflected the desire of many Englishmen of finding a way to incorporate the lower classes into the life of the nation. As Disraeli put it in March, 1867: "The working class question is the real question and that is the thing that demands to be settled."[12]

Between 1850 and 1870 there was a general improvement in wages and working conditions. The factory legislation, which sections of the British middle class had so strongly opposed in the first half of the century, was now more or less accepted.[13] The period of prosperity after 1850 had been marked by the growth of trade unions, and during the 1860's the debate on the proper role of these unions was the most important aspect of the British concern for the social question. Among the leaders of the business community, unions were generally regarded as harmful for the economy and dangerous to the morals of the workers. These suspicions seemed to have been verified by an outbreak of union violence in Sheffield in 1866. More than any other incident, these so-called Sheffield outrages focused the attention of British opinion on the unions. Employers wanted to seize this opportunity to break the unions by means of restrictive legislation. Union leaders, on the other hand, were determined to demonstrate the falseness of the charges leveled against the union movement as a whole. In February, 1867, a Royal Commission was set up to

12 Quoted by T. Tholfsen, "The Transition to Democracy in Victorian England," *International Review of Social History*, VI, No. 2 (1961), 226. For a summary of British internal affairs in the late 1860's, see E. L. Woodward, *The Age of Reform* (Oxford, 1938), pp. 155 ff. and 586–95.
13 Woodward, *The Age of Reform*, p. 590.

study the union movement and to make recommendations concerning legislative means for controlling the relations between capital and labor.[14] This Commission was just at the end of its investigations when Engel and Brentano arrived in Britain in August, 1868.

Brentano and Engel spent two months together studying the English situation. Brentano's interests seem quickly to have diverged from those of his teacher.[15] Engel appears to have been primarily interested in observing England's technological achievements, whereas Brentano wanted to study social problems. Brentano, therefore, was unwilling to spend all of his time in the interviews with British industrialists which the Prussian Ministry of Commerce had arranged. Because he wanted to see the social problem from the worker's viewpoint, he went to see John Malcolm Ludlow, the author of a recent book on the British working class which Brentano had read before leaving Germany.[16] Ludlow received him graciously and provided him with introductions to working class groups throughout England. According to Brentano's account in *Mein Leben,* after he and Engel had spent several weeks touring England, he became convinced that the future of the British labor movement lay not in industrial partnerships or co-operatives but in the trade unions.[17] Brentano decided to spend the winter in England studying these unions and so did not accompany Engel when the latter left for Berlin in September.

It is clear, however, that Brentano's description of his stay in England rather exaggerates the abruptness of the break from his earlier ideas. His interest in unions had been aroused even before he left Germany. In the early summer of 1868 he wrote an article

[14] On the Royal Commission, see Woodward, *The Age of Reform,* p. 593; Beatrice and Sidney Webb, *The History of Trade Unionism* (rev. ed.; London, 1926), pp. 259–64; and H. W. McCready, "British Labour and the Royal Commission on Trade Unions, 1867–1869," *University of Toronto Quarterly,* XXIV, No. 4 (July, 1955), 390–409.

[15] Brentano, *Mein Leben im Kampfe um die soziale Entwicklung Deutschlands* (Jena, 1931), pp. 45 ff. Hereafter cited as *Mein Leben.*

[16] The book was *The Progress of the Working Class 1832–1867* (London, 1867) by Ludlow and Lloyd Jones. Immediately after publication it appeared in a German translation. On this work see N. C. Masterman, *John Malcolm Ludlow* (Cambridge, 1963), pp. 198 ff.

[17] *Mein Leben,* p. 47.

on unions for the Prussian Statistical Bureau's periodical. Here his treatment was sympathetic to unionism, although he still felt that industrial partnership was the key to the social question.[18] An even clearer indication of the gradual nature of the shift in his ideas can be found in a memorandum which he sent to Bishop von Ketteler in November, 1868.[19] In his autobiography, Brentano vaguely described this memorandum as a proposal to set up an organization in Germany similar to the Christian Socialists in England.[20] In fact, the memorandum was entitled "A Proposal for the Founding of the First Society to Promote and Support Production Associations and Industrial Partnerships." This memorandum to Ketteler shows clearly the transitional nature of Brentano's ideas in 1868. In the first place, his proposal and the letter accompanying it indicate his disappointment with the progress of co-operatives and industrial partnership systems in England. He found them weak and spreading very slowly. His appeal to Ketteler was primarily designed to overcome this weakness.[21] Brentano suggested that Ketteler sponsor a society whose purpose would be to gather capital and buy business enterprises which would be converted into industrial partnerships or co-operatives. Should Ketteler accept these ideas, Brentano declared that he was ready to devote himself wholeheartedly

18 "Der Kongress der Trades' Unions zu Manchester vom 3. bis 6. Juni 1868," *Zeitschrift des königlichen preussischen statistischen Bureaus*, VIII, Nos. 4–9 (April–September, 1868), 239–43. In the introduction to *Arbeitergilden*, I, viii–ix, Brentano said he still distrusted the unions when he wrote this article.

19 See Bernhard Pfister, "Lujo Brentano," *Lujo Brentano: Grusswort und Reden bei der Feier der 110. Wiederkehr seines Geburtstages (14. Dezember 1954)* (Berlin, 1956), pp. 29–45. The memorandum may be found in Heinrich Schreiner, "Das sozialpolitische Verständnis der frühen katholischen Schriftsteller im neunzehnten Jahrhundert: eine kritische und vergleichende Würdigung des sozialkritischen und sozialpolitischen Gedankengutes von Baader, Buss, Reichenperger und Ketteler" (unpub. diss., Munich, 1955). The Ketteler papers are in the diocesan archive in Mainz. The relevant materials, however, could not be located when I attempted to use them there. A fragment of Brentano's letter to Ketteler and Ketteler's reply are in the Brentano Papers. The memorandum is also cited by Otto Pfülf, *Bischof von Ketteler (1811–1877): Eine geschichtliche Darstellung* (Mainz, 1899), I, 54.

20 *Mein Leben*, p. 48.

21 Schreiner, "Das sozialpolitische Verständnis," pp. v–vi.

to their realization.[22] It is interesting to note that although trade unions had nothing to do with his practical proposals, Brentano added a brief account of union developments and a defense of unions against their German and British critics. Ketteler's answer was prompt, but not encouraging. He praised Brentano's ideas and also his industrial partnership brochure. The bishop could not, however, promise any active support for the plan.[23]

It seems clear that in the winter of 1868 Brentano had not yet made up his mind about unions. Although his first reaction to the unions was sympathetic, he was still deeply involved in studying them and had not thought through their practical implications.[24] In any case, the *Denkschrift* to Ketteler was the last time Brentano advocated any sort of partnership system. In the first months of 1869 he became convinced that the trade unions provided the answer to the social question.

When Brentano decided to turn to John Malcolm Ludlow for an introduction to the conditions of the British working classes, he could hardly have made a more fortunate choice. As a leading Christian Socialist, an official of the worker protective organizations called "friendly societies," and an advocate of trade unionism, Ludlow had contacts with every aspect of the worker movement. Equally important, he seems to have taken a great liking to the young German scholar, and their correspondence indicates a warm mutual friendship which lasted until Ludlow's death in 1911.[25] For his part, Brentano was deeply impressed by Ludlow

22 *Ibid.*
23 Ketteler to Brentano, November 17, 1868, quoted in *ibid.*, p. xviii. In his speech on the social question at the German bishops' conference at Fulda in 1869, Ketteler referred to Brentano's partnership work; see *ibid.*, p. 182.
24 This account of Brentano's development is based on a letter he wrote to Ketteler in March, 1871, quoted in "Das sozialpolitische Verständnis," pp. xix–xx.
25 Ludlow's letters to Brentano reveal a greater degree of friendship and intimacy than any other correspondence in the Brentano Papers. It is difficult to tell if their relationship was a unique one for Brentano because the Brentano family removed all personal letters from his *Nachlass* before giving it to the Bundesarchiv. It is possible that they missed Ludlow's letters because they were in English. For an evaluation of Ludlow's character, see Charles Raven, *Christian Socialism 1848–1854* (London, 1920), p. 58, and P. H. J. H. Gosden, *The Friendly Societies in England 1815–1875* (New York, 1961), pp. 193–94, 196. On Ludlow's relationship to Brentano, see Masterman, *Ludlow*, pp. 203–5.

and never ceased to stress the extremely important role which Ludlow played in the formation of his ideas.[26]

In a number of important ways Ludlow was the perfect intermediary between Brentano and the British labor movement. Since Brentano was still a Catholic in 1868, he and Ludlow were drawn together by their common Christianity.[27] Furthermore, Ludlow and Brentano probably shared a common psychological attitude toward the working classes, which they seem to have viewed with a mixture of fear, compassion, and responsibility. Perhaps most important, Ludlow provided Brentano with an example of a uniquely unselfish social consciousness, totally devoted to the material, moral, and intellectual betterment of the workers. In Ludlow and his associates, Brentano saw men who were actually bridging the gap between what Disraeli called the "two nations." Brentano felt they could take much of the credit for the relative tranquillity of British social developments.[28] Living in imperial Germany, where the gap between rich and poor was ominously large, Brentano never ceased to admire this achievement.[29]

Ludlow's career as a social reformer began in 1848 when he was active in the English Christian Socialist movement. At this time he hoped to reconstruct society through co-operatives, an attempt which he abandoned in the mid-1850's when it was clear that the British working classes were not prepared for the self-sacrifice and discipline that co-operation demands. Ludlow did not, however, give up his ideals of co-operation, but set about educating the workers for some future realization of these goals. This was the purpose of the Working Men's College, where Ludlow, Charles Kingsley, Thomas Hughes, and Frederic Mau-

---

26 For example, see *Mein Leben*, pp. 47–48.

27 See Brentano, *Die christlich-soziale Bewegung in England* (Leipzig, 1883), p. 3. Here Brentano stressed the difference between socially-conscious British Protestantism and the conservative Catholicism on the continent.

28 On the Christian Socialists, see Brentano's essay cited above, n. 27; Raven, *Christian Socialism*; G. Binyon, *The Christian Socialist Movement in England* (London, 1931); the more critical account in J. Saville, "The Christian Socialists of 1848," in *Democracy and the Labour Movement,* ed. J. Saville (London, 1954), pp. 135–59; and T. Christensen, *Origin and History of Christian Socialism 1848–1854* (Aarhus, 1962).

29 See Brentano's speech, *Die Stellung der Gebildeten zur sozialen Frage* (Berlin, 1890), pp. 4 ff.

rice held highly successful evening courses. The influence of this institution on the social history of nineteenth-century Britain was considerable, not only because of the educational opportunity it offered the workers, but also because it had a great effect in bringing members of the upper classes into sympathetic contact with the workers' problems.

Despite Ludlow's hope that society could be rebuilt "upon the lines of a world-wide self-governing brotherhood," he was a firm supporter of the British trade unions.[30] He realized the difficulties of establishing a co-operative society, and just as he attempted to educate the workers at an evening college, so he felt that unions would be an educational force for the ultimate realization of a co-operative society. Ludlow never lost sight of the transitory nature of unions, however. As he once said: "I want trade unionism to expand into humanity and finally lose itself in it."[31]

When Brentano approached him for an introduction to British working-class movements, Ludlow decided to emphasize the unions. Like most alert social reformers in the late sixties, he realized that unionism was the most important social issue of the day. Furthermore, since Brentano had already advocated the partnership system, Ludlow could assume that the young German realized the advantages of co-operation.[32] As we shall see, Ludlow was extremely successful in convincing Brentano of the usefulness of unions. However, he was shocked to see that as Brentano's faith in unionism grew, his interest in co-operatives waned. After Brentano left London in 1869, Ludlow felt obliged to complain that, whereas Brentano had gone "head over heels into trade unionism," he remained "almost as innocent as a babe as to the real strength and vitality of the cooperative movement as a coordinate force with trade unionism within the working class. . . ."[33]

Brentano's increasing disinterest in co-operatives reflected the

[30] Raven, *Christian Socialism,* p. 64.

[31] Quoted in *ibid.,* p. 249.

[32] In a letter of May 10, 1873, Ludlow wrote to Brentano: "You and Max Hirsch both came here originally full of cooperation of some kind or other, and distrusting the trades unions, and I urged you both to look well into the latter as the more important of the two for the moment."

[33] Ludlow to Brentano, June 21, 1869.

fact that in the 1860's co-operation was a rather moribund movement.[34] As Brentano wrote to Ketteler in November, 1868, only consumer co-operatives seemed to be doing well, and these, he felt, had little relevance for Germany.[35] Perhaps Ludlow was able to overlook these weaknesses in the co-operative movement because he had faith in man's natural propensity to co-operate. Brentano, however, did not share this view of human nature. The contrast between the vigor of unionism and the infirmity of co-operation was enough to convince him that the future of the labor movement belonged to the unions.

Brentano's practical introduction to the British unions was through William Allan (1813–74), the secretary of the Amalgamated Society of Engineers.[36] Allan, of working-class origin, rose in the union movement because of his supreme organizational skill. In 1852 there had been an unsuccessful strike by the Engineers which resulted in a grave decline in membership and funds. After this experience, Allan decided to de-emphasize strikes as a means of improving wages and working conditions and to concentrate instead upon building a powerful union organization which could provide its members with many of the benefits of a modern insurance company. Together with this emphasis on organization and financial strength, Allan sought to make the unions respectable and to gain for them full legal recognition of their rights. With the success of these efforts, the

[34] See the Webbs' *History of Trade Unionism,* p. 226, on the weakness of co-operation in the late sixties. In the early 1870's the industrial partnership system set up by Engel in Berlin and the British model upon which it was based both returned to more orthodox modes of production. See H. Frommer, *Die Gewinnbetheilung, Staats- und sozialwissenschaftliche Forschungen* (Leipzig, 1886), VI, 31–34, 120–21.

[35] Schreiner, "Das sozialpolitische Verständnis," p. viii.

[36] On Allan and the Engineers, see the Webbs, *History of Trade Unionism,* pp. 217–19, 234–40, and James B. Jeffreys, *The Story of the Engineers 1880–1945* (Letchworth, England, n.d.). For Brentano's account of Allan, see *Mein Leben,* p. 49, and *Arbeitergilden,* I, xi, and 133–232. For the discussion of unions throughout this chapter, I am indebted to Hugh Clegg of Nuffield College, Oxford. Mr. Clegg provided me with a very enlightening conversation on unionism and allowed me to read in manuscript the book which has since appeared as Hugh A. Clegg, Alan Fox, and A. F. Thompson, *A History of British Trade Unions Since 1889. Vol. 1: 1889–1910* (Oxford, 1964). See also the recent survey of unions by Henry Pelling, *A History of British Trade Unionism* (Baltimore, 1963), especially pp. 49–52.

Engineers became the model for the other Amalgamated Societies of workers which grew up in the 1860's and 1870's. The Engineers' example was followed by the Carpenters' union, led by Robert Applegarth, another man who helped to introduce Brentano to the British unions. As the Webbs have expressed it: "In Allan and Applegarth . . . the traducers of Trade Unionism found themselves confronted with a combination of high personal character, exceptional business ability, and a large share of that official decorum which the English middle class finds so impressive."[37]

The importance of Allan and Applegarth within the union movement was greatly increased by the central role they played in the investigations of the Royal Commission.[38] In their appearances before the Commission, Allan and Applegarth sought to speak for the union movement as a whole. They stressed the insurance company aspects of the Amalgamated Societies, and their opposition to strikes, to the restraint of trade, and to violence of any kind. They attempted, in short, to make the unions acceptable elements in the bourgeois world. It was of great importance for the development of Brentano's views of unions that his first relationship with them came under these circumstances.

Brentano's main contact with the Royal Commission itself was through Frederic Harrison (1831–1923).[39] Harrison was a friend of Ludlow's and one of the most important middle-class champions of the union movement. One of the two pro-union members of the Commission, he struggled courageously on the unions' behalf. Due in part to his efforts, the Commission's report recognized the peaceful nature of unions, although its recom-

[37] Webbs, *History of Trade Unionism*, p. 240. On Applegarth, see Pelling, *History of Trade Unionism*, pp. 53–54.

[38] *Reports of the Commissioners Appointed to Inquire into the Organization and Rules of Trades Unions and other Associations: Minutes of Evidence* (London, 1867); Webbs, *History of Trade Unionism*, p. 264 ff.; and Pelling, *History of Trade Unionism*, p. 67.

[39] See Harrison's *Autobiographic Memoirs* (2 vols.; London, 1911) and the article by A. Cochrane in the *Dictionary of National Biography 1922–1930* (Oxford, 1937), pp. 406–8. For his view of unions, see his article "The Trades Unions Bill," *Fortnightly Review*, N.S., VI (July–December, 1869), 30–45. For Harrison's role on the commission, see McCready, "British Labour and the Royal Commission."

mendations did not fulfill all of the unions' demands for legal recognition. During November and December, 1868, the period in which Brentano's ideas on unionism were crystallizing, Harrison worked on a minority report for the Commission, in which he defended the unions' position. In his report, Harrison pictured the unions as an example of successful business acumen. He argued that the unions were in effect merely "an extension of the principle of free trade."[40] Brentano read Harrison's report in manuscript and fully endorsed his conception of unions.

At precisely the time Brentano was becoming acquainted with the practice of trade unionism, there was published in Britain a revision of classical economics that was of critical importance for the theory of unions. In the tradition of the Manchester economists, the collective bargaining of workers for an increase in wages was regarded as ineffective because of what was called the "wages fund." Simply stated, this meant that at any given time only a certain amount of wealth was present in the economy with which to pay for labor, and the price of this labor was dependent on the laws of supply and demand. Should a union succeed in getting a wage increase, this increase would be rendered meaningless either by a corresponding rise in prices or by a flight of capital from the affected industry, which would result in a decline in the demand for labor and therefore a decline in wages. This is more or less the argument Brentano himself used against unions in his pamphlet on industrial partnership.[41] The wages fund idea was particularly important in Germany because it was accepted not only by liberal economists but also played a central role in Lassalle's attempt to establish an independent labor movement. Lassalle, like Brentano in 1868, argued that collective bargaining was useless because it could not bring about a real increase in wages.[42]

40 McCready, "British Labour and the Royal Commission," pp. 406–7.

41 Das Industrial Partnership System: Ein Versuch zur Lösung der Arbeiterfrage (Augsburg, 1868), p. 25. Brentano probably acquired his ideas on the wages fund from Helferich, who defended the fund theory in the late 1860's. In this respect Helferich deviated from his teacher, Hermann, who suggested revisions in the concept of the fund. After 1869 Brentano emphasized the importance of Hermann for his own views. See Arbeitergilden, II, 201–2, and Mein Leben, p. 64.

42 Hermann Oncken, Ferdinand Lassalle: Eine politische Biographie (Stuttgart, 1920), pp. 278 ff.

In a book published in the first months of 1869, the British economist William Thomas Thornton attacked the wages fund theory and argued that it was indeed possible for unions to effect a real wage increase.[43] Thornton's arguments received the backing of John Stuart Mill, the recognized dean of liberal economics, in an article in the May, 1869, *Fortnightly Review*. Mill expressed his revised opinion in a statement often quoted by Brentano:

> The doctrine hitherto taught by all or most economists (including myself), which denied it to be possible that trade combinations can raise wages, or which limited their operations in that respect to the somewhat earlier attainment of a rise which the competition of the market would have produced without them—this doctrine is deprived of its scientific foundations, and must be thrown aside.[44]

Both Mill and Thornton had reservations about unions, but both of them by and large supported union demands.

It is extremely difficult to gauge the impact of the Thornton-Mill argument on the development of Brentano's thought. In *Mein Leben*, Brentano stressed the practical aspects of his British experiences and did not mention being influenced by this theoretical critique of the wages fund. In the articles he wrote on unions during the early 1870's, Brentano tended to overemphasize his own minor additions to Thornton's and Mill's argument, rather than his indebtedness to them. Brentano had a habit of stressing his own originality, sometimes to the extent of ignoring his intellectual debts. In his critique of the wages fund, however, he followed Thornton and Mill closely enough to permit little doubt that the essential elements of his work were derived from them.[45]

The impact of Mill's revision of classical economics on Bren-

---

43 W. T. Thornton, *On Labour: Its Wrongful Claims and Rightful Dues. Its Actual Present and Possible Future* (2d. ed.; London, 1870). The preface to the first edition is dated December, 1868. For the impact of Thornton's book on public opinion, see Pelling, *History of Trade Unionism*, p. 69.

44 John Stuart Mill, "Thornton on Labour and its Claims," *Fortnightly Review*, N.S., V (May 1, 1869), 517.

45 For the critique of the wages fund by Brentano, see *Arbeitergilden*, II, 196–218.

tano was undoubtedly heightened by the similarity of their positions within the history of European liberalism. Brentano himself spoke of their "similarity of endeavor" and praised Mill as a "model to be emulated while travelling a common path."[46] This common path was determined by the fact that both men realized that liberalism had to be revised to meet the new problems of the day. Like Mill, Brentano followed Comte's critique of the abstract economic methods of the later classical economists, and tried to lead liberal economics back to a more historically-oriented method.[47] Equally important, both Mill and Brentano realized that liberalism could not allow the problem of the working class to remain unsolved. A few weeks before Engel and Brentano had arrived in England, for example, Mill had spoken of the "hundred evils" which had grown up with industrialism and had asserted that "the old relation between workmen and employers is out of joint."[48] Finally, Mill hoped that the trade unions would be able to place the relationship between capital and labor on a sounder basis. Like Brentano, he was influenced by Harrison's report to the Royal Commission, with which he expressed his agreement.[49]

Mill's obvious importance for Brentano's intellectual development raises the question of the relative importance of Brentano's practical experiences with unions and his awareness of the innovations in economic theory which made a theoretical justification of unions possible. One scholar has argued that Mill's critique of the wages fund was a necessary prerequisite for Brentano's

[46] Brentano to Georg Knapp, May 17, 1874, quoted in Gerhard Wittrock, *Die Kathedersozialisten bis zur Eisenacher Versammlung 1872* (Berlin, 1939), p. 96. When Knapp wrote a critical review of Mill's *Autobiography*, Brentano came close to severing relations with him. *Ibid.*, p. 42.

[47] In *Arbeitergilden*, II, 310 ff., Brentano gave a description of his method, which was based on Mill's account of Comte in his *Auguste Comte and Positivism* (London, 1866). Brentano accepted Comte's notion that it was necessary to give the social sciences a historical dimension because of the importance of man's past, and that general truths could be formulated in the social sciences by a combination of inductive (mainly historical) and deductive methods. See Mill, *Auguste Comte*, pp. 83–86.

[48] Quoted from a speech by Mill on July 22, 1868, by S. MacCoby, *The English Radical Tradition 1783–1914* (London, 1952), p. 169.

[49] McCready, "British Labour and the Royal Commission," p. 408.

conviction that unions could solve social problems.[50] It seems more reasonable to conclude, however, that Brentano's acceptance of unionism was not due to Mill and Thornton alone, but rather to experiences within a climate of opinion of which they were very much a part. Mill and Thornton provided just one aspect of a historical situation in Britain that was particularly favorable to a display of the best points of unionism. Their ideas, therefore, can be seen as the theoretical analogue to the pro-union sentiments of Ludlow and Harrison and the practical achievements of Allan and Applegarth.

3 —

For almost a decade after 1869 Brentano was completely absorbed by his vision of social reform through unions. To some degree, this was due to the fact that Brentano's views became the subject of a bitter debate which tended to turn his ideas into arguments and thus hinder the evolution of his thought. However, the most important reason for his long adherence to unions as a solution to the social question must be sought in his own conception of unionism, which combined his experiences in England in 1868–69 with his earlier belief in economic liberalism. This synthesis of unionism and classical economics provided the real strength for Brentano's convictions and was his contribution to the debate on *Sozialpolitik* in Germany, which we will examine in the next chapter.

Brentano left London in May, 1869, after having spent nine months studying the British unions. For the next three years he worked on the material he had gathered in England and published two major studies of unionism: first, in 1870, an account of the relationship between unions and the medieval guilds; then his two-volume *Arbeitergilden der Gegenwart,* which appeared in 1871 and 1872.[51]

50 Werner Barich, *Lujo Brentano als Sozialpolitiker* (diss., Berlin, 1936), pp. 17, 45–50. Barich sought to prove Brentano's dependence on Mill by a rather complicated chronological argument which tried to show that Brentano did not accept unions until after he had read Mill's article. In my opinion, the critical stage in Brentano's relationship to unionism was the winter of 1868.

51 In 1870 a long article based on Brentano's work on unionism was published anonymously in the *North British Review,* LIII (October, 1870), 89–114. Although Brentano was referred to in the third person in the article, he was evidently the author. See *Mein Leben,* p. 56; *Arbeitergilden,* I, xiv.

Brentano was introduced to the problem of the historical relationship between unions and the medieval guilds while he was studying the British unions in 1868. The idea that there was some connection between the guilds and the unions was prevalent among the advocates of unionism in Britain, and Brentano undoubtedly discussed the question with them.[52] Shortly after his return to Germany he was given the opportunity of publishing his thoughts on the subject. In April, 1869, Toulmin Smith, a British expert on guilds, died and left his collection of guild documents unfinished and without an introduction. Brentano was recommended by a friend of Ludlow's to provide the introduction, which he completed in the winter of 1869, and which also appeared separately in an issue of some 750 copies.[53] In this work he attempted to demonstrate that the unions were the "successors of the old guilds." Although he admitted that the unions were not the direct heirs of the guilds, he argued that both institutions originated during times of economic disorganization, times in which the weak were oppressed by the strong and sought refuge from this oppression in some kind of collective action.[54]

Although Brentano's conclusions about the relationship of unions and guilds are based upon rather questionable historical analysis,[55] two aspects of his first book deserve to be considered. First, in his attempt to designate the guilds as the predecessors of the unions, Brentano, like many other nineteenth-century thinkers, seems to have been looking to the middle ages for models of organizations lacking in the modern world. Unlike most of the followers of this tradition, however, his concept of guilds in no way suggested a re-creation of medieval institutions

---

[52] *Mein Leben,* p. 54. For Ludlow's analysis of the relationship between guilds and unions, see his essay "Trade Societies and the Social Science Association," *Macmillan's Magazine,* February and March, 1861. Brentano noted the connection between guilds and unions as early as his memorandum to Ketteler, quoted in Schreiner, "Das sozialpolitische Verständnis," p. vii.

[53] Toulmin Smith, ed., *English Guilds* (London, 1870). Brentano's introduction was published as *On the History and Development of Gilds and the Origin of Trade Unions* (London, 1870).

[54] *Ibid.,* 102–3. In his *Arbeitergilden* (II, 314), Brentano suggested that this was an empirically verified law of human behavior.

[55] For a critique of Brentano's position, see Charles Gros, *The Gild Merchant* (Oxford, 1890), I, 167–72. On Gros, see *Mein Leben,* pp. 189–90.

as a solution to contemporary problems. Second, it should be noted that Brentano's historical interest in the guilds was very limited. He was interested in them because of what he felt to be their relationship to unionism, but for no other reason. In Brentano's work on guilds, as throughout much of his career, historical research was subordinated to the practical interests of the present.

Brentano used his introduction to *English Guilds* as the historical background for his *Arbeitergilden der Gegenwart*. This was the work which established his reputation in Germany, and it is here that we find the clearest formulation of his concept of unionism. As has been mentioned, one of the central achievements of Brentano's work was his successful integration of classical economics and unionism. Throughout the 1870's he continued to adhere to the basic elements of liberal economics that he had learned at Göttingen. Consider, for example, the view of state intervention presented in the first volume of the *Arbeitergilden*. Brentano acknowledged that at times the state must act to protect the weak and those unable to help themselves,[56] a position comparable to the relatively general acceptance of the factory laws in Britain. According to Brentano, however, state intervention could not hope to correct the basic problems brought on by industrialism; at best it could cure some of the symptoms of social and economic evils.[57] Only the unions could alleviate both the symptoms and the cause of social unrest.

Closely connected with his view of the limits of the government's role in the economy was Brentano's belief in economic freedom. An important reason for his acceptance of unionism was his conviction that the unions were compatible with a free economy. Although he realized that unions would modify economic freedom, Brentano felt that the laws of supply and demand would still function. Unions would merely give the workers equal strength in the struggle with the employers over the relative size of profits and wages. In other words, Brentano felt that unions would equalize but not destroy the free market economy. He does not seem to have envisioned a situation in which the unions would be strong enough to dictate to the employers and thus disturb the laws of the market.

[56] *Arbeitergilden,* I, 123–27.
[57] *Arbeitergilden,* II, 21.

Brentano was willing to modify the doctrines of classical liberalism in only one important respect: his awareness of social problems made him doubt the liberal economists' faith in economic individualism, which he felt was based on the erroneous assumption of human equality. In fact, individual competition favored the gifted and the wealthy, but put the average worker in an inferior position. It was the task of social reform to find economic equality for all.[58] To do this Brentano was willing to sacrifice economic individualism and to support the collective action of workers.

Brentano's conviction that unions could solve the social question without government intervention and without tampering with the free economy allowed him to argue that his proposals left intact the essential elements of classical economic theory. He believed that the teaching of the classical economists was not contradicted, but supplemented, by the trade unions. He expressed this idea in a phrase he frequently repeated during the 1870's: "The British unions are the necessary and natural fulfillment [Ergänzung] of economics on the basis of complete freedom."[59] It will be recalled that Brentano's experiences with the British unions appeared to confirm this view: Allan and his colleagues seemed to have accepted the classical view of economics. Brentano believed that they sought only the right to organize, not a revision of the economic structure.[60]

In addition to their apparent harmony with economic liberalism, unions were attractive to Brentano because they seemed to provide an essentially conservative answer to the social question. Brentano did not believe that social injustice was a necessary part of the existing social order. For him the social question was the result of an inequality of economic opportunity which unions could rectify. He was, in his words, interested in the improvement of the condition of "the workers as workers," nothing

58 *Arbeitergilden*, II, 50–52.
59 *Arbeitergilden*, II, 326. In *Mein Leben* (p. 83) Brentano wrote: "Because I wanted our economic life protected from all attempts at revolutionary change (attempts which were bound to fail), I demanded that the principle of freedom which governs contemporary economics be extended to the workers and thus be logically, honestly and consistently completed."
60 Webbs, *History of Trade Unionism*, p. 239.

more.[61] Thus, in contrast to men like Lassalle and Marx, who sought to improve the lot of the workers by a reconstruction of the social order in which the working class absorbed the rest of society, Brentano wanted progress within the framework of the existing social structure.[62] He was attracted to a labor leader like Allan precisely because Allan's policy was to work within the present social system.

Brentano felt that the conservative character of the unions was reaffirmed by their educational programs and their emphasis on honesty and morality.[63] He viewed unionism not only as a way of settling questions of wages, but also as a means of spreading culture to the lower classes.[64] Like Ludlow and Harrison, Brentano was convinced that the unions were important vehicles for moral as well as material progress.

Finally, it should be noted that Brentano had almost no interest in the political aspects of the labor question. As we have pointed out, Brentano became committed to the essentially apolitical doctrines of classical liberalism during the mid-1860's.[65] He tended, therefore, to view problems in economic, and to a lesser degree, cultural terms. As we shall see, his indifference to the political dimensions of social unrest was reinforced by his experience in German academic life and was shared by a large number of his contemporaries in imperial Germany. Here again, the British unions seemed to conform to his position. As one unionist wrote to Brentano: "In such a matter as trade unionism, politics of the ordinary kind do not much enter."[66] The Engineers, for example, had a by-law forbidding the discussion of

---

[61] Quoted by Ludwig Nieder, "Lujo Brentano und die deutschen Arbeiter," *Deutsche Arbeit*, I, No. 12 (December, 1916), 583.

[62] Brentano contrasted his position to Marx's in *Mein Leben*, p. 50.

[63] *Arbeitergilden*, I, 156, and II, 55.

[64] According to Brentano: "The *Arbeiterfrage* is in no way only a question of wages, but also a question of culture." The final goal of social reform must be "a society in which all mankind partakes in all the blessings of culture." *Arbeitergilden*, II, 219, 339.

[65] For a stimulating discussion of the apolitical character of classical liberalism, see Sheldon Wolin, *Politics and Vision: Continuity and Innovation in Western Political Thought* (Boston, 1960), pp. 286–351.

[66] Lloyd Jones to Brentano, January 30, 1873. See also H. Pelling, *The Origins of the Labour Party* (London, 1954), pp. 2 ff.

political subjects at their meetings.[67] Brentano often contrasted the unions with the Chartist movement, which he regarded as the unheeded serpent in the British Eden. He felt that the Chartists, like the German Social Democrats, wished to overthrow the existing order through the political tyranny of the majority over the minority. He was not opposed to suffrage reforms, but his political remarks were always parenthetical.[68] He clearly did not want the workers to be forced to fight for control of the state in order to solve their difficulties. He was convinced that the unions offered a solution to the social question which avoided both state interference and democratic political action.

In summary, then, it can be seen that Brentano was attracted to the British unions because he saw them as offering an essentially conservative, gradualist solution to the social question, consistent with the limits of his conception of social reform and with his political and economic ideas. The unions' role in a peaceful resolution of social conflicts seemed to be further insured by the development in England of arbitration boards which sought to solve industrial disputes without strikes or lockouts. As early as 1868 Brentano had noted these arbitration institutions with approval,[69] and in February, 1872, he returned to England specifically to study them. The arbitration boards appeared as the capstone of his system in the conclusion to the second volume of his *Arbeitergilden*.[70] He had long recognized the wastefulness and undesirability of strikes and now could point to the arbitration boards at work in England as a system which allowed workers and employers to reach an agreement without any work stoppage. These organs presupposed the union movement because, according to Brentano, in order for them to work properly the workers had to be organized. Furthermore, both workers and employers had to have experience with the harmful

---

[67] *Arbeitergilden*, I, 231, and the Webbs, *History of Trade Unionism*, p. 242. There are indications that the trade union leaders were more politically active than Brentano seems to have realized. However, they always maintained the position that "we have no desire to make our societies channels for political agitation." Pelling, *History of Trade Unionism*, p. 63.

[68] *Arbeitergilden*, II, 327.

[69] Brentano, "Kongress der Trades Unions," as cited in n. 18 above.

[70] *Arbeitergilden*, II, 245–308.

character of lockouts and strikes in order to be willing to make the sacrifices necessary for compromise agreements.

Brentano's vision of organized interests settling their differences within a framework of economic rather than political institutions is reminiscent of the corporate tradition popular in Germany from the beginning of the nineteenth century. This tradition was renewed by the *Genossenschaft* theory of Otto von Gierke at precisely the time Brentano was first studying the unions. It is impossible, however, to link Brentano with any specific elements of this tradition. Gierke's book, for example, came out in the fall of 1868, after Brentano had left Germany.[71] It is probable that Brentano did not read it until his ideas were fairly well formed, because he did not cite Gierke in his 1870 book on the guilds, and he referred to this work for the first time in volume one of the *Arbeitergilden*. Although Gierke and Brentano were later colleagues at Breslau, their correspondence suggests a friendship which in part rested upon a reticience to engage in intellectual exchanges.[72] While it cannot be proven that Gierke was entirely without influence on Brentano's conception of labor organizations, it seems clear that the latter's ideas were essentially the result of his own experiences with English theory and practice.

Brentano was one of the first Germans to realize the enormous significance of unions as a means of improving the worker's position in an industrial society. Although unions in both Germany and England developed along lines which Brentano could not have foreseen in the early 1870's, they did indeed fulfill his expectations by providing the workers with the means of attaining a greater share in the wealth and progress created by their labor. As a tireless advocate of the workers' right to collective bargaining, Brentano played a significant role in the practical

[71] Otto Gierke, *Rechtsgeschichte der deutschen Genossenschaft* (Berlin, 1868). The preface is dated July, 1868. On Brentano and Gierke, see Georg Römer, "Lujo Brentano in den geistigen Strömungen seiner Zeit" (unpub. diss., Munich, 1954), pp. 216–29. Although Römer gives an acute analysis of the differences between Brentano and Gierke, he assumes that Gierke influenced Brentano's thought. I have found no evidence to support this assumption. Throughout Römer's work a similar lack of concrete historical analysis detracts from its value.

[72] The letters from Gierke in Brentano's papers are mostly concerned with personal or professional affairs. A card from Gierke of October 25, 1895, expresses his desire to remain friends despite their scholarly differences.

and legal acceptance of unions in Germany. Furthermore, in his lectures and writings he recognized that one of the major weaknesses of modern society was the cultural gap between the working classes and the rest of society, against which Ludlow and the Christian Socialists had struggled in England. Surely one of the reasons that this gap, with all of its ominous political and social consequences, remained in imperial Germany was that the warnings of men like Brentano were not sufficiently heeded.

There are, however, certain aspects of Brentano's work on unionism that cannot pass without critical comment. In the first place, Brentano presented a somewhat incomplete picture of British unionism in 1868. Like many later historians, he allowed the powerful and respectable Amalgamated Societies to dominate his view of the unions. This was at least in part due to the efforts of the leaders of these societies, who in 1868 were seeking to represent the union movement as a whole to the Royal Commission. In fact, in the late sixties the Amalgamated Societies represented a minority within British unionism. In many industries the control of the unions rested entirely with the local organizations, which were frequently very vigorous in their pursuit of the workers' interests. Even in some of the local branches of the large unions like the Engineers there was a good deal more militancy than Brentano seems to have realized.[73] His absorption with the Amalgamated Societies also led him to overlook the fact that his solution to the *Arbeiterfrage* was only effective for skilled workers like engineers. It is clear that when Brentano spoke of the problems of the "workers," he was actually addressing himself to the problems of men like the engineers and the carpenters, not to the mass of unskilled industrial laborers.[74]

[73] This interpretation is based on the work by Clegg, cited above, n. 36. See also the important article by G. D. H. Cole, "Some Notes on British Trade Unions in the Third Quarter of the Nineteenth Century," *Essays in Economic History*, ed. E. M. Carus (London, 1962), III, 202–21; and Pelling, *A History of Trade Unionism*, p. 76. During the investigations of the Royal Commission even Harrison was shocked by some of the evidence on union activity (Pelling, p. 68).

[74] Significantly, Marx errs in precisely the opposite direction. In contrast to Brentano, Marx regarded all workers as downtrodden, unskilled proletarians and overlooked the fact that the working class was becoming more, not less, diversified in skill, living standards, and so on. On this point, see R. Dahrendorf, *Class and Class Conflict in Industrial Society* (Stanford, 1959), pp. 48–51.

If Brentano greatly underestimated the militancy of British unionism, he also overestimated the effectiveness of arbitration in settling industrial disputes. In fact, arbitration only worked in England in very special cases. The instance Brentano studied—the Nottingham Hosiery Board—reflected the peculiar problems of that industry, whose highly competitive nature made it advantageous for the employers to agree to pre-determined wages.[75]

Brentano can also be criticized for basing his work on the untested and highly questionable assumption that the English experience was absolutely relevant for Germany. Although Brentano's *Arbeitergilden* volumes were devoted entirely to British developments, he began with a clear statement of the value of his findings for Germany:

> Economic developments in England are not only of English, but of universal significance. . . . We have become accustomed to seeing the economic phenomena there repeating themselves in Germany only modified by our particular circumstances.[76]

In the polemics in which Brentano was later involved, this overemphasis on the importance of the British model was frequently mentioned. It was a criticism to which Brentano was particularly sensitive and one which he always rejected.[77] The criticism, however, was not entirely without foundation. Brentano spent far too little time analyzing Germany's "particular circumstances." He was wrong in believing that economic developments in one country are of universal significance, and that Germany would necessarily follow the British pattern in labor relations. It was an error to overlook the extent to which labor relations, social reform, indeed even the character of industrialism itself, are determined by the political and social structure of the individual country. It is important to note, however, that this overemphasis on British affairs did not arise merely through some individual intellectual weakness of Brentano's, but was an integral part of his economic thought and historical position. Eco-

---

[75] Clegg, *et al., A History of British Trade Unions,* I, 24 ff.

[76] *Arbeitergilden,* I, vii–viii.

[77] For example, see Brentano's essay, "Zur Reform der deutschen Fabrikgesetzgebung," *Jahrbücher für Nationalökonomie und Statistik,* XIX, Nos. 3 and 4 (1872), 1–2.

nomic liberalism of the kind he followed tended to ignore politics and to view the world in essentially non-political terms. With this emphasis on economics Brentano's views inevitably blurred the deep-seated differences of politics and society which separated Germany and England.[78] Furthermore, as has frequently been pointed out, Brentano's estrangement from the political developments in Germany put him in a position not only to accept this form of economics but also to accept a model outside the German scene.

Brentano's failure to perceive the political and social differences between the English and German situation had unfortunate consequences for his effectiveness as a social reformer. He failed to see that the relative placidity of English social relations in the seventies and eighties was due not only to unions but also to a willingness on the part of the British to seek solutions for the political dimension of the social question. Therefore, Brentano's conviction that unions could solve German social problems left unanswered some of the essential political questions that were a part of social tensions in a quasi-authoritarian state like Germany. This weakness in Brentano's outlook gradually emerged when, after 1869, he sought to apply the insights he had gained in Britain to German social problems.

[78] It is interesting to note how Brentano's British friends shared his conviction that German developments would follow the British pattern. See, for example, a letter from Harrison to Brentano of June 5, 1878, in which Harrison compared the situation in Germany with an earlier period in British labor relations. Note also Marx's comment, quoted above, p. 22.

# CHAPTER III

# The Debate on Social Reform
# in Germany
# 1869-1872

## 1 –

Soon after Brentano returned to Germany in the spring of 1869, he found that the interest he had developed in social reform was shared by a number of his contemporaries, who were also seeking answers to what was now recognized as the "social question."

This increasingly widespread concern for what the Germans call *Sozialpolitik*[1] was in part a result of the maturation of the German economy that had taken place since the mid-nineteenth century. After 1850, particularly in the years immediately preceding the depression of 1873, the dynamism of the economy had a significant impact on German national life.[2] As industrialism matured, many Germans turned to a consideration of social

---

[1] There is no simple English equivalent for *Sozialpolitik*. The German word has a more practical implication than "social thought," and does not suggest solely government action as does "social policy." For our purposes *Sozialpolitik* can be taken to mean a theory or policy concerning the social or economic relationship between classes or social groups, with at least the implication that this theory or policy has practical relevance for the regulation or improvement of these relationships. See F. Lütge, "Der Begriff Sozialpolitik: Ein neuer Versuch," *Jahrbücher für Nationalökonomie und Statistik*, CXXXVII (1932), 481–514, and G. Albrecht, *Sozialpolitik* (Göttingen, 1955), especially pp. 9–33.

[2] On the development of the German economy before 1850, see F. Lütge, *Deutsche Sozial- und Wirtschaftsgeschichte: Ein Überblick* (2d ed., Berlin, 1960), pp. 427–44. For German industrial growth after 1850, see Jürgen Kuczynski, *Die Geschichte der Lage der Arbeiter unter dem Kapitalismus. Vol. I: Die Geschichte der Lage der Arbeiter in Deutschland von 1789 bis in die Gegenwart* (6th ed.; Berlin, 1954), Part I, pp. 165 ff. and 175. I have used Kuczynski's statistics throughout this study; unfortunately his orthodox

problems because they felt that economic change was destroying the entire fabric of society. In 1872, for example, the liberal historian Alfred Dove expressed the uneasiness of his generation when he warned of the dangers involved in the new economic forms: "The ultimate bonds which have held men—both employer and employee—together will be carelessly ripped asunder. Mass will face mass, and then the battle [*Massenschlacht*] will begin."[3]

Dove's anxiety over the effects of industrialism coincided with the fears of those who believed that the seeds of revolution were inherent in the historical development of the nineteenth century. "The era of revolution," wrote Jacob Burckhardt in 1871, "extends to our own day and we are, relatively speaking, perhaps only at the beginning or in the second act; it must be realized that the apparently placid decades from 1815 to 1848 were only an intermission in the great drama."[4] In the early seventies, fear of revolution in Germany was heightened by the presence of the German workers' party founded in 1869, which declared its allegiance to the Socialist International. Moreover, the Paris Commune of 1871 provided an example of the terrors of revolution which had a great impact on German social reformers.[5] The

---

Leninist approach makes his analysis of this statistical information highly doubtful. On the expansion of the economy after 1850, see also W. Sombart, *Die deutsche Volkswirtschaft im neunzehnten Jahrhundert* (Berlin, 1913), p. 81.

[3] Quoted by Friedrich Meinecke in "Alfred Dove und der klassische Liberalismus im neuen Reich," the introductory essay to Meinecke's edition of Dove's *Ausgewählte Aufsätze* (Munich, 1925), I, xxvii.

[4] The phrase is from Burckhardt's lectures of 1870–71 on the French Revolution, quoted in Theodor Schieder, *Staat und Gesellschaft im Wandel unserer Zeit* (Munich, 1958), p. 11.

[5] The conservative social reformer Karl Rodbertus saw the Commune as a warning that "the German state is called upon to consider the social question once the national question has been solved." Quoted in Ernst Schraepler, *Quellen zur Geschichte der sozialen Frage in Deutschland* (Berlin and Frankfurt, 1957), II, 1. On the Commune's impact, see also W. Vogel, *Bismarcks Arbeiterversicherung: Ihre Entstehung im Kräftespiel der Zeit* (Braunschweig, 1951), p. 19, and W. Pöls, *Sozialistenfrage und Revolutionsfurcht in ihrem Zusammenhang mit den angeblichen Staatsstreichplänen Bismarcks* (Lübeck and Hamburg, 1960), pp. 27 ff. Brentano once wrote that the Commune played a role for his generation comparable to that of the Chartists for the Christian Socialists in England, *Die Christlich-Soziale Bewegung in England* (Leipzig, 1883), p. 51.

leader of the German Social Democrats, in a statement significantly similar to Burckhardt's, made clear the relevance of the Commune for Germany and for the entire nineteenth century:

> . . . if at the moment Paris has been repressed, then I remind you that the battle in Paris is only a skirmish, the main engagement lies ahead of us, before long the battle cry of the Paris proletariat . . . will become the battle cry of the entire European proletariat.[6]

In the early seventies concern for social problems, engendered by an uneasiness about the consequences of industrial expansion and by a fear of social revolution, was given further impetus by Germany's political unification. As the Crown Prince noted in his diary in February, 1871: "The task when peace is concluded will be the solution of social questions."[7] Throughout German society men felt that the completion of the *Reichsgründung* liberated energies for the solution of internal problems. It was hoped that the relaxation of social tensions might be the domestic analogue to national unification.[8]

At the same time that economic progress, fear of revolution, and ideals of internal unity sensitized Germans to the need for reform measures, the initiative for social reform passed into the hands of three important groups in German society. In 1869 the hierarchy of both the Catholic and Protestant churches began to take a renewed interest in social reform and showed signs of transcending the prevailing *Caritas* tradition which we described in chapter 1.[9] Also, after 1870, socially-conscious individuals

---

[6] Quoted from a Reichstag speech by August Bebel on May 25, 1871, in Fritz Völkerling, *Der deutsche Kathedersozialismus* (Berlin, 1959), p. 15. For the impact of this speech on the conservatives, see H. Oncken, *Lassalle: Eine politische Biographie* (3d ed.; Stuttgart, 1920), p. 492.

[7] *Diaries of the Emperor Frederick*, ed. M. von Poschinger (London, 1902), p. 257.

[8] For example, see the speeches at the 1871 meeting of the Protestant "Inner Mission," quoted in W. Shanahan, *German Protestants Face the Social Question. Vol. I: The Conservative Phase, 1815–1871* (Notre Dame, 1954), p. 400, and Gustav Schmoller's speech in *Verhandlungen der Eisenacher Versammlung zur Besprechung der sozialen Frage* (Leipzig, 1873), p. 2.

[9] At the Fulda meeting of German bishops in 1869 it was decided that "the church must help solve the social question. . . ." Shanahan, *German Protestants*, p. 388, and Vigener, *Ketteler: Ein deutsches Bischofsleben des 19.*

began to assume important posts in the bureaucracy, thus beginning to form a nucleus within the administration which Bismarck would later use to implement his social program.[10] Most
significant for our purposes was the fact that in the late 1860's
and early 1870's a new generation of German academicians,
mainly professors of economics, began to publish important
works on social reform in Germany.[11]

Until the end of the sixties, the majority of German economists
did not appear overly interested in social problems.[12] This lack
of concern reflected the predominant position held in the academic study of economics by that highly abstract version of
laissez-faire liberalism which we have already observed in Helferich's lecture hall at Göttingen.[13] This economic liberalism

---

*Jahrhunderts* (Munich and Berlin, 1924), pp. 556 ff. A similar stand was
taken by the Protestants in 1871; see Shanahan, p. 398.

[10] In December, 1871, Theodor Lohmann wrote to a friend that "in government circles there is a consciousness of the necessity of doing something for
the workers and also the will to accomplish it." Quoted in H. Rothfels,
*Theodor Lohmann und die Kampfjahre der staatlichen Sozialpolitik* (Berlin,
1927), p. 26.

[11] The most important of the professors' contributions to the social question
were the following: Gustav Schmoller, *Zur Geschichte der deutschen
Kleingewerbe im 19. Jahrhundert* (1870); Brentano's *Arbeitergilden der
Gegenwart* (1871–72); Hans von Scheel, *Die Theorie der sozialen Frage*
(1871); Gustav Schönberg, *Arbeitsämter* (1871); and Adolf Wagner, *Rede
über die soziale Frage* (1871). For a further discussion of this literature see
Eugen Philippovich, "Das Eindringen der sozialpolitischen Ideen in die
Literatur," *Die Entwicklung der deutschen Volkswirtschaftslehre im neun-
zehnten Jahrhundert*, ed. S. Altmann (Leipzig, 1908), Vol. I, chap. 31; Hans
Gehrig, *Die Begründung des Prinzips der Sozialreform* (Jena, 1914); and H.
Berger, "Der Kathedersozialismus an der Universität Berlin in der Zeit von
1870 bis 1880," *Wissenschaftliche Zeitschrift der Universität Berlin, Gesell-
schafts- und sprachwissenschaftliche Reihe*, XI, No. 2 (1962), 309–32.

[12] In an interesting study of *The Origins of Social Liberalism in Germany*
(Chicago and London, 1963), Donald Rohr tried to demonstrate that there
was far greater interest in social reform among early nineteenth-century
German liberals than is usually maintained. Rohr demonstrates the depth
of this interest in men like von Mohl, Harkort, and Biedermann (pp. 121–
39, 147–54), but he does not succeed in proving that these men were
representative of the majority of German liberals.

[13] Philippovich, "Das Eindringen der sozialpolitischen Ideen," pp. 1–2;
Schraepler, *Quellen*, II, 5; and Brentano, *Mein Leben im Kampfe um die
soziale Entwicklung Deutschlands* (Jena, 1931), pp. 72–73. Hereafter cited
as *Mein Leben.*

received the support of a significant number of liberal politicians, journalists, and bureaucrats, until the mid-seventies.[14]

In the 1860's, however, students began to question the classical liberalism they found at the universities.[15] We have already seen how Brentano's reaction against this tradition led him to the British unions. Many of his contemporaries shared his conviction that liberal abstractions had little relevance for the urgent social problems of the present, and like him they searched for economic ideas more attune to the problems of an industrial Germany. However, most of Brentano's contemporaries sought their correctives to the errors of liberal economics, not in British developments, but in the historical school of economics, which had been coexisting with the dominant liberal tradition in German economics since the beginning of the century.

The historical tradition in German economics had been formulated in the early nineteenth century as a reaction against the Enlightenment.[16] Adam Müller, one of the first historical economists, attacked Adam Smith as an integral part of the Enlightenment and asserted an ethical, historical, and nationally-oriented view of economic phenomena against what he felt was the rationalistic, abstract individualism of Smith. Müller insisted that economics was not the struggle of individuals for profit, but was rather a spiritual matter which concerned the entire political community.[17] Later in the century Friedrich List restated the essentials of this critique of the classical economists without the romantic coloration Müller gave to his ideas. List,

---

[14] On Rudolf Delbrück, perhaps the best known of these liberal bureaucrats, see Rudolf Morsey, *Die oberste Reichsverwaltung unter Bismarck* (Münster, 1957), pp. 41 ff.

[15] For example, see Hans Hermann von Berlepsch, *Sozialpolitische Erfahrungen und Erinnerungen* (Mönchen-Gladbach, 1925), p. 16; Julius von Eckardt, *Lebenserinnerungen* (Leipzig, 1910), I, 271; and Gustav Schmoller, *Zur Geschichte der deutschen Kleingewerbe im 19. Jahrhundert* (Halle, 1870), pp. vi–vii.

[16] On the historical tradition in German economic thought, see Philippovich, "Das Eindringen der sozialpolitischen Ideen"; W. B. Cherin, "The German Historical School of Economics: A Study in the Methodology of the Social Sciences" (unpub. diss., Berkeley, 1933); and W. J. Fischel, "Der Historismus in der Wirtschaftswissenschaft dargestellt an der Entwicklung von Adam Müller bis Bruno Hildebrand," *Vierteljahrschrift für Sozial–und Wirtschaftsgeschichte*, XLVII, No. 1 (1960), 1–31.

[17] Fischel, "Der Historismus," p. 13.

like Müller, emphasized the national and historical basis of economic study.[18] This historical viewpoint penetrated the German universities at mid-century when, in the years between 1843 and 1853, Wilhelm Roscher (1817–94), Bruno Hildebrand (1812–98), and Karl Knies (1821–98) published important monographs which not only applied the ideas of Müller and List to academic economics, but also explored some of the methodological problems of the historical approach.[19]

Although Roscher, Hildebrand, and Knies had a decided impact on German economics, the advocates of a historical viewpoint remained a minority in Germany until the late 1860's, when the so-called young historical school began to form.[20] These men combined the historical orientation of Roscher, Hildebrand, and Knies with the ideas of Comte, Mill, and in some cases, Marx.[21] Furthermore, most of them were influenced by the account of contemporary French social theory which they found in Lorenz von Stein's influential works.[22] Perhaps most important, the "young historical school" was influenced by the fact that its members grew to intellectual maturity under the impact of the economic change, the fear of social unrest, and the ideals of domestic unification which we mentioned at the beginning of this chapter. The result was that the "young historical

[18] *Ibid.*, pp. 15–20.

[19] Wilhelm Roscher, *Grundriss zu Vorlesungen über die Staatswirtschaft* (Göttingen, 1843); Bruno Hildebrand, *Die Nationalökonomie der Gegenwart und Zukunft* (Frankfurt, 1848); Karl Knies, *Die politische Oekonomie vom Standpunkte der geschichtlichen Methode* (Braunschweig, 1853). For an analysis of the so-called older historical school, see M. Hüter, *Die Methodologie der Wirtschaftswissenschaft bei Roscher und Knies* (Jena, 1928); Cherin, "The German Historical School," pp. 1–34, and Fischel, "Der Historismus," pp. 21–29.

[20] Gehrig, *Begründung des Prinzips der Sozialreform*, pp. 139–62.

[21] For the intellectual influences on the historical school, see P. Anderson, "Gustav Schmoller," *Some Historians of Modern Europe*, ed. B. Schmitt (Chicago, 1933), pp. 420–42; F. Meinecke, "Drei Generationen deutscher Gelehrtenpolitik," in *Staat und Persönlichkeit* (Berlin, 1933). On Comte and the historicist tradition in Germany, see Ernst Troeltsch, *Der Historismus und seine Probleme* (Tübingen, 1922), pp. 390–420.

[22] Von Stein (1815–90) was an important influence on many of these young economists, particularly because of his *Der Sozialismus und Kommunismus des heutigen Frankreichs* (1842). See Philippovich, "Das Eindringen der sozialpolitischen Ideen," pp. 2–3, and H. Nitzschke, *Die Geschichtsphilosophie Lorenz von Steins* (Munich and Berlin, 1932), pp. 130–36.

school" accepted the historical economists' high regard for history and sought to use this historical approach to solve the problems of the present.

It is hardly surprising that these young economists sought an alternative to classical liberalism in the ideas of Müller, List, and Knies. The historical tradition's concern for empirical reality and its national orientation seemed far better equipped to solve the problems of German society than laissez-faire liberalism. Equally important, this tradition was much more in harmony with the spirit of the years of the *Reichsgründung* and with the entire temper of German intellectual life in the second half of the nineteenth century, which was increasingly permeated by historically and nationally directed disciplines.[23]

2 –

In the months after his return from England Brentano began to make contact with some of the younger economists in Germany.[24] In the fall of 1870, his book on *The History and Development of Gilds* was reviewed by a young professor from Halle, named Gustav Schmoller. Schmoller's almost unqualified praise for Brentano's work marked the beginning of a long and important friendship.[25] At the same time that Brentano was

[23] After 1850 both historical studies and jurisprudence developed attitudes towards history and the nation which now appeared in the "young historical school." Schmoller and his associates led German economics away from Anglo-French traditions and developed a "German school" with roots in the romantic and Hegelian movements. For a brilliant survey of this development in German intellectual history, see Heinrich Heffter, *Die deutsche Selbstverwaltung* (Stuttgart, 1950), pp. 349–72.

[24] Gustav Schmoller to Brentano, April 25, 1870, reprinted in W. Goetz, "Der Briefwechsel Gustav Schmollers mit Lujo Brentano," *Archiv für Kulturgeschichte*, XXVIII, No. 2 (1938), 320. Goetz published the correspondence between Schmoller and Brentano from 1870 to 1878 in the *Archiv*, XXVIII, No. 2 (1938), 316–54; XXIX, Nos. 1–2 (1938), 147–83; XXIX, No. 3 (1939), 331–47; and XXX, No. 1 (1941), 142–207. This will hereafter be cited as Goetz, plus volume and page number. When necessary, Goetz's version has been collated with the originals of Schmoller's letters to Brentano in the Brentano Papers. On Brentano's contact with his colleagues, see also Adolf Wagner to Brentano, April 27, 1870. Unless otherwise noted all unpublished letters are from the Brentano Papers.

[25] Schmoller's review was in the *Literarisches Centralblatt*, November 19, 1870. See Brentano to Schmoller, January 3, 1871, Goetz, XXVIII, 326.

beginning to make a name for himself in the German academic world, his view of the political situation in Germany was radically altered by the Franco-Prussian War. Early in 1870 he was still considering emigrating to England.[26] But for Brentano, as for many of his contemporaries, Prussia's impressive victory over France removed all doubt about the direction of Germany's future. By September, 1870, Brentano supported Bismarck and was outspoken in his enthusiasm for the Prussian victories.[27] He had made his peace with a Prussian-led Germany. As he wrote to his mother on January 17, 1871: "All of human history shows that everything which we call law, either in domestic or foreign affairs, is nothing but the formalization of existing power relationships."[28]

In the spring of 1871 Brentano joined the University of Berlin as a *Privat Dozent*. At the same time, the first volume of his *Arbeitergilden der Gegenwart* was published, and he was recognized as a member of the new generation of economists who were calling into question the principles of classical liberalism.[29] Before considering the details of Brentano's relationship with his German colleagues, it is necessary to analyze his intellectual position in 1871 with reference to the development of historical economics in Germany.

In examining the development of Brentano's ideas in the 1860's, we saw how he began to employ historical research in his attempt to find answers to the problems of social reform. We also saw that his interests in history was always subordinated to his desire to solve practical questions and to illuminate contemporary situations.[30] In comparison with most members of the

[26] John Ludlow to Brentano, January 8, 1870.

[27] John Ludlow expressed his dismay over the change in Brentano's attitude in a letter of September 5, 1870. The British liberals had been favorable to Prussia until the battle of Sedan, after which they became pro-French. On Ludlow's attitude, see N. C. Masterman, *John Malcolm Ludlow* (Cambridge, 1963), pp. 207–8.

[28] *Mein Leben*, p. 62. In the early seventies Brentano and his brother Franz quarrelled over the *Reichsgründung*. See Emilie to Lujo Brentano, January 10, March 12, 1871, Franz Brentano Papers. I am indebted to Professor Franziska Mayer-Hillebrand for this reference.

[29] See Gustav Schönberg's review of the first volume of the *Arbeitergilden*, *Zeitschrift für die gesamte Staatswissenschaft*, XXII, No. 4 (1871), 695–720.

[30] Brentano clearly expressed this view in a letter to Schmoller of May 4, 1878, Goetz, XXX, 191–93.

"young historical school," Brentano assigned historical method a subsidiary role in his research. More important, he did not share his colleagues' belief in the state's responsibility in solving social questions.[31] Brentano's early anti-Prussianism and his retention of a considerable portion of the liberal suspicion of state intervention set him apart from those followers of Müller and List whose enthusiasm for the state reflected their wholehearted participation in the *Reichsgründung*.[32] Finally, Brentano's view of the structure of economic action was significantly different from that of his colleagues. He retained an essentially liberal view of economics, in which the laws of supply and demand regulated conflicting interests. His notion of social reform did not imply a final reconciliation of these conflicting interests, but rather the creation of institutions like the unions through which economic conflict would be equalized and compromises could be encouraged. In contrast to this view, many of the young historical economists doubted that the conflict of economic interests was necessary and looked forward to the termination of these conflicts through state-initiated social action.[33]

Brentano uncovered the root of his differences with the "young historical school" when he wrote to Schmoller in 1878:

> I feel that your views would be different in many respects if you had lived for a longer time in a country [England] where you could have seen the great things freedom can accomplish, where you could have experienced the influence freedom can have on the character of a nation. . . .[34]

---

31 See Brentano's remarks on the state in the *Verhandlungen der Eisenacher Versammlung zur Besprechung der sozialen Frage*, p. 29. In the 1920's Brentano was given an honorary degree from the University of Manchester. His citation, which is in the Brentano Papers, credited him with "an almost English distrust of the state."

32 For example, see Schmoller's viewpoint on this subject in Anderson, "Gustav Schmoller," pp. 417 ff.

33 Schmoller, *Über einige Grundfragen der Sozialpolitik und der Volkswirtschaftslehre* (Leipzig, 1904), p. 68. On Wagner, see E. Thier, *Rodbertus, Lassalle, Adolf Wagner* (diss., Leipzig, 1930), pp. 69 ff. For a contrast between Brentano's views of industrial arbitration and those of Wagner and Schmoller, see J. Teuteberg, *Geschichte der industriellen Mitbestimmung in Deutschland* (Tübingen, 1961), pp. 285–86.

34 Brentano to Schmoller, November 4, 1878. Copy in the Brentano Papers.

Throughout most of his career, Brentano's regard for England, expressed in that synthesis of classical economics and trade unionism described in the last chapter, set him apart from the majority of his colleagues, whose social and economic views were formulated under the influence of very different traditions.

However important Brentano's disagreements with his contemporaries were to become in later years, in 1871 they were almost entirely concealed by what seemed to be broad areas of agreement. Most obviously, Brentano and his colleagues believed that social problems had to be solved within the existing social order. They shared a feeling of urgency in attaining a solution to these problems, both because they desired social justice and because they feared that the status quo might be destroyed by revolution. Brentano and his German contemporaries rejected a completely negative attitude towards government-sponsored social reform. Furthermore, although their programs differed considerably, most of the "young historical school" accepted Brentano's support for labor organizations and arbitration as one possible solution for social strife.[35]

In addition to this common concern for social justice and an elementary agreement as to how it might at attained, Brentano and his colleagues were held together by their common membership in the German academic community. Most German professors, like Brentano, came from families with wealth and social position. Their backgrounds and frequently their marriages connected them with the commercial, industrial, and agricultural elites of Germany.[36] Furthermore, the academic world was an exclusive and self-conscious community with an immense amount of social prestige. The German professor dominated the intellectual life of his nation far more than his western European

[35] Schmoller's address at Eisenach, *Verhandlungen*, pp. 78–95. Schönberg, *Arbeitsämter* (1871).

[36] Paulsen, *The German Universities*, pp. 128, 187. On the social composition of the German academic community see the data gathered by C. von Ferber in *Die Entwicklung des Lehrkörpers der deutschen Universitäten und Hochschulen, 1864–1954*, Vol. III of *Untersuchungen zur Lage der deutschen Hochschullehrer*, edited by H. Plessner (Göttingen, 1956), pp. 163–84. For an extremely critical picture of German academic life during the Second Empire, see Dieter Fricke, "Zur Militarisierung des deutschen Geisteslebens im Wilhelminischen Kaiserreich: Der Fall Leo Arons," *Zeitschrift für Geschichtswissenschaft*, VII, No. 5 (1960), 1069–1107.

counterparts and was ranked socially among the highest strata of society.[37] Most interesting for our purposes was the rather unique relationship between the German professor and his government. During the nineteenth century, bureaucratic control of the universities increased, and in most German states a separate department was set up for university affairs. Professors were selected by this department and were considered state officials.[38] This gave the state a considerable amount of control over the university and increased the political and social homogeneity of the faculties. Not even the most moderate socialist, for example, was allowed to hold a university chair.[39]

As professors, Brentano and the young historical economists were subject to these pressures for conformity, and it is indeed to their credit that they maintained a sympathy for the workers and an awareness of the interests of the lower classes. In one important respect, however, their perception of the full implications of the German social question was hindered by their membership in the German academic community. After 1871 most German professors shunned party politics. As one scholar put it: "He who devotes himself to the quest for truth cannot be a party man."[40] Most German academicians were convinced that it was impossible to reconcile political action with disinterested scholarship.[41] On one hand, this attitude reflected the concrete realities

37 Friedrich Paulsen, *The German Universities and University Study* (New York, 1906), p. 4. See also Golo Mann, "The Intellectuals: Germany," *Encounter*, IV, No. 6 (June, 1955), 42–49. For an indication of the continuing prestige of the academic world in contemporary Germany, see the figures given in K. M. Bolte, *Sozialer Aufstieg und Abstieg* (Stuttgart, 1959), pp. 30 ff.

38 Paulsen, *The German Universities*, pp. 74 ff., and F. Lilge, *The Abuse of Learning: The Failure of the German University* (New York, 1948), p. 19. Brentano once remarked that the Minister of Culture was "all powerful" in his control over the German university (*Mein Leben*, p. 282). It is interesting to note that although Brentano was often outspoken in his criticism of the Ministry's policies, he did not attack the principle of bureaucratic control. An example of this was his attitude during the famous Spahn controversy at the University of Strassburg, as described in K. Rossmann, *Wissenschaft, Ethik und Politik* (Heidelberg, 1949), especially p. 22.

39 Paulsen, *The German Universities*, pp. 105–6. See also the discussion of the Aron case in Fricke, "Zur Militarisierung des deutschen Geisteslebens."

40 Paulsen, *The German Universities*, p. 355.

41 One of the clearest examples of this attitude was Heinrich von Treitschke.

of imperial Germany: the quasi-authoritarian structure of the German state and the interest-group character of the German parties.[42] On the other hand, the attitude was the product of a long tradition in German intellectual life, a tradition with roots in the late eighteenth and early nineteenth centuries, when political life did not exist in Germany, and when the German intellectual could only participate in the affairs of his nation as the supplier of ideals or as an adviser to the king and bureaucracy. In the middle third of the century there were signs that German academicians had broken with this tradition. In the 1840's and 1850's "political professors" were in the vanguard of the liberal movement. However, with the defeat of the liberals' political program in the 1860's, the professors either left public life or confined their activity to the pursuit of national rather than domestic political ideals. It is one of the most significant facts of modern German history that after the founding of the Empire most German intellectuals reverted to the apolitical role they had played in the early nineteenth century. Indeed, non-participation in party politics became a virtue and even a prerequisite for authentic scholarly production.[43] The result was what Friedrich Meinecke once called the "gap between the political and the intellectual life of Germany." "The student of politics," Meinecke wrote, "has always remained outside of the real political life of the nation."[44]

The solutions for the social question offered by the members of the "young historical school" reflected this apolitical attitude. Gustav Schmoller, for example, wanted a socially-conscious bureaucracy, inspired and advised by professors like himself, which would guarantee social justice because of its neutral position above the parties. From a similar point of view, Adolf Wagner

---

See Andreas Dorpalen, *Heinrich von Treitschke* (New Haven, 1957), p. 229, and also the remarks in J. Knoll, *Führungsauslese in Liberalismus und Demokratie: Zur politischen Geistesgeschichte der letzten hundert Jahre* (Stuttgart, 1957), p. 18.

[42] See Theodor Schieder, "Die geschichtlichen Grundlagen und Epochen des deutschen Parteiwesens," *Staat und Gesellschaft im Wandel unserer Zeit* (Munich, 1958).

[43] For a few suggestive remarks on this attitude in German intellectual life, see W. Stark, *The Sociology of Knowledge* (Glencoe, Ill., 1958), pp. 7–8.

[44] F. Meinecke, "Drei Generationen deutscher Gelehrtenpolitik," p. 136.

hoped for a social monarchy that would protect the worker's interests.[45]

Brentano's acceptance of the apolitical posture of the German professors was conditioned by certain features of his intellectual make-up already apparent in 1869. His training and experience led him to employ essentially economic categories in his examination of social problems, and it was for this reason that the trade unions appealed to him. Throughout his career, Brentano continued to search for solutions to the social question that did not require parliamentary action. Furthermore, like his German colleagues, he came to regard party politics as incompatible with his scholarly search for truth.

We have already pointed out that the economic orientation of Brentano's thinking caused him to overlook the essential fact that the effectiveness of the British unions as a solution to the social question rested on a constitutional structure which Germany did not possess. His acceptance of the German academic community's apolitical attitude aggravated this weakness in his approach to German social problems. Brentano's union proposals, like Schmoller's reform-oriented bureaucracy and Wagner's social monarchy, left untouched some of the major sources of social discontent in Germany. Throughout the imperial era, social tensions were related to political and constitutional questions. These questions could only be confronted politically, and the attitude of many German professors towards politics, which Brentano came to share, made such a confrontation impossible.

### 3 —

By 1870, the academic social reformers in the "young historical school" began to realize that they belonged to a new generation of economists. During 1870 and 1871, many of them exchanged letters on the possibility of co-operative action on behalf of social reform.[46] In Berlin and in Leipzig, professors met to discuss how

---

45 C. Brinkmann, *Gustav von Schmoller und die Volkswirtschaftslehre* (Stuttgart, 1937), pp. 96, 99, and E. Thier, *Rodbertus, Lassalle, Adolf Wagner,* p. 73.

46 Gustav Schönberg to Gustav Schmoller, June 27, 1870; Adolf Wagner to Schmoller, November 20, 1870, cited in G. Wittrock, *Die Kathedersozialisten,* pp. 25, 81. See also Schmoller to Brentano, February 5, 1871, reprinted in Goetz, XXVIII, 329.

their common concern with social problems might have concrete effects.[47] In December, 1871, these tentative steps toward co-operative public action were given new impetus by a harsh attack on the "young historical school" published by the liberal jour-nalist Heinrich Oppenheim in the *Nationalzeitung*.[48]

In his article, Oppenheim referred to the socially-conscious professors as *Kathedersozialisten*, a term usually translated as "socialists of the chair," but perhaps more meaningfully ren-dered as "academic socialists." The label proved to be the most lasting part of Oppenheim's article; from that point on, Bren-tano and his colleagues were known as *Kathedersozialisten*. Un-doubtedly Oppenheim used the word "socialist" because he realized its polemical value. However, he also felt that these professors could be called socialists in a meaningful sense of the word: "We regard as socialists," Oppenheim wrote, "anyone who proposes a system of state action to solve the social question."[49] In this respect, he continued, no significant differences existed between the "beer hall" socialists and the academic reformers.[50] As another liberal journalist expressed the same point: "Zum Bebel und zum Liebknecht fehlt ihnen nur der Muth."[51] By putting the *Kathedersozialisten* in the same category with the socialist agitators, Oppenheim threw down a challenge the pro-fessors could not ignore and began the debate on a level of distortion and bitterness which it was never able to transcend.

Oppenheim's article expressed most of the criticisms which the so-called Manchester school would direct against the *Katheder-sozialisten* during the next two years. Although Oppenheim did not reject all forms of state-sponsored social reform, he regarded government intervention with suspicion.[52] Furthermore, he dis-trusted unions, although he was unwilling to recommend state

47 Wittrock, *Die Kathedersozialisten*, p. 90.
48 Oppenheim's article, entitled "Manchesterschule und Kathedersozialismus," was published on December 7, 1871. It is reprinted in Oppenheim's book, *Der Kathedersozialismus* (Berlin, 1872).
49 Quoted in Else Conrad, *Der Verein für Sozialpolitik und seine Wirksamkeit auf dem Gebiet der gewerblichen Arbeiterfrage* (Zurich, 1906), p. 37.
50 Oppenheim, *Der Kathedersozialismus*, p. 2.
51 "To be like Liebknecht and Bebel, they lack only courage." The remark was made by W. E. Eras and is quoted in N. Schüren, *Die Katheder-sozialisten und die Manchesteregoisten* (Leipzig, 1873), p. 24.
52 Oppenheim, *Der Kathedersozialismus*, pp. 34, 51–62.

action against them. Finally, he resented the academic social reformers' criticisms of the German business community, which he regarded as the chief source of German liberalism.[53] The debate on *Sozialpolitik* which began with Oppenheim's article was continued in other liberal papers such as the *Breslauer Zeitung* and the *Ostsee Zeitung* by journalists and politicians like Ludwig Bamberger, W. E. Eras, and Alexander Meyer.[54]

The main objects of the liberal attack were those *Kathedersozialisten* who held extreme statist views, men like Adolf Wagner and Hans von Scheel. Brentano was not mentioned in Oppenheim's article of December, 1871, but he considered himself obligated to defend his colleagues. He spent most of the month of December trying to find a periodical in Berlin that would accept his rejoinder to Oppenheim.[55] After having been refused by the *Nationalzeitung, Preussische Jahrbücher,* and *Das neue Reich,* his article was enthusiastically accepted by Julius von Eckardt, editor of the *Hamburger Correspondent,* whose views on the social question resembled Brentano's.[56] For the next two years von Eckardt was a close associate of the *Kathedersozialisten,* and his paper gives the best available chronicle of their side of the polemic.[57]

Brentano's article against Oppenheim in January, 1872, was the first of a series of polemics which he wrote against the German "Manchesterites" during the next two years.[58] In 1873, Brentano and Ludwig Bamberger exchanged critiques which

[53] Oppenheim, *Der Kathedersozialismus,* p. 45.

[54] On the debate, see H. Gehrig, *Die Begründung des Prinzips der Sozialreform, passim.*

[55] Brentano to Schmoller, December 10, 1871, Goetz, XXIX, 340.

[56] Brentano published his answer to Oppenheim, "Abstrakte und realistische Volkswirte," in the *Correspondent* of January 11, 1872. On Brentano's relationship with Eckardt, see *Mein Leben,* p. 76, and Eckardt, *Lebenserinnerungen,* I, 272. Both of these accounts are incorrect about the first meeting of the two men, which took place in December, 1871. See Brentano to Schmoller, December 31, 1871, Goetz, XXIX, 342.

[57] For example, see the following *Correspondent* articles: "Der Freihandel und die soziale Frage," April 13, 1872; "Die Freiheit der Wissenschaft und die 'liberale' Volkswirtschaft," May 9, 1872; and G. Schönberg, "Die Polemik der Freihandel-Schule," June 7 and 8, 1872.

[58] A typical example of Brentano's polemics against the liberals was his exchange with Alexander Meyer in the *Breslauer Zeitung* of November and December, 1872, reprinted in *Über Einigungsämter* (Leipzig, 1873).

exemplified the tone of the debates between liberals and *Kathedersozialisten*. According to Bamberger, Brentano's work on the unions,

. . . oscillated between a romanticized defense of the thousand little privileges of the old guilds and wild proposals for a complete reorganization of society in the style of a most audacious innovator.[59]

Brentano found the work on the labor question in which Bamberger criticized the *Arbeitergilden* "an amusing attempt to create an impression with unlimited superficiality and really astonishing ignorance."[60]

In spite of the acidity of this exchange, the differences between Brentano and his opponents were largely matters of emphasis rather than principle. For example, Brentano shared the liberal's commitment to the view of a free economy subject to the laws of the market. He did, however, believe that unions could improve the workers' condition within such a structure.[61] Bamberger argued that proposing unions to cure social ills was like prescribing medicine for an incurable disease, since economic phenomena were governed by rigid natural laws.[62] Brentano attacked this viewpoint from two directions. First, he repeated his arguments against the wages fund theory, demonstrating that real wages could be increased through collective bargaining.[63] Second, he made some studies of the beneficial effect of actual wage increases on the performance of workers.[64]

In the last analysis, perhaps the most important issue dividing Brentano and Bamberger was their assessment of the character of

[59] Ludwig Bamberger, *Die Arbeiterfrage unter dem Gesichtspunkte des Vereinsrechtes* (Stuttgart, 1873), p. 62.

[60] Brentano, *Die "wissenschaftliche" Leistung des Herrn Ludwig Bamberger* (Leipzig, 1873), p. 72.

[61] At one point Brentano wrote that "the underlying difference between myself and the liberals is a difference with regard to the possibility of effective manipulation of economic life." *Ibid.*, p. 53.

[62] Ludwig Bamberger, Theodor Barth, and Max Broemel, *Gegen den Staatssozialismus* (Berlin, 1884), p. 10.

[63] Brentano, "Zur Lehre von den Lohnsteigerungen," *Zeitschrift für die gesamte Staatswissenschaft*, XXXII (1876), 466–78.

[64] *Mein Leben*, p. 106, and Brentano's pamphlet, *Über das Verhältnis von Arbeitslohn und Arbeitszeit zu Arbeitsleistung* (Leipzig, 1876).

the German working class. Brentano, largely because of his experiences with the British unions, regarded the German labor movement as potentially moderate and respectable. Perhaps Bamberger drew his image of the workers from his experiences in 1848, when the lower classes either broke with their bourgeois leaders and became radical social revolutionaries or joined with the forces of reaction against the revolution. In any case, Bamberger argued that Brentano's unionism might work in England, but that the German workers were far less trustworthy than their British counterparts. To allow them to organize was to endanger the social order.[65] This distrust of the workers was an important source of Bamberger's pessimism over the possibility of social improvement.

Brentano countered these accusations against the German workers by pointing out that England had also had a revolutionary, anti-state, working-class movement in Chartism. He felt that the Chartists, like the German Social Democrats, wanted to overthrow the existing order. They had collapsed when the British middle classes granted them their just demands.[66] Brentano argued that the German workers turned to socialism only because the liberal parties refused to consider the workers' needs. He promised a reconciliation of workers and Reich on the basis

---

[65] Bamberger, *Die Arbeiterfrage*, pp. 14–15. A more extreme expression of the increasing distrust of the working classes can be found in the work of Heinrich von Treitschke, who joined the attack on the *Kathedersozialisten* in 1874. Treitschke's arguments were not based on doctrinaire liberalism, but rather on his conviction that society was inevitably aristocratic. As such, his opposition to social reform adumbrated the views expressed by men like Baron von Stumm after 1890. On Treitschke's polemic with Schmoller and Brentano, see A. Dorpalen, *Heinrich von Treitschke*, pp. 198 ff.; Brentano's letters to Schmoller of July 6, 21, and September 28, 1874, Goetz, XXIX, 332–35; Treitschke to Brentano, February 28, March 11, 1874; and Brentano to Treitschke, October 30, 1876 (Brentano Papers). Treitschke's views are reprinted in his *Zehn Jahre deutscher Kämpfe* (Berlin, 1897). For Treitschke's position in the development of German attitudes towards the social question, see J. Knoll, *Führungsauslese in Liberalismus und Demokratie*, p. 117, and the excessively hostile remarks by Jürgen Kuczynski in *Die Geschichte der Lage der Arbeiter unter dem Kapitalismus*, I, Part II, 269–77.

[66] Brentano, "Die englische Chartistenbewegung," *Preussische Jahrbücher*, XXXIII, Nos. 5 and 6 (1874), 431–47, 531–50.

of the existing social order if the liberal parties would support the necessary social reforms.[67]

One of the most remarkable features of the polemics between Brentano and the German "Manchester" school was the disparity between the issues involved and the bitterness of tone and harshness of style. To explain this, it is necessary to look beyond the issues of state intervention and unions and consider the context within which the polemic developed.

The main burden of the attack on the *Kathedersozialisten* was borne by men from the left wing of the National Liberal Party: Oppenheim, Bamberger, Eras, Meyer, and others. These men represented the economic interests in Germany—mainly finance and banking—which had the most to lose from a revision of the Reich's liberal economic policies. Bamberger, for example, had been a highly successful banker during his years of exile after 1848, and he retained some of his connections with the banking establishment.[68] Moreover, there was an important political reason why these liberals defended classical economics and opposed social reform. They regarded the writings of the *Kathedersozialisten* as the beginning of an alliance between the workers and the conservatives. They feared that this alliance would be based on state-sponsored social reform and would be directed against the economic and political achievements of the bourgeoisie.[69] This specter of a conservative–worker alliance had

[67] Brentano, "Die liberale Partei und die Arbeiter," *Preussische Jahrbücher*, XL, No. 1 (1877), 112–22.

[68] On Bamberger, see Walter Bussmann, "Zwischen Revolution und Reichsgründung: Die politische Vorstellungswelt von Ludwig Bamberger," *Schicksalswege deutscher Vergangenheit*, ed. W. Hubatsch (Düsseldorf, 1950), pp. 203–33; W. Kelsch, *Ludwig Bamberger als Politiker* (diss., Berlin, 1933); Hermann Oncken, "Ludwig Bamberger," *Preussische Jahrbücher*, C (1900), 63–94. On the left wing of the National Liberal party, see the following: L. Krieger, *The German Idea of Freedom* (Boston, 1957), p. 347; Ludwig Maenner, "Deutschlands Wirtschaft und Liberalismus in der Krise von 1879," *Archiv für Politik und Geschichte*, IX, No. 11 (1927), 357–60; G. Franz, "Der Parlamentarismus," *Jahrbuch der Ranke Gesellschaft*, III (1957), 89; E. Schraepler, "Die politische Haltung des liberalen Bürgertums im Bismarckreich," *Geschichte in Wissenschaft und Unterricht*, V, No. 9 (September, 1954), 529–44.

[69] Oppenheim, *Der Kathedersozialismus*, pp. 2–3, 44; Bamberger, *Die Arbeiterfrage*, p. 11; and *Aus Eduard Laskers Nachlass*, ed. W. Cahn (Berlin, 1902), pp. 81–82.

been present in the liberal consciousness since the failure of the revolution of 1848. It was kept alive in the 1860's and early 1870's by occasional indications that Bismarck was willing to consider such an anti-liberal coalition.

This fear of a conservative–worker reconciliation was probably increased after 1870 by the liberals' awareness of the precariousness of their own alliance with Bismarck, a fact made clear by the government's opposition to liberal demands in the debate over the military budget, which had ended in a liberal defeat just a few days before Oppenheim's first anti-*Kathedersozialisten* article.[70] Only within this context of tension and insecurity does the bitterness of the liberal attack on the academic social reformers become understandable. Only in such an atmosphere could a man of Bamberger's intelligence regard so innocuous a book as Brentano's *Arbeitergilden* as "pure class-hatred propaganda."[71]

Just as the bitterness of the liberal attack on the *Kathedersozialisten* cannot be understood without reference to the condition of German liberalism in the early seventies, so the character of Brentano's response must be seen in the light of his intellectual and professional situation. If there were real points at issue between the liberals and some of the right wing *Kathedersozialisten,* we have said enough to show that the differences between Brentano and his liberal opponents were rather slight. We have argued that Brentano was harshly condemned by men like Oppenheim and Bamberger because the tensions of their political position produced a feeling of insecurity which caused them to react with vigor against the slightest disagreement. Obviously, Brentano's response to the liberals was conditioned by the vigor of their attack. At the same time, however, his reaction can also be viewed as reflecting some tensions within his own career in the early seventies. In the winter of 1872 Brentano was called to Breslau as a professor *extraordinarius* of economics. Breslau was one of the centers of "Manchester" liberalism in Germany, and the young professor was subjected to repeated attacks from the

70 Wittrock, *Die Kathedersozialisten,* pp. 124–25, and G. Stoltenberg, *Der deutsche Reichstag 1871–1873* (Düsseldorf, 1955), pp. 81–82.
71 Bamberger to Eduard Lasker, September 26, 1872, reprinted in P. Wentzke, *Deutscher Liberalismus im Zeitalter Bismarcks. Vol. II: Im neuen Reich* (Bonn and Leipzig, 1926), p. 60.

liberal press, which he had to face more or less without his colleagues' support. The intensity of these attacks probably caused Brentano to become increasingly belligerent in his response.[72] Furthermore, as an *extraordinarius*, he was one step below a full professor. This academic inferiority, together with the continued liberal attacks, seems to have made Brentano somewhat insecure and hypersensitive. It is worth noting that the year 1873, the time of his bitterest polemic against Bamberger, was also the time during which he seemed to be the most overwrought and pessimistic about his academic future at Breslau.[73]

Although these irritating features of his life in the early seventies may have increased Brentano's willingness to engage in public debates, there were also some rather more permanent factors which contributed to his penchant for polemic. First, he was an epistemological optimist. His few methodological statements during the early years of his career stressed the fact that, given the proper method and the proper attitude, the truth was available to all men. Obviously, the primary question such a theory of knowledge suggests is why then do men so often disagree? Brentano was sometimes willing to explain disagreements in terms of faulty method, but more often he felt that those who failed to see the logic of his position did so because their motives were impure. Throughout his career, Brentano charged that his opponents fell into error because they represented some selfish interests which distorted their view of reality. He regarded himself as a disinterested observer who was obliged to defend with moral vigor the results of his detached, scholarly search for truth.[74]

Secondly, the source of Brentano's polemical attitude must be considered in the light of his political position in Germany. As we have seen, Brentano felt vitally interested in social problems and was convinced that solutions to these problems must be

---

[72] *Mein Leben*, pp. 85–86; and Brentano to Schmoller, December 3, 1872, Goetz, XXIX, 149.

[73] See Brentano's letters to Schmoller during 1873, Goetz, XXIX, 159–76.

[74] On Brentano's method, see his *Arbeitergilden der Gegenwart* (Leipzig, 1872), II, 308–39, and his later views in *Wie studiert man Nationalökonomie?* (Munich, 1911).

found. At the same time, his attitude toward political action, aggravated by the political structure of the German Empire, deprived him of any direct influence on public affairs.[75] Perhaps Brentano poured into his publications and academic activities the passions that in some nations could be canalized into political activity. As one of his students has written: "Lujo Brentano addressed his classes as he would have political meetings and they responded with cheers and countercheers."[76] This politization of his scholarly activities may well have added to the intense and sometimes frenetic quality of Brentano's polemics.

Perhaps this point can be illustrated by considering for a moment the polemic which Brentano had with Karl Marx in 1872. Ninety years later, one is struck by the triviality of the issue involved—in this case the proper wording of a quotation by Gladstone. One is also struck, however, by the curious similarity of tone and style displayed by these two most different of men. Perhaps this similarity reflected the fact that both men spent their lives absorbed by practical problems, yet both of them had to seek in the passion of their theoretical quarrels some consolation for their exclusion from the world of practical achievements.[77]

The next chapter will be concerned with the efforts of Brentano and his colleagues to find a means through which they could exert some influence on the internal development of imperial Germany. The failure of these efforts must be kept in mind to explain the vigor with which Brentano debated issues which he could not influence.

---

[75] Perhaps the classic statement of the political frustrations of the German professor is the testament of the great historian Theodor Mommsen: " . . . in the deepest part of my being and what I can call the best that is in me, I have always been an *animal politicum* and have wanted to be a citizen. That is not possible in our nation. . . ." Reprinted in A. Heuss, *Theodor Mommsen und das 19. Jahrhundert* (Kiel, 1956), p. 282.

[76] J. Schumpeter, *A History of Economic Analysis* (New York, 1953), p. 802. Ludwig Curtius makes a similar point in *Deutsche und antike Welt: Lebenserinnerungen* (Stuttgart, 1951), p. 125.

[77] *Mein Leben*, pp. 56–57, and the collection of Brentano's articles against Marx, *Meine Polemik gegen Karl Marx* (Berlin, 1890).

# CHAPTER IV

# The "Verein für Sozialpolitik" and the Problem of Scholarship and Politics 1872-1879

## 1 —

In the first months of 1872 the so-called *Kathedersozialisten* began to consider some form of collective action in their debate with the liberals. By the spring of that year the conflict had been extended until almost all of the "young historical school" were included. The polemic reached a high point in March and April when Oppenheim attacked Adolf Wagner, and the latter answered in an embittered, anti-Semitic pamphlet.[1] In May, 1872, Julius von Eckardt wrote to Wagner and suggested that the most prominent social reformers get together privately to consider an anti-liberal counter-offensive.[2] Wagner accepted Eckardt's proposal and began at once to secure support from his colleagues. When he wrote to ask Schmoller's help on May 20, Wagner could already count on the agreement of Brentano, Ernst Engel, and Gustav Schönberg.[3]

---

[1] A. Wagner, *Offenen Brief an Herrn H. B. Oppenheim* (Berlin, 1872); G. Wittrock, *Die Kathedersozialisten bis zur Eisenacher Versammlung 1872* (Berlin, 1939), pp. 137–40; E. Conrad, *Der Verein für Sozialpolitik und seine Wirksamkeit auf dem Gebiet der gewerblichen Arbeiterfrage* (Zurich, 1906), pp. 42–44. Hereafter cited as Conrad, *Verein*.

[2] J. von Eckardt, *Lebenserinnerungen* (2 vols.; Leipzig, 1910), I, 274, and Wittrock, *Die Kathedersozialisten*, p. 165.

[3] Conrad, *Verein*, p. 56. See also F. Boese, *Geschichte des Vereins für Sozialpolitik 1872–1932*, *Schriften des Vereins für Sozialpolitik* (Berlin, 1939), CLXXXVIII, 2–3.

The leading *Kathedersozialisten* met in Halle on July 13 and 14, 1872. Besides Brentano, Schmoller, Wagner, and Eckardt, Bruno Hildebrand, Wilhelm Roscher, Georg Friedrich Knapp, and others attended.[4] Schmoller, who had been a professor at Halle since 1864, assumed the role of host. At thirty-four, Schmoller was one of Germany's most promising young economists. In contrast to the eloquence and ardor with which Brentano presented his ideas, Schmoller was reserved and soft-spoken. He avoided polemic whenever possible and always stood ready to conciliate his more quarrelsome colleagues. It was at the Halle meeting that Schmoller's qualities of leadership first became apparent. The finesse with which he handled both allies and opponents made him the natural leader of the *Kathedersozialisten,* a position he was to enjoy almost until his death in 1917.[5]

The main result of the Halle meeting was the decision to call a larger meeting at Eisenach in the fall, where like-minded professors, bureaucrats, and businessmen could formally discuss the social problems of the day. The feeling at Halle was that if it proved successful, the Eisenach convention could lead to a more permanent organization. The Halle meeting laid down two criteria for participation in the Eisenach gathering: an interest in *Sozialpolitik* and a disavowal of extreme laissez-faire liberalism.[6]

There is very little evidence to suggest what kind of an organization the men at Halle hoped would develop from the Eisenach convention. Both Schmoller and Brentano evidently wanted an organization which would educate German public opinion on social problems and, if possible, provide information and inspiration for the Reichstag.[7] There were, however, certain

---

4 Conrad, *Verein,* p. 57, and Boese, *Geschichte des Vereins,* p. 3.

5 On Schmoller, see the remarks in Eckardt, *Lebenserinnerungen,* I, 278, and Franz Eulenburg, "Zur Erinnerung an Gustav Schmoller und Adolf Wagner," *Historische Vierteljahrschrift,* XIV, No. 3 (1919–20), 430–38. For a brief account of Schmoller and the *Verein,* see A. Ascher, "Professors as Propagandists: The Politics of the *Kathedersozialisten," Journal of Central European Affairs,* XXIII, No. 3 (October, 1963), 282–302. Ascher emphasizes the *Verein's* attitudes towards foreign policy.

6 Conrad, *Verein,* p. 57. The invitation to Eisenach was reprinted in the *Hamburger Correspondent* on September 7, 1872.

7 In his memoirs Eckardt argued that Brentano and Schmoller clashed at Halle over the procedure and purpose of the Eisenach meeting. Eckardt sug·

differences between Brentano and Schmoller already apparent at Halle. In contrast to Brentano, Schmoller wanted to work with as large a group as possible, even if significant disagreements existed.[8] Moreover, unlike Brentano, he seems to have been opposed to having the Eisenach meeting take definite stands on controversial issues. Thus, in the months preceding Eisenach, Schmoller resisted Brentano's efforts to have printed resolutions delivered beforehand to the participants in order to facilitate their taking a position on the points discussed. It was only when he saw how moderate Brentano's resolutions actually were that he agreed to have them printed.[9]

For Brentano, the most important issue at Halle seems to have been the role Adolf Wagner was to play in any future organization of the *Kathedersozialisten*. Wagner was the most conservative of Brentano's colleagues. His solution for social problems consisted almost exclusively of state intervention. Unlike Brentano, Schmoller, and the other members of the "young historical school," Wagner had an essentially unhistorical, statistical view of economics. Furthermore, he was outspoken, even vicious, in dealing with those who disagreed with him. Thus, Wagner and Brentano combined differences of opinion and a similarity of polemical temperament that made a clash between them almost unavoidable.[10] At Halle, Wagner seems to have been isolated,

---

gested that Brentano wanted a vigorous, political organization while Schmoller wanted a purely scholarly body. From the other available evidence it would appear that Eckardt is rather overstating the position of both men at Halle. *Lebenserinnerungen*, I, 275. See Brentano, *Mein Leben im Kampfe um die soziale Entwicklung Deutschlands* (Jena, 1931), pp. 73, 93. Hereafter cited as *Mein Leben*. On the similarity of their views, cf. Brentano's statement to Frederic Harrison in a letter of March 2, 1873 (Harrison Collection, London School of Economics), and Schmoller's remarks to Wilhelm Roscher, reprinted in *Briefwechsel zwischen Wilhelm Roscher und Gustav Schmoller*, ed. W. Biermann (Greifswald, Germany, 1922), p. 23.

8 Schmoller to G. F. Knapp, December 21, 1872, quoted in Wittrock, *Die Kathedersozialisten*, p. 214.

9 See Brentano's and Schmoller's correspondence in September, 1872, reprinted in W. Goetz, "Der Briefwechsel Gustav Schmollers mit Lujo Brentano," *Archiv für Kulturgeschichte*, XVIII, No. 2 (1938), 351–54, and XXIX, No. 1–2 (1939), 147. Hereafter cited as Goetz with volume and pages.

10 Wittrock, *Die Kathedersozialisten*, p. 148. On Wagner, see the remarks in *Ferdinand Tönnies-Friedrich Paulsen Briefwechsel* (Kiel, 1961), p. 15, and the rather extreme account in E. Clark, "Adolf Wagner: From National Economist to National Socialist," *Political Science Quarterly*, LV, No. 3

and his attempts to galvanize his colleagues into a group agitating for monarchial socialism were largely ignored. Wagner left Halle deeply annoyed at the treatment he had received and without enthusiasm for future co-operation.[11] Schmoller eventually succeeded in soothing his feelings and in gaining his support for the Eisenach meeting, but Wagner never overcame his feeling of alienation from the other *Kathedersozialisten*.[12] He finally lost interest in the activities of his colleagues and by the late 1870's was involved in Adolf Stoecker's Christian Social Movement, a vehicle for social action more congenial to his political views and his temperament.

The gathering planned at Halle took place on October 6 and 7, 1872.[13] The speeches at the Eisenach convention expressed in rather moderate terms the program of the academic social reformers. In a speech on factory legislation, Brentano called for some state regulations of the working conditions of women and children. He concluded his address by asking those present to support measures which would enable the workers to build their hopes for the future on the basis of the existing social order.[14] In his speech on unions, Schmoller defended the labor organizations and called for sympathy and understanding for the workers' demands.[15]

The most interesting remarks at Eisenach were contained in Schmoller's introductory address. "Since most of us are scholars," Schmoller began, "and we usually stand far removed from public life, we must justify why we have called together this distin-

(September, 1940), 378–411. A recent article by an East German historian also concentrates on Wagner's career: H. Berger, "Der Kathedersozialismus an der Universität Berlin in der Zeit von 1870 bis 1880," *Wissenschaftliche Zeitschrift der Universität Berlin, Gesellschafts- und sprachwissenschaftliche Reihe*, XI, No. 2 (1962), 309–32.

11 *Mein Leben*, p. 78, and Brentano to Schmoller, August 1, 1872, Goetz, XXVIII, 346. Wittrock, *Die Kathedersozialisten*, pp. 169 ff., rather overdramatizes Wagner's isolation and makes him a victim of a plot between Brentano and Schmoller. It seems more likely, however, that Wagner's ideas simply did not reflect the opinion of the group.

12 Wittrock, *Die Kathedersozialisten*, p. 174.

13 *Verhandlungen der Eisenacher Versammlung zur Besprechung der sozialen Frage am 6. und 7. Oktober 1872* (Leipzig, 1873). See also *Mein Leben*, p. 79; Conrad, *Verein*, pp. 58 ff., and Boese, *Geschichte des Vereins*, p. 7.

14 *Verhandlungen*, p. 28.

15 *Ibid.*, pp. 78–95.

guished assembly." He then spoke of the deep gap between rich and poor in Germany which introduced the distant but unmistakable danger of social revolution. In the face of this danger, Schmoller continued, men have come to doubt the absolute validity of liberal economics. At the same time, the *Reichsgründung* had created a state to which all Germans could turn for leadership in the search for social peace and progress. In this situation, the function of the Eisenach meeting was to find a way to further social reform by educating the public and by influencing legislation. "What we seek here," Schmoller said, "is a basis for the reform of our social conditions and a general agreement for ideas which have been frequently expressed, but which have still not found acceptance by the public."[16]

Schmoller neglected to mention, however, how such a "basis for the reform of our social conditions" was to be achieved. The failure to apply any criteria for participation in the Eisenach meeting other than an interest in social reform and disavowal of laissez faire meant that men from every part of the political spectrum attended. Schmoller tried to avoid serious disagreements by insisting that the proper subjects for discussion were not questions of principle but concrete reform proposals.[17] The notion that men as far apart politically as, for example, Wagner and Brentano, could discuss concrete proposals without reference to questions of principle seems rather farfetched. Furthermore, the Eisenach convention was discouraged by its organizers from voting on any questions raised by the speakers. This measure was quite obviously a palliative, which perhaps obscured the tremendous differences of opinion at the meeting, but added little to a feeling of equanimity. Also, the lack of formal voting detracted from any collective influence the convention might have had on German public life. Schmoller summed up the significance of the Eisenach meeting rather better than he intended when he wrote to a friend: "Discussion is to be our major concern."[18]

In fact, the major achievement of the Eisenach congress was the perpetuation of its own ambiguities of organization and purpose. In May, 1873, an Executive Committee elected at

16 Schmoller's speech is reprinted in his *Zur Sozial- und Gewerbepolitik der Gegenwart: Reden und Aufsätze* (Leipzig, 1890), pp. 2 ff.
17 *Ibid.*, p. 3.
18 Biermann, ed., *Briefwechsel*, p. 22.

Eisenach set up an organization which came to be called the *Verein für Sozialpolitik*.[19] This organization became the forum for the *Kathedersozialisten,* and although its direct influence on German politics was negligible, the *Verein* did play a central role in the academic and intellectual life of imperial Germany.

The most immediate effect of the Eisenach congress and the formation of the *Verein* was to clarify the *Kathedersozialisten*'s debate with the liberals. The first liberal reaction to Eisenach was quite critical. The meeting was attacked in the liberal press and the idea persisted that the professors were in some way the secret accomplices of Bismarck in an anti-capitalist, anti-bourgeois alliance.[20] The existence of the *Verein* alleviated some of the fears upon which the liberal attack was based, however, and after a few months a gradual process of reconciliation between the *Verein* and the liberal's *Kongress deutscher Volkswirte* began.[21] This process started when Rudolf Gneist, an active member of the *Kongress,* was elected chairman of the *Verein.* Although Gneist resigned after only two years, his presence in the *Verein* probably served to quiet some of the liberals' distrust.[22] More important than Gneist's role in the *Verein* was the fact that the *Verein* almost unanimously rejected the ideas of those men who openly advocated a conservative-proletarian alliance. At the Eisenach meeting, Rudolf Meyer, editor of the conservative *Berliner Revue,* was bitterly criticized by the majority of participants. In 1874 Meyer and Hermann Wagener were sent by Bismarck to observe the *Verein*'s annual meeting. When they were prevented from exercising any influence on the proceedings, they left completely disillusioned.[23]

---

[19] Conrad, *Verein,* pp. 62 ff. For the statutes of the *Verein,* see *Schriften des Vereins für Sozialpolitik* (Leipzig, 1874), IV, 121 ff.

[20] *Mein Leben,* pp. 80, 93; von Eckardt, *Lebenserinnerungen,* I, 283; Conrad, *Verein,* pp. 61–62; and Schmoller to Brentano, November 12, 1872, Goetz, XXIX, 148.

[21] On the *Kongress,* see L. Krieger, *The German Idea of Freedom* (Boston, 1957), pp. 407–13.

[22] Boese, *Geschichte des Vereins,* pp. 16–17, and Wittrock, *Die Kathedersozialisten,* pp. 211–14.

[23] On Meyer at Eisenach, see von Eckardt, *Lebenserinnerungen,* I, 279; Karl Rodbertus, *Briefe und socialpolitische Aufsätze,* ed. R. Meyer (Berlin, n.d.), p. 246, and *Verhandlungen der Eisenacher Versammlung,* pp. 98–102. On his role in 1874, see *Mein Leben,* p. 97; K. Feibelmann, *Rudolf Hermann Meyer: Ein Beitrag zur politischen Ideengeschichte des neunzehnten Jahr-*

At the same time that the *Verein* was expressing its hostility to the "social conservatives," closer co-operation with the *Kongress* was discussed. At the end of the *Verein* meeting in 1874, Ernst Engel proposed that a committee be set up to negotiate with the liberals about some form of co-operation. The membership voted to turn the matter over to the Executive Committee.[24] In the months after the 1874 meeting, members of the *Verein* and *Kongress* discussed possible ways in which they might end their quarrels and achieve some sort of collaboration.[25] Brentano furthered this cause in a series of letters to Eduard Lasker, a political ally of Bamberger and Oppenheim, who had never allowed himself to become involved in the polemics against the *Kathedersozialisten*.[26] In October, 1875, the Executive Committee of the *Verein* accepted an agreement with the *Kongress,* and it was decided that each organization would hold its meeting in alternate years so that men could belong to both organizations. Neither organization was willing, however, to sacrifice its independent existence.[27]

Co-operation was almost destroyed when Bamberger attacked the *Kathedersozialisten* in a Reichstag speech on January 7, 1876.[28] Bamberger apologized, however, and in accordance with the agreement, *Verein* members attended the *Kongress* meeting in 1876, and some *Kongress* members came to the 1877 *Verein* meeting.[29]

---

*hunderts* (Würzburg, 1933), p. 82; R. Meyer, "Bericht über den Kongress des Vereins für Sozialpolitik im Jahre 1874," *Die Zukunft*, XII (August, 1895), 395–406; and Brentano to Schmoller, October 16, 1874, Goetz, XXIX, 335. In 1875 Meyer returned to the *Verein* alone and was completely ignored; see *Schriften des Vereins*, XI (Leipzig, 1876), 6–14.

[24] *Schriften des Vereins für Sozialpolitik* (Leipzig, 1875), IX, 151–56.

[25] *Mein Leben*, p. 95.

[26] P. Wentzke, *Deutscher Liberalismus im Zeitalter Bismarcks* (2 vols.; Bonn and Leipzig, 1925–26), II, 137 ff. and 143–44, reprints the correspondence between Schmoller, Lasker, and Brentano for 1875 and 1876.

[27] *Mein Leben*, p. 96, and Conrad, *Verein*, pp. 75–78. See also Brentano to Schmoller, May 12, 1875, Goetz, XXX, 142–43.

[28] *Stenographische Berichte über die Verhandlungen des deutschen Reichstages*, 2d Legislative Period, 3rd Session, Vol. II (Berlin, 1876), pp. 960–64. Brentano to Schmoller, January 28, January 30, 1876, Goetz, XXX, 151, 154–55.

[29] See A. Held, "Der volkswirtschaftliche Kongress und der Verein für Sozialpolitik," *Schmollers Jahrbuch*, I, No. 1 (1877), 159–77, and "Die

By 1876, therefore, the polemic between the liberals and the *Kathedersozialisten* was over. Their co-operation proved fruitless, however, because after 1876 the attention of socially-conscious Germans was turned away from the debates of professors and journalists toward the practical measures that were beginning to take shape in the Chancellor's office. By the time the liberals terminated their agreement with the *Verein* in 1881, both sides had forgotten their earlier polemics and were engaged in a reappraisal of their own ideas in the light of an axial shift in German domestic politics.

## 2 —

The agreement with the liberals in 1876 proved to be a mixed blessing for the *Verein*. When the liberal attacks ceased, the *Verein* lost the common enemy which had been its chief source of unity.[30] After 1876 Brentano and his colleagues were far more willing to bring to the surface the differences within their own ranks. Furthermore, at the same time that the agreement with the *Kongress* made the members of the *Verein* more conscious of their disunity, this disunity was accentuated by the changes which were taking place in the German political scene during the late 1870's.

The year 1876 marked a turning point in Brentano's role in the debate over *Sozialpolitik* in Germany. During the early seventies, when he was publicly battling extreme liberals like Bamberger, and when he was faced with what seemed to be a consistently liberal government economic policy, Brentano stressed the revisions he had made in his own liberal viewpoint, such as his advocacy of unions, factory legislation, and so on.[31]

fünfte Generalversammlung des Vereins für Sozialpolitik zu Berlin am 8.–10. Oktober 1877," *ibid.*, No. 4 (1877), pp. 791–802; Brentano to Schmoller, October 30, 1876, Goetz, XXX, 164.

[30] For Brentano's views on the divisions within the *Verein*, see *Mein Leben*, pp. 82–84. See also G. Wittrock, *Die Kathedersozialisten*, p. 3, and H. Gehrig, *Die Begründung des Prinzips der Sozialreform* (Jena, 1914), pp. 207–8.

[31] In 1873 Brentano seems to have come closest to his colleagues' view of the state; in that year he wrote to Schmoller that the question of state intervention did not interest him as long as there was social progress. However, one suspects that even at this high point of co-operation with the "young historical school," he was rather overstating his apathy to state intervention. See Goetz, XXIX, 155.

The end of the debate with the "Manchesterites" and a tendency on the part of the government to abandon its laissez-faire policies caused Brentano to reaffirm his belief in the values of a free economy and reawakened in him his distrust of all extensive state action. This change in Brentano's viewpoint after 1876 is rather characteristic of his intellectual development: at no time did he renounce or abandon his earlier views, but instead subtly changed the emphasis of his work from social reform to economic freedom.[32]

The first sign of a shift in the government's attitude toward social reform came in 1876 when Rudolf Delbrück, the leading exponent of economic liberalism within the bureaucracy, resigned from government service.[33] In April, 1876, one of the first overt steps was taken in Bismarck's social program by the passage of a new insurance law.[34] The most significant aspect of this law was the concept of compulsory coverage upon which Bismarck's later program was to be based. The law prescribed that the individual must be insured, but gave him the choice of belonging to a privately-owned but government-approved fund [Kasse] or to a government fund administered on the local level.[35]

Although it was impossible for Brentano to perceive the full implications of the insurance law of April, 1876, he did grasp the significance of the compulsory insurance principle. He attacked this principle in an article published early in 1877, in which he

[32] In the later seventies Brentano was frequently accused of having changed his mind about social questions. He always denied these charges. See, for example, "Die Arbeiter und die Produktionskrisen," *Schmollers Jahrbuch*, II, No. 3 (1878), 566–67. Hereafter cited as "Produktionskrisen."

[33] E. Eyck, *Bismarck: Leben und Werk* (Erlenbach-Zurich, 1944), III, 190.

[34] The most complete work on Bismarck's social program is Walther Vogel, *Bismarcks Arbeiterversicherung: Ihre Entstehung im Kräftespiel der Zeit* (Braunschweig, 1951). See also H. Rothfels, *Theodor Lohmann und die Kampfjahre der staatlichen Sozialpolitik* (Berlin, 1927), and Rothfels' article, "Bismarck's Social Policy and the Problem of State Socialism in Germany," *Sociological Review*, XX, Nos. 1 and 3 (January and July, 1938), 81–94, 288–302; both of these works give a highly positive view of Bismarck's efforts within the context of his social thought. For a more critical interpretation, see E. Eyck, *Bismarck*, III, *passim*.

[35] Vogel, *Bismarcks Arbeiterversicherung*, pp. 21–23. The law is reprinted in Brentano, *Die Arbeiterversicherung gemäss der heutigen Wirtschaftsordnung* (Leipzig, 1879). This book will be hereafter cited as *Arbeiterversicherung*.

formulated for the first time the argument that he was to employ against Bismarck's insurance plans for the next four years.[36] Brentano began this article with a historical account of the problem of worker protection. As in the *Arbeitergilden,* the main purpose of this historical background was to prepare the way for his conclusions concerning the problem at hand. Brentano argued that his examination of past systems of worker protection showed that in order to be effective these systems had to correspond to the contemporary economic order.[37] The present economic order, he continued, is based upon the principle of freedom, a principle which would be violated by compulsory insurance. The result of this law would actually be to leave the worker in a weaker position than before: he was to be compelled to make premium payments, while his ability to pay, that is, his employment, was to be subject to the changes of a free market.[38] Thus, if the worker lost his job, he was in danger of losing all of the benefits from his previous payments simply because he could no longer keep up his premiums.

Brentano's hostility to the insurance law of 1876 came in part from his dislike of government interference with the free economy. An equally important source of his opposition, however, was his realization that this insurance scheme might severely hamper the development of unionism in Germany. In the first place, he saw that the danger of losing his benefit payments would make the worker extremely reluctant to engage in strikes. Second, the existence of government-operated insurance funds would provide serious competition for the unions' own welfare programs, which, Brentano felt, were at the very core of their existence.[39]

Just as in the *Arbeitergilden,* Brentano tried to show that unionism provided a far better answer to social problems than government action. Unions, he maintained, were able to give the necessary insurance protection to the workers within a free economic system. As in his earlier works, he pointed to the

---

[36] Brentano, "Gewerbeordnung und Unterstützungswesen," *Schmollers Jahrbuch,* I, No. 3 (1877), 471–501.

[37] *Ibid.,* pp. 472–84.

[38] *Ibid.,* p. 495.

[39] *Ibid.,* pp. 498–99. For the effect of this law on the unions, see J. Reindl, *Die deutsche Gewerkschaftsbewegung* (Altenberg, 1922), p. 59.

British unions as the proof for his conviction that unionism allowed a synthesis of freedom and security.[40] Brentano was particularly impressed by the fact that the British unions, unlike the German government's plan, provided unemployment insurance as well as sickness and disability benefits.

Brentano's insistence that any insurance scheme include unemployment compensation among its benefits undoubtedly came not only from his high regard for the British unions but also from the unemployment prevalent in Germany as a result of the depression of 1873.[41] Brentano examined this question in an article called "The Workers and Production Crises," which he published in 1878.[42] He regarded depressions as primarily the result of overproduction due to a shift in demand. He accepted such crises as an inevitable part of a free economy in which the consumer may shift his demand for goods without regard for the supply. Furthermore, he doubted that depressions could be avoided in a planned economy because of the tendency of human nature to buy and sell unpredictably.[43]

Brentano restated his position on insurance in a book entitled *Worker Insurance According to the Contemporary Economic Order,* which was published in 1879.[44] In this book Brentano, like Bamberger and Oppenheim earlier in the decade, directed his critique against socialists of both right and left. He argued that Lassalle, Mehring, and Adolf Wagner were all equally wrong in their common demand for a planned economy.[45] Brentano agreed with these men that the worker's present position was extremely insecure and that security was an essential part of any solution to the social question.[46] However, he felt that security could be given the worker without surrendering economic freedom, which was one of the "basic principles of all

40 *Ibid.,* p. 490.
41 For the impact of the depression on Germany, see H. Rosenberg, "Political and Social Consequences of the Great Depression of 1873–1896 in Central Europe," *Economic History Review,* XIII (1943), 58–73.
42 Brentano, "Produktionskrisen."
43 *Ibid.,* p. 575. For a critique of Brentano's views from a Marxist standpoint, see J. Kuczynski, *Studien zur Geschichte der zyklischen Überproduktionskrisen in Deutschland 1873–1914* (Berlin, 1961), pp. 171 ff.
44 Brentano, *Arbeiterversicherung,* as cited above, n. 35.
45 *Ibid.,* p. 15.
46 *Ibid.,* pp. 17–19.

of modern public life."[47] After examining all the existing forms of insurance and pronouncing them to be ineffective, Brentano concluded by pointing to the effective insurance system in British unions and by calling upon the German workers to form trade unions on the English model. It is worth noting that in 1879 he realized the weakness of existing German unions, but felt an authentic German movement was still possible. As in the *Arbeitergilden*, he emphasized his conviction that such a movement had to grow spontaneously and could not be imposed by the government.[48]

In the months following the publication of Brentano's book on social insurance, the direction of Bismarck's legislation became increasingly clear.[49] In 1881, when some of the most important measures had already been proposed and when government opposition to liberal economics was explicitly stated,[50] Brentano gave his defense of a free economic system its most extreme formulation. In a book on the insurance laws published in that year, he essentially repeated his earlier plea for unemployment coverage and the free economic order.[51] In this work Brentano made his antipathy toward government intervention much more explicit. By this time he seems to have realized that Bismarck's compulsory, state-directed insurance plan was only one facet of an extension of government control over economic life:

> It is simple to summarize what the fulfillment of all [Bismarck's] measures will mean: The economic life of every individual will be inexorably caught up in the life and development, the action and impulses of the state, and the individual will be dependent upon the rule of bureaucracy.[52]

Brentano felt that such a concentration of power in the hands of the state was harmful in itself and was also dangerous because it tempted the worker to gain economic control by seizing political

47 *Ibid.*, p. 90.
48 *Ibid.*, pp. 222–23.
49 Vogel, *Bismarcks Arbeiterversicherung*, chap. 11.
50 On Bismarck's relationship to the liberal parties, see O. Quandt, *Die Anfänge der Bismarckischen Sozialgesetzgebung und die Haltung der Parteien* (Berlin, 1938), pp. 31–44 and 73–74. Quandt's usefulness is greatly impaired by his National Socialist outlook.
51 *Der Arbeiterversicherungszwang, seine Voraussetzungen und seine Folgen* (Berlin, 1881), pp. 66–67.
52 *Ibid.*, p. 94.

power. Whether such a course led to socialism of the left or of the right, he predicted that its result would be disastrous.[53]

Brentano's increased emphasis on economic freedom inevitably led to disagreements with the more conservative members of the *Verein*. In an earlier chapter his views of the state and of the nature of economic activity were contrasted with those of his colleagues. Beginning in 1876, at the precise moment when the *Verein* no longer faced a common enemy, Bismarck's new domestic policies provided an issue through which Brentano's differences with his colleagues might be brought to the surface.[54]

In 1877 Brentano rejected an invitation to co-operate on a new periodical with some of the more conservative members of the *Verein*.[55] In that same year he echoed the liberal criticism of the early seventies when he characterized Adolf Wagner and some of the other conservative *Kathedersozialisten* as being "closest to the Social Democrats" because they advocated state control of the economy.[56] In 1878 Brentano's relationship with Wagner, never a very friendly one, was broken off because Brentano expressed his agreement with an article directed against Wagner's views in the liberal *Nationalzeitung*.[57]

The most significant of Brentano's changing relationships in the late 1870's was his friendship with Gustav Schmoller. Because the two men were bound by ties of personal affection, we can observe their intellectual differences gradually taking shape without the polemical bitterness that usually marked Brentano's disagreements. Furthermore, because Schmoller was the most influential—indeed, almost the paradigm—of the "young historical school," an analysis of Brentano's critical dialogue with him is extremely helpful in making clear Brentano's relationship to this intellectual movement.[58]

---

53 *Ibid.*, pp. 107–8.
54 On the differences in the *Verein*, see above n. 30, and E. Philippovich, "Das Eindringen der sozialpolitischen Ideen in die Literatur," *Die Entwicklung der deutschen Volkswirtschaftslehre im neunzehnten Jahrhundert*, ed. S. Altmann (Leipzig, 1908), I, 49.
55 Brentano to a journalist named Golomek, December 9, 1877. Unless otherwise noted all unpublished letters are in the Lujo Brentano Papers.
56 Brentano to E. Lasker, July 9, 1877.
57 Brentano to Schmoller, April 11, 1878, Goetz, XXX, 188; Wagner to Brentano, April 5 and 8, 1878, and a draft of Brentano's reply of April 6, 1878.
58 Schmoller had a great deal of influence in the Ministry of Education and was able to exert a significant amount of control over academic appoint-

In the early seventies Brentano and Schmoller were not only close personal friends, but also considered themselves to be in essential agreement on social and economic questions.[59] Their disagreements emerged in the later seventies for a variety of reasons. In the first place, the end of the polemics in which they had closely co-operated removed a bond of unity.[60] An equally important reason was the fact that before the middle of the decade both Brentano and Schmoller held rather ambivalent views on *Sozialpolitik* and economic freedom. We have already mentioned how until 1876 Brentano stressed the ways in which he had modified his liberal outlook. By the same token, in the early seventies Schmoller retained some liberal elements in his thought.[61] However, around the middle of the decade, Schmoller and Brentano both began to shift the emphasis in their ideas: as Brentano became more liberal, Schmoller became more conservative.[62]

Schmoller first clarified some of the characteristics of his thought in an article significantly entitled "The Social Question and the Prussian State."[63] This article contained two of the essential elements in Schmoller's view of society and economics, both of which lay at the basis of his differences with Brentano. First, he showed a marked distrust for the effects of both political and economic freedom. Schmoller did not actually deny the

---

ments, which he tended to use in favor of those who agreed with his general point of view. This fact rather increases Schmoller's value as a typical member of the "young historical school." See F. C. Lane, "Some Heirs of Gustav von Schmoller," in *Architects and Craftsmen in History: Festschrift für Abbott Payson Usher*, ed. J. Lambie (Tübingen, 1956), p. 10.

59 *Mein Leben*, p. 82. Brentano to Schmoller, February 4, 1871, Goetz, XXVIII, 327. On October 19, 1872, Brentano wrote to his friend Alfred Boretius that he felt he and Schmoller agreed on most matters.

60 It is clear that the polemics of the early seventies created a strong tie between them. See, for example, Schmoller's defense of himself and of Brentano, reprinted in *Über einige Grundfragen der Socialpolitik und der Volkswirtschaftslehre* (Leipzig, 1904), pp. 14 ff.

61 C. Brinkmann, *Gustav Schmoller und die Volkswirtschaftslehre* (Stuttgart, 1937), pp. 44, 66.

62 Brentano and Schmoller were both conscious of this development: Brentano to Lasker, July 9, 1877; and Schmoller to Brentano, April 21, 1878, Goetz, XXX, 189–90.

63 "Die Sozialfrage und der preussische Staat," reprinted in *Zur Social- und Gewerbepolitik der Gegenwart* (Leipzig, 1890), pp. 37–63.

value of parliamentary government or of economic freedom, but he did warn that they frequently led to the exploitation of the weak by the strong.[64] Freedom, as Schmoller wrote elsewhere, doesn't matter; progress does.[65] Second, in this article he clearly stated for the first time that the bureaucracy was the agency best suited to mediate between various conflicting interests in society. Schmoller pictured the monarch and his bureaucrats as the professional representatives of the state and as the "only neutral element in the conflict of social classes." This neutrality enabled them impartially to settle social and economic disputes.[66]

Brentano reacted to this article by pointing out that his friend was rather overestimating the value of the modern German bureaucracy. He suggested that Schmoller had "perhaps been influenced too much by the image of the bureaucracy in the days of Friedrich Wilhelm I."[67] Any further disagreement was averted, however, by the polemic between Schmoller and Treitschke which began in 1874. Brentano actively supported Schmoller's defense of social reforms in this polemic and was therefore not inclined to pursue their differences.[68] Nevertheless, when he sent a copy of Schmoller's article to Lasker in the fall of 1875, he felt obliged to note that whereas he and Schmoller agreed on economic matters, the latter attached greater value to the role of the state.[69]

In October, 1876, Brentano finished a book entitled *Labor Relations and Contemporary Law*.[70] This work was supposed to be a restatement of his earlier ideas and was published in lieu of a second edition of the *Arbeitergilden*.[71] However, it reflected Brentano's increasing emphasis on the necessity of defending the existing free economic order. Now Brentano stressed even more

[64] *Ibid.*, pp. 49–50; Brinkmann, *Schmoller*, p. 82.
[65] Schmoller, *Über einige Grundfragen*, p. 68.
[66] Schmoller, "Die Sozialfrage und der preussische Staat," p. 62; Brinkmann, *Schmoller*, p. 97, correctly emphasized the importance of this statement.
[67] Brentano to Schmoller, January 16, 1875, Goetz, XXIX, 342.
[68] On the debate, see Schmoller, *Über einige Grundfragen*, pp. 1–211, and A. Dorpalen, *Heinrich von Treitschke* (New Haven, 1957), pp. 198–203. See above, chap. 3, n. 65.
[69] Brentano to Lasker, November 21, 1875, reprinted in P. Wentzke, *Deutscher Liberalismus*, II, 138–39.
[70] *Das Arbeitsverhältnis gemäss dem heutigen Recht* (Leipzig, 1877). Hereafter cited as *Arbeitsverhältnis*.
[71] *Mein Leben*, p. 100.

than he had in 1871 that his support for the unions came from the fact that only through unions could the free economy be preserved and social justice guaranteed.[72]

Brentano wrote to Schmoller that "the best thoughts in [this book] belong to you," and sent him a copy.[73] Schmoller delayed commenting on the work for almost three months and finally gave his opinion at the end of January, 1877.[74] This letter first brought the differences between the two men out into the open.[75] Schmoller filled his letter with repeated praise but made clear his disagreement on two important points. In the first place, he objected to the fact that a book entitled "Labor Relations and Contemporary Law" should be concerned almost exclusively with British trade unions.[76] As Schmoller wrote somewhat later: "You don't have our time as a whole in mind, but always solely British developments, which appear to you to be the ideal and from which you deduce."[77] Secondly, Schmoller felt the book was too dogmatic and protested that Brentano frequently defended his position merely by showing it to be compatible with abstract liberal principles.[78]

Despite Brentano's efforts to avoid deepening the rift between them, Schmoller restated his criticisms of Brentano's views in July, 1877.[79] In August they met in Strassburg, where they seem to have had some success in reconciling their differences.[80] Within a year, however, their quarrel was renewed. This time the occasion was Brentano's break with Adolf Wagner. Schmoller defended Wagner and hinted that Brentano's hostility toward him came from the increasing "Manchesterite" tendency of Bren-

---

[72] *Arbeitsverhältnis,* p. 340.

[73] Brentano to Schmoller, October 30, 1876, Goetz, XXX, 165.

[74] Schmoller to Brentano, January 28, 1877, Goetz, XXX, 152–54. Goetz incorrectly dated this letter January 28, 1876.

[75] *Mein Leben,* p. 101.

[76] Schmoller to Brentano, January 28, 1877, Goetz, XXX, 152.

[77] Schmoller to Brentano, December 29, 1878.

[78] Schmoller to Brentano, January 28, 1877, Goetz, XXX, 153. See also *Mein Leben,* pp. 102–3.

[79] Schmoller to Brentano, July 13, 1877, Goetz, XXX, 153. Schmoller's remarks were directed against Brentano's article on "Die liberale Partei und die Arbeiter," *Preussische Jahrbücher,* XL, No. (1877), 112–22.

[80] See the letters from August and September, 1877, reprinted in Goetz, XXX, 180 ff.

tano's own thought.[81] By the fall of 1878 their disagreement had been heightened by their differences over Bismarck's insurance program. Schmoller supported all aspects of Bismarck's new internal policy: the tariff, the insurance laws, even the anti-Socialist bill.[82] Since he was becoming increasingly convinced that the state was the proper vehicle for social reform, Schmoller regarded Brentano's defense of the liberal economic order as both unhistorical and dogmatic.[83] In his reply to these charges Brentano called the Prussian state bureaucracy "organized brutality" and pointed to the dangers of government control. "I love freedom too much," Brentano wrote, "to see it destroyed by either socialist or absolutist despotism."[84]

In November, 1878, Brentano and Schmoller exchanged a series of letters in an effort to get to the root of their disagreement.[85] In this exchange, the issues which divided them were clearly exposed: their views of the state, of Prussia, of liberalism, and of the importance of the liberal model. Schmoller, a bureaucrat's son and a loyal supporter of the *Reichsgründung*, saw these issues very differently than Brentano did.[86] After these letters Brentano and Schmoller spoke less and less about their differences. They realized that their friendship was threatened and they endeavored to avoid a permanent rupture. They were not, however, ever able to return to the warmth of their cooperation of the early seventies. A hint of distrust began to cloud

---

81 Schmoller to Brentano, April 21, 1878, Goetz, XXX, 190.

82 For Schmoller's views on the tariff, see his address to the *Verein* in 1879, *Verhandlungen von 1879, Schriften des Vereins* (Leipzig, 1879), XVI, 19–20; Schmoller's view of the insurance program is analyzed in W. Vogel, *Bismarcks Arbeiterversicherung*, pp. 71 ff.; on his judgment of anti-Socialist measures, see J. Elberskirch, *Die Beurteilung des Sozialismus durch die historische Schule der Nationalökonomie* (diss., Cologne, 1930), pp. 77–78. For Schmoller's evaluation of Bismarck's entire career, see his *Charakterbilder* (Munich and Leipzig, 1913).

83 Schmoller to Brentano, November 2, 1878, Goetz, XXX, 202–7.

84 Brentano to Schmoller, November 4, 1878, from a copy in the Brentano Papers.

85 See the letters of November 2 and 4, 1878, cited in nn. 83 and 84, and Schmoller to Brentano, November 11, 1878. For the two men's later views on these letters see Brentano in *Mein Leben*, pp. 96–98, and Schmoller, "Lujo Brentano zum 70. Geburtstag," *Schmollers Jahrbuch*, XLI, No. 1 (1915), 365–70.

86 This point is stressed by Brentano in *Mein Leben*, pp. 98–99.

Brentano's relationship with Schmoller in the 1880's.[87] When Schmoller gave an unfavorable review to a book by one of Brentano's students in 1887, Brentano delivered a scathing reply, and their correspondence was broken off for several years.[88]

3 —

Brentano's debate with Schmoller was part of a general crisis which emerged within the *Verein für Sozialpolitik* after 1876. As we have described it, the *Verein* combined elements of both a scientific and a political organization. In its requirements for membership and in its procedure, the *Verein* resembled an academic society. At the same time, however, many members hoped that it would have some effect on German public life. Issues of contemporary importance were scheduled for discussion, and after the initial meeting members were allowed to vote on resolutions presented at the end of each formal address. In 1873 there was even talk of dispatching a committee to present these resolutions to the Reichstag.[89] This combination of scholarly and political aspect provided the framework for the conflict within the *Verein* in the late 1870's, when Bismarck's legislation created the issues which brought the political differences within the organization to the surface. By 1879 it was no longer possible for the *Verein* to continue to synthesize its scholarly and agitational characteristics.

As late as June, 1878, Brentano and Schmoller agreed that despite obvious differences of opinion among the members, there remained broad areas of agreement upon which future work could be based.[90] In the following months it became increasingly clear that they had rather underestimated the strength of the divisive factors. Because of the arrangement made in 1876 with the *Kongress deutscher Volkswirte,* the *Verein* did not meet in

---

87 John Ludlow to Brentano, March 12, 1885.

88 Schmoller, "Lujo Brentano zum 70. Geburtstag," and *Mein Leben,* pp. 134–35; see below, chap. 5.

89 *Schriften,* IV, 49. It should be noted that a significant number of the *Verein's* members never were interested in seeking practical influence. In 1874, for example, the voting on resolutions was almost abandoned because so few members remained to participate. *Schriften,* IX, 135.

90 Schmoller to Brentano, June 13, 1878, and Brentano's reply, June 15, 1878, Goetz, XXX, 196. A similar feeling was expressed by Adolf Held in a letter to Brentano on June 17, 1878.

1878. This lapse prolonged the illusion of unity by making it possible to avoid a debate on the anti-Socialist laws. The *Verein*'s Executive Committee tried to side-step the entire issue by communicating to the members that it was the business of the *Verein* to seek positive reforms, not to consider such questions as police tactics against Socialists.[91] This refusal to take a stand on the anti-Socialist legislation is an indication of the increasing narrowness of the *Verein*'s conception of *Sozialpolitik,* as well as of that lack of political awareness which we have already pointed to as a major weakness in the *Kathedersozialisten*'s approach to social questions.

The *Verein* could not avoid a debate on the question of tariff policy, which was quickly coming to the center of public attention in 1878. The Executive Committee set a meeting for the spring of 1879, because the customary autumn date would have fallen after the Reichstag's discussion of the tariff.[92] This decision suggests that the leaders of the *Verein* retained the hope that their deliberations would influence the legislators in Berlin, a hope that undoubtedly encouraged those who wanted the *Verein* to play a more active role in current affairs. In any case, the members recognized the importance of the issue, and even during the preparation for the gathering there were indications that the debate on the tariff would be more vigorous than at any earlier meeting.

The problem of free trade versus protectionism served to crystallize the political divisions within the *Verein.* As early as 1877, conservatives and liberals, supporters and opponents of Bismarck, seized this issue as the one over which they were prepared to air their differences.[93] In 1879 the protectionists grouped around Schmoller who, as usual, was supporting the government's policies. The advocates of free trade were led by Ernst Nasse, who had replaced Gneist as the *Verein*'s chairman.[94] Unfortunately, we have no evidence on Brentano's posi-

---

91 Conrad, *Verein,* p. 67, and F. Boese, *Geschichte des Vereins,* p. 32. Brentano seems to have rather exaggerated the importance of this episode, *Mein Leben,* p. 122.

92 Conrad, *Verein,* pp. 68 ff., and Boese, *Geschichte des Vereins,* pp. 34 ff.

93 *Schriften des Vereins* (Leipzig, 1878), XIV, 123 ff.

94 On Nasse, see Boese, *Geschichte des Vereins,* pp. 34–35. Schmoller stated his views in a letter to Brentano of March 29. 1879.

tion, since a serious illness prevented him from taking part in the debate.

As anticipated, the meeting of April, 1879, was long and stormy. The debate was heated and the speakers were frequently interrupted by shouts of disagreement or encouragement. In short, the *Verein* seemed to have lost its scholarly restraint and to be on the verge of developing into a political organization. After hours of speeches and seemingly endless debate, the meeting ended with a narrow and rather inconclusive victory for the protectionists.[95]

The bitterness engendered at the 1879 meeting provided the impetus for a reconsideration of the form and function of the *Verein*. This reconsideration was furthered by the feeling among many members that the initiative for *Sozialpolitik* in Germany had now been assumed by Bismarck, whose policies would be determined without reference to the divided and equivocal opinions of the *Verein*. Nasse delayed for a full year after the debate on the tariff before calling a meeting of the Executive Committee. At this meeting it was decided that the *Verein* would turn to questions of less contemporary political significance. In a communication announcing a meeting for the fall of 1881 the committee stressed that the *Verein* was abandoning agitation and would henceforth concentrate on the publication of scholarly monographs and the detached consideration of practical issues. In his opening address to the 1881 meeting, Nasse emphasized this scholarly orientation, adding that the *Verein* should confine itself to providing the legislator and bureaucrat with accurate information. The *Verein,* Nasse cautioned, should be an organization devoted to the promotion of "discussions of the problems of *Sozialpolitik* which would be objective, scholarly, and as independent as possible from the conflict of parties and interests."[96] It was also decided that resolutions could no longer be

---

95 The minutes of the meeting are reprinted in *Schriften des Vereins für Sozialpolitik*, XVI (Leipzig, 1879). See also Boese, *Geschichte des Vereins*, pp. 37–41; Conrad, *Verein*, p. 68; and *Mein Leben*, p. 112.

96 *Verhandlungen von 1881, Schriften des Vereins für Sozialpolitik* (Leipzig, 1882), XXI, 1–3. Boese, *Geschichte des Vereins*, p. 44, and Conrad, *Verein*, p. 69. Brentano noted this shift in a letter to his brother, April 27, 1881 (Franz Brentano Papers). See also the letters from Nasse to Brentano, March 7, 1881, and October 12, 1884.

submitted to the *Verein* for approval. Voting would be confined to questions of organization and procedure.[97]

The debate over the tariff in 1879 marked a clear turning point in the history of the *Verein*. Thereafter, the scholarly aspects of the organization were emphasized. The annual meetings became less important and more attention was devoted to the monographs published in the *Schriften des Vereins für Sozialpolitik*.[98] At the same time, the preponderance of professors in the *Verein* increased.[99] In the years after 1879 the *Verein*'s greatest significance came to be its role in the life of the German academic community.[100]

The *Verein*'s popularity among German academicians can be explained in terms of the professors' attitude towards politics, which we have already described. Although membership engendered a certain sense of involvement in contemporary affairs, it did not require commitment to a coherent program or action which might interfere with the scholar's highly valued detachment. Once political action was regarded as incompatible with scholarship, there remained nothing political for scholars to do but talk, and hope that someone with power would listen. That is precisely what was done in the *Verein* for the next half century. As Schmoller put it: "We have never required allegiance to a social program from our members. We soon gave up voting. We have had faith that . . . through the power of truth and justice we could have wide effects."[101]

Although there is very little information on Brentano's view of

[97] *Schriften*, XXI, 3.

[98] More than forty years later, when the *Verein* again faced a crisis in development, Heinrich Herkner recalled the great significance of the shift of emphasis in the 1880's. *Verhandlungen von 1922, Schriften des Vereins* (Munich and Leipzig, 1923), CLXIII, 86.

[99] L. Seyffardt, *Erinnerungen* (Leipzig, 1900), p. 269, and G. Wittrock, *Die Kathedersozialisten*, p. 185.

[100] See H. St. Marc, "Étude sur l'Enseignement de l'Économie politique dans les Universités des Pays de la langue Allemande," *Revue d'Économie Politique* (1892), VI, 439. Conrad, *Verein*, pp. 74–75. See also A. Oncken, "New Tendencies in German Economics," *Economic Journal*, XI, No. 35 (September, 1899), 468–69; W. B. Cherin, "The German Historical School of Economics" (unpub. diss., Berkeley, 1933), p. 21.

[101] *Zwanzig Jahre deutscher Politik (1897–1917): Aufsätze und Vorträge* (Munich and Leipzig, 1920), p. 24. For Schmoller's views on the differences between scholarship and agitation see Brinkmann, *Schmoller*, p. 11.

the transformation of the *Verein* in 1879, there is some indication that he was rather dissatisfied with its purely scholarly orientation.[102] In later years, he frequently blamed Schmoller for having changed the *Verein* from a practical organization into an academic society for the education of bureaucrats.[103] It is important to note, however, that he had no real alternatives to offer. The combination of practical activity and scholarship, which the *Verein* failed to institutionalize, was in fact a conflict Brentano was unable to resolve in his own career.

Brentano had been concerned about the relationship between practical activity and scholarship from the outset of the *Verein*. Just a few days after the Eisenach meeting of 1872 he published an article entitled "The Point of Departure and Lasting Principles of the So-called *Kathedersozialisten*."[104] Here he first formulated what proved to be the underlying tension in the *Verein* and in his own career:

> Before Eisenach the *Kathedersozialisten* were a scientific school, now they are, according to many, a party. For not a few people the word party has an unpleasant sound. People ask, how can scholars be true to their science if they constitute themselves as a party?[105]

The goal of scholarship, Brentano continued, is the ruthless pursuit of truth, but a party must represent special interests which would inhibit this search. Brentano accepted the dichotomy between scholarship and party politics and he made no attempt to reconcile the two. Instead he tried to assure his readers that the *Kathedersozialisten* would never allow anything to impede their devotion to the truth.[106]

Eight years later Brentano again expressed his thoughts on the scholar and politics. The occasion was an article by Schmoller

---

102 This is suggested by Ernst Nasse in a letter to Brentano of October 12, 1884.

103 *Mein Leben,* pp. 93, 122. Brentano expressed the same idea in a eulogy he wrote of Schmoller, which, as far as I know, has never been published (Brentano Papers).

104 "Der Ausgangspunkt und die dauernde Grundlage der sogenannten Kathedersozialisten," *Hamburger Correspondent,* November 10, 1872.

105 *Ibid.*

106 A further indication of Brentano's attitude can be found in the introduction to his *Arbeitergilden der Gegenwart* (Leipzig, 1871), I, xvii.

entitled "Science, Party Principles and the Practical Goals of German Politics."[107] In this essay Schmoller offered his view of the scholar's relationship to the world of political action:

> Like the chorus in Greek tragedy, [science] should not act, rather it should stand away from the center of the stage, guide the actors by its observations and measure their action according to the highest ideals of the time.[108]

Brentano attacked Schmoller's choice of a metaphor rather than its meaning, by showing the various contradictory and unenlightened positions taken by the chorus in Greek plays,[109] and he offered his own model from ancient drama:

> The role of science should be that of the seer Tiresias, who measures the character's action according to principles derived from the complete development of things. . . . Like Tiresias, science should base its advice, not on ideals—that is, men's wishes—but on the will of gods—that is, on laws derived from a study of the nature of things. . . .[110]

Brentano does not seem to have realized that Tiresias was perhaps superior to the chorus in his foreknowledge, but that like it, his unwillingness to act put him at the mercy of events. Neither Brentano nor Schmoller could solve the problem of how the intellectual and the practical, the scholarly and the political were to coexist and interact. Unhappily, this was a failure shared by almost their entire generation in the German academic community.

In a manner significantly analogous to the development of the *Verein*, Schmoller resolved the tension between scholarship and politics in his own career by narrowly limiting the scope of his political involvement. Perhaps one of the reasons for the unusual placidity of Schmoller's academic activity was the fact that he was able to fit his political views into his total view of social reform. As we have mentioned, he came to view the bureaucracy as the proper vehicle for social action. He conceived of his role (and

---

107 Schmoller, "Die Wissenschaft, die Parteiprinzipien und die praktischen Ziele der deutschen Politik," reprinted in *Zur Social- und Gewerbepolitik der Gegenwart: Reden und Aufsätze* (Leipzig, 1890), pp. 183–203.
108 *Ibid.*, p. 192.
109 *Mein Leben*, pp. 113–14.
110 *Ibid.*, p. 114.

that of the entire *Verein*) as one of gradually accumulating the necessary facts and making this data available to the appropriate bureaucrats.[111]

Brentano was neither temperamentally nor intellectually suited for an approach to social reform as gradual and indirect as Schmoller's. Unlike Schmoller, he was not satisfied with slowly amassing facts; he wanted to formulate laws that could be applied to general problems.[112] Equally important, he did not believe that bureaucratic measures could solve social problems, but insisted that unionism was the only answer. Unions, however, could be furthered only by popular support and action. Thus, the character of Brentano's reform proposals precluded his acceptance of an advisory view of social reform like Schmoller's. However, as we have seen, Brentano shared Schmoller's distrust of practical agitation and his aversion to party politics. The result of Brentano's inability to combine his theoretical statements with consistent action was his failure to realize in practice the fruits of his theoretical endeavors.

Brentano's failure to reconcile scholarship and politics was reflected in an ambivalence in his personality: at times he expressed a desire to withdraw from all practical activity, and yet he was also driven by an equally strong urge to take part in public affairs and to aid in the realization of his reform proposals. In surveying the course of his brilliant academic career, one is aware of a feeling of discontent underlying his success, a feeling which seems to have had its roots in his unwillingness to live placidly in the world of scholarship and his reluctance to become unequivocally involved in the world of politics.[113]

This ambivalence appeared very early in Brentano's career. In 1873 he wrote to Schmoller that he was considering resigning

---

[111] Brinkmann, *Schmoller*, p. 115; for a later statement of Schmoller's distrust of parliamentarianism, see his 1911 essay, "Der deutsche Reichskanzler," reprinted in *Zwanzig Jahre deutscher Politik (1897–1917): Aufsätze und Vorträge*, pp. 81–90.

[112] As Brentano once wrote to Schmoller: "Only the general aspects of particular events seem to me to be of scientific importance. The rest is as immaterial as the color of Salome's stockings." Brentano to Schmoller, October 27, 1878, Goetz, XXX, 199.

[113] For the striking similarity between Brentano's position and that of Max Weber, see Marianne Weber, *Max Weber: Ein Lebensbild* (Heidelberg, 1950), pp. 257–58.

from the Executive Committee of the *Verein*. His decision was in part based on a disagreement with the majority of this committee, but it is significant that Brentano added a second reason for his resignation: "I am ill-suited for practical activity, only through quiet, solitary work can I accomplish something."[114] He went on to say that his activities in the *Verein* kept him from his real task, which was to apply exact scientific methods to the study of economics. In the past, economics had been greatly impeded by its involvement in party politics and polemics. These were, Brentano concluded, "errors we should avoid."[115]

After an appeal from Schmoller to reconsider, Brentano decided to remain on the committee.[116] Less than a week later, he wrote to Schmoller in a very different key. A printer's strike had broken out in Breslau and Brentano wanted a declaration from the *Verein* in favor of the strikers.[117] He himself became so deeply involved in the controversy that he was called upon to explain his conduct to the Ministry of Education.[118] When he was unable to get the *Verein* to take collective action, Brentano complained: "What good does it do to always talk about agitation when every good opportunity for collective action is thrown away. . . ?"[119]

It is worth pointing out that in 1873, almost at the same time that Brentano was thinking in terms of "quiet solitary work," he was engaged in his bitter polemic against Ludwig Bamberger. Brentano's description of this conflict leaves little doubt that he pursued his opponent with great relish.[120]

In the 1870's Brentano's ambivalence between practical activity and scholarship also had a political dimension. We have already considered his warnings about the dangers of combining scholarship with political action. During the seventies, however, he seems to have considered himself a member of the left wing of

114 Brentano to Schmoller, February 1, 1873, Goetz, XXIX, 155.
115 *Ibid.*, p. 156.
116 Schmoller to Brentano, February 3, 1873, *ibid.*, p. 157.
117 Brentano to Schmoller, February 6, 1873, *ibid.*, p. 158. On the strike, see Brentano's article, "Geschichte und Wirken eines deutschen Gewerkvereins," *Schmollers Jahrbuch*, VI, No. 3 (1882), 993–1001.
118 *Mein Leben,* pp. 88–89. On Brentano and the strike, see *Schriften*, IX, 58.
119 Brentano to Schmoller, February 19, 1873, Goetz, XXIX, 164.
120 *Ibid.*

the National Liberal Party.[121] In this connection it is important to remember that in the 1870's the word "party" usually referred to a common adherence to political principles rather than to a political organization.[122] Although Brentano later denied that he had belonged to any political organization before 1899,[123] there is ample evidence that he was a member of the National Liberal *Wahlverein* in Breslau until 1878.[124]

Late in 1873 Brentano was asked by a liberal group from the Prussian city of Cottbus to be their Reichstag candidate. He wrote to Schmoller that "despite my anger over the recent additions to the industrial code and despite the pleasure I would get from venting this anger in the Reichstag, I had to decline because of my university duties."[125] In December, 1876, he ran for a municipal office in Breslau, but was defeated.[126] Later that same month, Moritz Müller, a liberal leader from Pforzheim, asked Brentano to run for the Reichstag, and he accepted.[127] Although Brentano agreed to send a declaration to be read to his voters in Pforzheim, he privately stressed his reluctance to run and was apathetic over victory.[128] At no time did he consider leaving Breslau to visit the area he was going to represent.

Brentano almost immediately regretted his decision to run. One of the reasons for this was Müller, whose letters became

[121] Brentano to Lasker, November 21, 1875, reprinted in Wentzke, *Deutscher Liberalismus*, II, 139.

[122] T. Nipperdey, *Die Organisation der deutschen Parteien vor 1918* (Düsseldorf, 1961), pp. 9–11.

[123] Brentano, "Zum Jubiläum des Vereins für Sozialpolitik," *Frankfurter Zeitung*, July 8, 9, 10, 1897.

[124] In the Brentano Papers there is a draft of a letter to the Breslau National Liberal *Wahlverein* written November 23, 1877, in which Brentano announced his resignation. Judging from a letter from Brentano to Lasker on December 3, 1877, this letter of resignation was never sent. Brentano did resign, however, one year later. *Mein Leben*, p. 96.

[125] Brentano to Schmoller, December 12, 1873, Goetz, XXIX, 178. Brentano's statement suggests that he regarded the Reichstag as a forum in which he might express his opinions, not as a legislative institution.

[126] Brentano to Schmoller, December 16, 1876, Goetz, XXX, 168.

[127] M. Müller to Brentano, December 17, 1876, and Schmoller to Brentano, December 21, 1876.

[128] There is a draft of this declaration in the Brentano Papers. Müller had it printed in the *Pforzheimer Anzeiger*, No. 302 (clipping in the Brentano Papers).

increasingly vague and eccentric.[129] Furthermore, on December 21, 1876, Schmoller wrote to Brentano that he doubted if Müller could get him elected. Müller, Schmoller explained, had neither party organization nor popular support in Pforzheim.[130] As soon as he received this letter, Brentano wrote to Müller questioning the wisdom of his candidacy.[131] From this point on the situation became almost farcical: Müller revised Brentano's private letters and published them; it became clear that another and far more powerful liberal candidate was also going to run in Pforzheim; faced with certain defeat, Brentano resigned from the race, a resignation Müller refused to accept or even to announce; Brentano finally communicated his resignation to his opponent's headquarters.[132]

This brief episode is a significant, if somewhat exaggerated, example of the style of politics in the 1870's. It was not unusual, for example, for candidates not to visit their constituencies in years when elections did not seem to be too hard fought.[133] Furthermore, Brentano's abortive Reichstag candidacy brought into focus his own feelings about the significance of politics. As he wrote to Schmoller early in 1877: "No one can be happier than I am over not having been elected. I only accepted the nomination because of a feeling of duty and that has been satisfied."[134] This combination of duty and apathy is characteristic of the ambivalence of Brentano's political attitude. The low regard for the legislative process which this attitude implies was unfortunately widespread among Brentano's colleagues in the German academic community.

Almost immediately after the Pforzheim affair, Brentano be-

---

[129] August Bebel, who had known Müller in the 1860's, recalled him as a "somewhat eccentric but vigorous, and in his own way, well-meaning jewelry manufacturer." Bebel, *Aus meinem Leben* (Stuttgart, 1910), I, 115.

[130] Schmoller to Brentano, December 21, 1876.

[131] Brentano to Müller, December 22, 1876, reprinted in the *Pforzheimer Anzeiger*, No. 302.

[132] Brentano to Schmoller, January 4 and February 1, 1877, Goetz, XXX, 170–71. My account of Brentano's candidacy is based on the letters and clippings in the Brentano Papers. In *Mein Leben* (p. 107), Brentano stated that his scholarly activity prevented him from accepting the mandate offered by that "outstanding man" Moritz Müller.

[133] Nipperdey, *Die Organisation der deutschen Parteien*, pp. 36–37.

[134] Brentano to Schmoller, January 4, 1877, Goetz, XXX, 170.

gan to speak more and more of devoting himself solely to scholarship. Faced with his increasing isolation within the *Verein* and an increasingly uncongenial political atmosphere in Germany,[135] Brentano sought to settle his ambivalence between scholarship and practical activity by turning away from the practical. In the summer of 1877, he complained of the fruitlessness of his activities, and called a withdrawal from contemporary affairs a "question of my scholarly existence."[136]

In 1879 Brentano's dissatisfaction with German domestic politics prompted him to try to make a definite break with nonscholarly activity. "How sad are our current affairs," he wrote:

> I would prepare a critique of Bismarck if I thought it would do any good, but after careful consideration I am convinced that I should keep my resolution not to concern myself with contemporary affairs any longer. If I could read Assyrian, I'd start a book on the ancient Assyrian economy, if only to forget the economic policies of modern Germany.[137]

For the next few years at least, Brentano abandoned his search for a solution to the problem of scholarship and politics. But, as we shall see, this conflict remained characteristic of his career. In a few years the pull of contemporary affairs brought him from his study, again ready to do battle for the causes he considered just.

[135] As early as 1876, Brentano gave Ludlow a pessimistic account of German affairs, to which Ludlow referred in a letter of March 3, 1876.

[136] Brentano to Schmoller, August 10, 1877, Goetz, XXX, 179. He expressed a similar sentiment to Alfred Boretius in a letter of March 3, 1876. At about the same time Brentano's friend Adolf Held wrote to John Ludlow that he was also going to give up politics. N. C. Masterman, *John Malcolm Ludlow* (Cambridge, 1963), p. 215.

[137] Brentano to Schmoller, January 1, 1879, and November 15, 1881. Early in 1879 Brentano did write some articles defending the Printers' Union, but he refused to use his name or involve himself personally. See Brentano's correspondence with R. Härtel, January, 1879.

# CHAPTER V

# Liberalism Re-Examined:
# A Decade of Doubt and Revision
# 1879-1889

## 1 —

The years 1878–1879 saw a significant realignment in German domestic affairs. The effects of the depression of 1873, Bismarck's increasing disenchantment with his liberal allies, and a growing fear of the Social Democrats led to the important legislation of the late seventies: the anti-Socialist law, the protective tariff, and the beginning of state welfare programs. At the same time, economic self-interest and a common fear of social revolution provided the basis for an alliance between the leaders of heavy industry and the owners of large estates, an alliance that found expression not only in the behavior of the political parties, but also in the bureaucratic and military establishments.[1] Although this reconciliation of industry and agriculture proved unable to provide a stable basis for Bismarck's internal policy until 1887, the Chancellor was still able to dominate the German domestic scene. His opponents were in disarray: the Center Party was willing to bargain, the liberal parties were beset with internal divisions and self-doubt, and the Socialists were driven underground by the repressive legislation of 1878. In comparison with

[1] On German politics in the late 1870's, see E. Eyck, *Bismarck: Leben und Werk* (Erlenbach-Zurich, 1944), III, 278–314; Hans Rosenberg, "Political and Social Consequences of the Great Depression of 1873–1896 in Central Europe," *Economic History Review*, XII (1942), 58–73; and two stimulating articles by Eckart Kehr: "Zur Genesis des königlichen preussischen Reserveoffiziers," *Die Gesellschaft*, V, No. 2 (1928), 492–502, and "Das soziale System der Reaktion in Preussen unter dem Ministerium Puttkamer," *Die Gesellschaft*, VI, No. 2 (1929), 253–74.

the crises that marked the period after 1890, German domestic politics from 1879 to 1889 possessed a surface stability, a false calm.

The political mood of the eighties was complemented by a pervasive feeling of economic stagnation. Although the period following the great depression of 1873 was by no means one of continuous decline, many Germans tended to regard the period as one of chronic depression.[2]

The political, social, and economic condition of Germany in the 1880's had a pronounced effect on the development of *Sozialpolitik*. We have already seen how some members of the *Verein für Sozialpolitik* came to feel that Bismarck's social legislation eliminated the main task of the *Verein*.[3] At the same time, the widespread pessimism about the future of the German economy and the increasing fear of foreign competition led to a transformation of the meaning of the "social question." Under the impact of the economic expansion before 1873, social reformers had been concerned with how the lower classes might best share in the fruits of economic growth. In the 1880's, however, many reformers turned their attention to a search for ways of providing the workers with some measure of security in the face of economic contraction.

As we have seen, Brentano's assessment of German politics in 1879 led him to withdraw from public debate and devote himself exclusively to scholarship. Nevertheless, the eighties were restless years for him. The absence of enemies deprived his ideas of their former focus. He turned from his preoccupation with labor problems to work on economic history, tariff policy, and industrial organization. These new interests reflected the paling of Brentano's commitment to his earlier views on *Sozialpolitik* and the first crisis in his faith in the possibility of liberal social reform in Germany.

Brentano's only important lapse into practical activity came as a result of his taking over Schmoller's chair at Strassburg when the latter moved to Berlin in 1882.[4] He accepted his new

---

2 Rosenberg, "Political and Social Consequences," pp. 60–61.

3 See Schmoller's remarks to this effect in *Verhandlungen von 1890, Schriften des Vereins für Sozialpolitik* (Leipzig, 1890), XLVII, 3.

4 On Brentano's move to Strassburg, see *Mein Leben im Kampfe um die soziale Entwicklung Deutschlands* (Jena, 1931), pp. 115 ff. Hereafter cited as *Mein Leben*.

position with enthusiasm and attempted to fulfill the major purpose of the university at Strassburg, which was to bring German culture to Alsace.[5] Gradually, however, Brentano became aware of what he felt to be a central difficulty in the process of Germanization: industrial relations in Alsace were still governed by a French law of 1864 and were not subject to the German industrial code. This meant that in economic matters the administration in Alsace favored the interests of the employers. The result, Brentano argued, was the alienation of the Alsatian workers, whose sympathies would otherwise have been pro-German. He sought to focus national attention on this problem in 1887, when he provided the *Nationalzeitung* with some material for an article on the Alsatian labor question.[6] In the same year Heinrich Herkner, a student of Brentano's, published an account of labor relations in Alsace's cotton mills which was extremely critical of the Alsatian industrialists.[7] Brentano's activities made his position at the university difficult. Therefore, when he was offered a chair at Vienna in 1888, he accepted.[8]

A further result of Brentano's activity in Alsace was to bring to a head his already tense relations with Schmoller. As early as 1885, he seems to have regarded his former friend and ally with distrust. This feeling grew over the next few years.[9] When Herkner's book appeared, Schmoller regarded it as a reflection on his own career in Strassburg and answered with a sharply critical review. He accused Herkner of being blinded by the ideal

[5] On Brentano's experiences in Strassburg, see his *Elsässer Erinnerungen* (Berlin, 1917). An excellent summary of the political and constitutional condition of Alsace-Lorraine is Hans Ulrich Wehler, "Elsass-Lothringen von 1870 bis 1918: Das 'Reichsland' als politisch-staatsrechtliches Problem des zweiten deutschen Kaiserreiches," *Zeitschrift für die Geschichte des Oberrheins,* CIX (1961), 133–99.

[6] *Nationalzeitung,* March 23, 1887; see also Brentano's *Mein Leben,* pp. 130–31.

[7] Heinrich Herkner, *Die öberelsässische Baumwollindustrie* (Strassburg, 1887); see also Herkner, "Der Lebenslauf eines Kathedersozialisten," *Die Volkswirtschaftslehre der Gegenwart in Selbstdarstellungen,* ed. F. Meiner (Leipzig, 1924), pp. 12–13.

[8] *Mein Leben,* pp. 138 ff.

[9] In a letter of March 12, 1885, John Ludlow called attention to Brentano's distrust of Schmoller. This distrust is clear in a letter of Brentano to Schmoller of May 6, 1887. For Schmoller's view of this letter, see his letter to Brentano of June 18, 1887, reprinted in *Mein Leben,* p. 134.

of Britain, "drawn from the lectures and writings of his mentor." Schmoller's review evoked a harsh response from Brentano which caused a temporary rupture in their relationship.[10]

Brentano accepted the chair of economics at Vienna in part because he felt that he could help his brother Franz, who had lost his chair of philosophy there as a result of religious difficulties.[11] When his efforts on his brother's behalf appeared fruitless, Brentano became increasingly dissatisfied with Vienna and in 1889 accepted a chair at Leipzig, where he remained until he was called to Munich in 1891. The restless nature of Brentano's academic career in the eighties is probably in part cause, in part symptom of the transformation in his thought, which we will analyze in this chapter.

2 —

A few months after Brentano's arrival in Strassburg he was asked to write the chapter on the labor problem for an introductory *Handbuch* on economics edited by Gustav Schönberg.[12] Brentano's essay was more or less a brief restatement of his ideas up to that time. Just as in his works of the late 1870's, he was critical of state-directed social action.[13] He repeated his demand for a liberal solution to social problems which recognized the worker's legitimate demands without reorganizing the existing economic order.[14] As usual, he turned to the unions as the basis for such a solution.[15] It is significant, however, that for the first time in print Brentano considered the actual record of German unionism. He could point to only two unions which had developed according to the English pattern: the Printers' Union with 8,800 members and the Milliners' Union with 3,000.[16] Thus, after

10 *Mein Leben,* pp. 134–35. Schmoller's review appeared in *Schmollers Jahrbuch,* XI (1887), 1338–41.

11 *Mein Leben,* pp. 138 ff. Letter of Franz to Lujo Brentano, July 19, 1887; Lujo to Franz, July 25, September 20, and October 5, 1887, Franz Brentano Papers.

12 G. Schönberg, *Handbuch der politischen Ökonomie* (Tübingen, 1882). See the review in *Schmollers Jahrbuch,* VI (1882), 1379–87.

13 Brentano, "Die gewerbliche Arbeiterfrage," in Schönberg, *Handbuch,* pp. 935 ff. Hereafter cited as "Gewerbliche Arbeiterfrage."

14 *Ibid.,* p. 944.

15 *Ibid.,* p. 954.

16 For Brentano's view of the Printers, see his letters to their leader Richard Härtel, especially in January, 1879, and his article "Geschichte und

twelve years of agitation, less than 12,000 workers in only two industries fulfilled Brentano's prerequisites. He found the other unions unacceptable because of their connections with either the Socialist or the left liberal parties. Brentano believed that these political connections, absent from his model British unions in the 1870's, prevented the development of the unions into moderate, economically-oriented interest groups.

Brentano's essay, however, contained no indication that he had abandoned his earlier point of view. Even though his account of the unions did not dominate the essay quite to the degree it might have ten years earlier, he concluded with a clear statement in favor of union developments.[17] Furthermore, Brentano was still unambiguously opposed to any state regulation of the disputes between workers and employers. He continued to maintain that management and labor had first to experience the wastefulness of labor struggles before they would be willing to compromise in an effective system of arbitration.[18]

Why did Brentano continue to restate his ideas on social reform in the face of such clearly unfavorable historical developments? The most obvious reason was the fact that during the seventies his ideas were expressed within the context of a polemic, a context which could not but make a man like Brentano assert himself with renewed vigor each time he was challenged. His skill as a debater was great, his logic penetrating and persuasive. He demonstrated again and again that in the existing economic order only a liberal solution to social problems was possible and that only unions were able to combine freedom and social justice. Ironically, Brentano's skill as a polemicist and the compelling logic and clarity he could give to his ideas may have made it easier for him to overlook the fact that these ideas were increasingly irrelevant in the German situation.

For another reason why Brentano failed to be shaken by the course of German events, we must look to his method and his view of economics. It will be recalled that he viewed economics as an exact science which could provide useful generalizations from the study of the past and present. His ideas on unions, he felt,

---

Wirken eines deutschen Gewerkvereins," *Schmollers Jahrbuch*, VI, No. 3 (1882), 993–1001. On the Printers, see the union publication *Der Verband der deutschen Buchdrucker* (Berlin, 1916).

17 "Gewerbliche Arbeiterfrage," pp. 958 ff., 991.

18 *Ibid.*, p. 969.

rested securely on generalizations of this kind. Furthermore, as we have seen, Brentano viewed events in primarily economic terms. His training and experience combined to prevent him from perceiving the political and social facts of German life which made improbable a process analogous to the development of British unionism. Thus, in the early 1880's Brentano still seems to have regarded the German economy, and therefore the German unions, as a few steps behind England in a process common to all industrial nations.[19]

The final reason for Brentano's failure to revise his ideas on unions until after 1882 is suggested by a consideration of his view of the German unions themselves.[20] Whatever illusions he may have had concerning the parallel development of Germany and England, he fully realized that existing German unions were quite different from their British counterparts. As early as 1870 Brentano referred to the "disagreeable activities of our unions, which are dominated by the political parties."[21] He regarded his account of the British unions in the *Arbeitergilden* as an attempt to show Germans what peaceful and conservative organizations unions really could be. Brentano expressed a similar sentiment in 1872 when he wrote in the *Preussische Jahrbücher* that his discussion of unions was limited to British developments because of the immaturity of German unionism.[22] His most candid statement on the condition of unions in Germany was made in a letter to the liberal journalist Alfred Boretius in the fall of 1872:

Many competent people seriously doubt whether the German unions can ever mature by themselves. I have doubts

[19] In 1878 Brentano wrote to Schmoller: "We are now only at the place England was in 1824." Letter of October 27, 1878, reprinted in W. Goetz, "Der Briefwechsel Gustav Schmollers mit Lujo Brentano," *Archiv für Kulturgeschichte*, XXX, No. 1 (1941), 201. Hereafter cited as Goetz with volume and page number.

[20] For the early period of German unionism, see Theodor Cassau, *Die Gewerkschaftsbewegung: Ihre Soziologie und ihr Kampf* (Halberstadt, 1925), and S. Nestriepke, *Die Gewerkschaftsbewegung* (3 vols.; Stuttgart, n.d.). On the Hirsch-Duncker unions see the sympathetic work by W. Gleichauf, *Geschichte des Verbandes der deutschen Gewerkvereine* (Berlin, 1907). Of particular interest for the 1860's and early 1870's is G. Mayer, *Johann Baptist von Schweitzer und die Sozialdemokratie* (Jena, 1909).

[21] Brentano to Schmoller, May 3, 1870, Goetz, XXVIII, 323.

[22] "Die Gewerkvereine im Verhältnis zur Arbeitsgesetzgebung," *Preussische Jahrbücher*, XXIX, No. 4 (1872), 586.

myself. For this reason [Ernst] Nasse believes the state should take over union developments. . . . Recently in *Preussische Jahrbücher* (vol. 29) I showed that I wouldn't exclude this possibility. I am afraid, however, that it is still too early for government aid for unions: if this aid comes too early it will spoil the entire affair. For that reason there should be still several years of sympathetic waiting.[23]

Brentano's relationship with the German unions in the seventies leaves some doubt as to what he meant by "sympathetic waiting." As we have seen, he did go out of his way to support the Printers' Union. Furthermore, he refrained from extreme public attacks on the Socialist unions. He did, however, engage in some bitter exchanges with the leaders of the *Deutsche Gewerkschaften,* the union movement sponsored by some members of the *Fortschrittspartei.*[24] This enmity is somewhat puzzling in view of the fact that the founder of these unions, Max Hirsch, was greatly influenced by British unionism and, like Brentano, was a friend of John Ludlow.[25] The reasons why Brentano disliked Hirsch and his organization are not entirely clear. He seems to have objected to the connections of these unions with a political party. Furthermore, he doubted the sincerity and effectiveness with which they represented the interests of the workers.[26] One cannot help but suspect that an added source of Brentano's hostility was his unwillingness to share with anyone his title of German paladin of the British unions.[27] Whatever

---

23 Brentano to Boretius, October 19, 1872, quoted in G. Römer, "Lujo Brentano in den geistigen Strömungen seiner Zeit" (unpub. diss., Munich, 1954), p. 124.

24 See Gleichauf's account cited above, n. 20.

25 In a letter of May 10, 1873, Ludlow drew attention to the similarity of Hirsch's and Brentano's development.

26 Brentano, "Die Hirsch-Duncker'schen Gewerkvereine: Eine Replik," *Schmollers Jahrbuch,* III, No. 2 (1879), 215–31. During the early seventies the Hirsch unions were beset by internal divisions and the lingering effects of a disastrous strike in 1869–70. See J. Reindl, *Die deutsche Gewerkschaftsbewegung* (Altenburg, 1922), pp. 39–40, 48 ff.

27 Brentano minimized Hirsch's knowledge of the British unions at every opportunity. For example, see his comments reprinted in L. Nieder, "Lujo Brentano und die deutschen Arbeiter," *Deutsche Arbeit,* I, No. 12 (December, 1916), 583; Lujo Brentano, "Zur Polemik über die deutschen Gewerkvereine," *Sozialpolitisches Centralblatt,* III, No. 8 (November 20, 1893), 93–94; and Brentano's letter of 1909 to Gustav Mayer, cited in Mayer, *Johann Baptist von Schweitzer,* pp. 242–43.

the reasons for his antipathy towards the *Deutsche Gewerk-schaften*, there seems little doubt that, with the exception of the Printers and the Milliners, these unions were closer to Brentano's ideals than any German organization. His attitude towards Hirsch and his unions is an example of how Brentano's polemical temperament tended to alienate him from men who should have been his allies in the struggle for reform in Germany.

Thus, Brentano continued to regard unionism as the best possible answer to social problems in spite of, rather than because of, the condition of German unions. This was in part due to his belief that the state of German unionism reflected the immaturity of the German economy. Equally important, there were certain ambiguities in the condition of German unionism which, when seen from Brentano's point of view, reinforced his conviction that the sorry state of German unions was only a passing phase.

It is significant that the main branches of German unionism were founded in 1868 while Brentano was in England.[28] Although both Ernst Engel and Max Hirsch kept him informed about union developments, there is no evidence that he displayed great interest in these events.[29] Brentano wrote much of his early work on unions in Aschaffenburg, far from the centers of German unionism. Furthermore, by the time he arrived in Berlin in 1870, much of the unions' original vitality was lost. The early seventies were, as one historian has put it, a "time of *Kinderkrankheiten*," during which the unions were hampered first by the effects of the Franco-Prussian War[30] and then by the depression of 1873.[31] By 1877 only about 49,000 (out of an approximate total of two million) workers belonged to centrally-organized unions, and of these the Printers, with 5,500 members, were the second largest group.[32] It was thus perfectly understandable that Brentano would regard the union movement as

[28] Nestriepke, *Gewerkschaftsbewegung*, I, 153–61.

[29] E. Engel to Brentano, October 6, November 18, December 27, 1868, and the letters from Hirsch to Brentano, October, 1868, to December, 1869.

[30] Cassau, *Die Gewerkschaftsbewegung*, pp. 13 ff.; Nestriepke, *Gewerkschafts-bewegung*, I, 172; and Gleichauf, *Geschichte des Verbandes*, pp. 14–15.

[31] Nestriepke, *Gewerkschaftsbewegung*, I, 172.

[32] These figures are from a table compiled in 1877 by August Geib. They are analyzed in Cassau, *Gewerkschaftsbewegung*, p. 14, and Reindl, *Die deutsche Gewerkschaftsbewegung*, p. 61.

immature and still malleable, even though in retrospect the main lines of union developments had become clear by 1878.

Another important element in Brentano's judgment of the German unions was the anti-union policy of the local and imperial governments. Although the right of workers to organize was guaranteed in the Imperial Industrial Code, it was always possible for governments to use certain clauses of this law to hamper union developments.[33] These efforts were greatly facilitated by the anti-Socialist legislation of 1878.[34] Brentano argued that the unenlightened policy of repression prevented the growth of a non-revolutionary worker movement. His point is not without validity and it enabled him to hope that if the German government, like the British government earlier in the century, removed all restrictions on worker organizations, the situation would be normalized and Socialist organizations would change into conservative, apolitical unions on the British model.

In sum, therefore, we can see that Brentano did not revise his position on unions during the seventies because he was forced to defend this position from attack, because his view of economics tended to confirm the validity of his arguments, and because what he felt to be the immaturity of German unionism allowed him to hope that the unions in Germany could still develop into organizations resembling those in Britain.

In the early 1880's certain factors which had impeded a revision of Brentano's ideas changed, and he began to reconsider his former theories. In 1884 he wrote to Schmoller that he was relieved that a disagreement with Schönberg precluded the publishing of his essay in the second edition of Schönberg's *Handbuch*. Brentano added that, because he had changed his mind on the worker question, he needed time to consider his new position.[35] This letter is one of the few instances in which Brentano admitted that he had revised his theories. The origins of this revision can be found in the changes that had been taking place in Brentano's view of the German situation since 1879.

[33] Nestriepke, *Gewerkschaftsbewegung*, I, 163–65, and Reindl, *Die deutsche Gewerkschaftsbewegung*, pp. 25–38.
[34] Nestriepke, *Gewerkschaftsbewegung*, I, 218–33, and Reindl, *Die deutsche Gewerkschaftsbewegung*, pp. 67 ff.
[35] Brentano to Schmoller, June 19, 1884. On Brentano's controversy with Schönberg, see Schönberg's letters of 1884 in the Brentano Papers.

The most obvious change in Brentano's position after 1879 was caused by his withdrawal from controversy. Without the pressures of debate he had time to think over his ideas and gain a certain flexibility which he had previously lacked.

Equally important, in the early 1880's Brentano became aware of certain aspects of the British union movement he had hitherto ignored. In the late seventies he criticized the government insurance program because it did not provide the unemployment protection necessary for real worker security. Sometime in the 1880's, he became aware that even the strongest British unions were unable to handle the mass unemployment caused by the lingering effects of the depression of 1873.[36] Also, as early as 1882 he began to get discouraging reports about the development of unions in Britain. In that year Ludlow wrote:

> The trade [union] world like all others had changed since then [1872], and your idealization of the Amalgamated Society of Engineers and its policy under Allan is, I should say, no longer true at all of contemporary trades unionism. . . . I think moreover that you would find that boards of arbitration (which have not multiplied much) are mutually incompatible with your favorite type of trades union, and are only adapted to localized trades.[37]

Although Brentano never publicly declared his disappointment with the British unions, such a report from a source as sympathetic and as reliable as Ludlow must have made an impression on him.

The final and perhaps most important cause of the shift in Brentano's ideas was his realization that there were some essential differences between the German and English situations. It is impossible to give an exact date for what was doubtlessly a gradually evolving awareness. The first hint that Brentano's views were changing can be found in a letter to Schmoller of September, 1884, in which he wrote that he was planning an article contrasting Germany and England.[38] Here, as in all

---

[36] *Über die Ursachen der heutigen sozialen Not* (Leipzig, 1889), pp. 20–21. In the late seventies and eighties there was a marked decline in the vitality of the British unions; see H. Pelling, *A History of British Trade Unionism* (Baltimore, 1963), pp. 83–85.

[37] Ludlow to Brentano, August 2–3, 1884.

[38] Brentano to Schmoller, September 30, 1884.

problems concerning Brentano's development in the eighties, we are hampered by a lack of evidence. In any case, a more explicit statement on Germany and England did not come until 1888, when Brentano published an essay in which he explored for the first time reasons why labor relations in Germany were not following the British pattern. In his view the differences between Germany and England resulted from two developments. First, he repeated his argument that the German government's failure to grant the workers the complete right to collective bargaining had prevented the growth of British-type unions and encouraged revolutionary sentiment.[39] Second, he pointed out that Germany's geographical and political position was far less favorable to the liberal development of labor relations than England's. Social relations in England had been more placid than in Germany because England had had centuries of national unity which mitigated modern social differences. Furthermore, Britain possessed an enviable geographical position which provided her with the security necessary for the gradual evolution of institutions that could solve social problems. In contrast to this, Germany's vulnerable geographical position and the necessities of maintaining her national strength gave an urgency to the solution of German social problems which was not a part of the British situation.

Brentano drew an important conclusion from these differences. Germany's position required "a shortening of the development of a new social order by means of conscious leadership from the ruling classes [Herrschenden]."[40] Therefore, in this essay he suggested that the government set up arbitration boards for the regulation of labor relations.[41] Only by participating in the determination of wages and hours could the worker be reconciled to the existing political and social order.[42] Brentano realized that these boards would suffer from the fact that they had not

[39] "Die beabsichtigte Alters- und Invalidenversicherung für Arbeiter und ihre Bedeutung," *Jahrbücher für Nationalökonomie und Statistik*, N.S., XVI, No. 1 (1888), 42–43.

[40] *Ibid.*, p. 45.

[41] *Ibid.*, p. 43. This article was prompted by a government proposal to set up organizations by profession to administer insurance. Brentano proposed that arbitration boards be made part of these organizations.

[42] *Ibid.*, p. 42.

grown up gradually as they had in Britain. However, given the German situation, government action was unavoidable.[43]

In another essay published in 1888 Brentano suggested the new vantage point from which he had come to view German social developments:

> All attempts which sought to go against the national, political and social developments of nations have ended in failure. . . . History shows that the successful statesman is he who recognizes the essential course of developments and, whether he likes it or not, places himself at the head of this course, conquers it and has it serve rather than conflict with the goals he considers necessary.[44]

Brentano was never totally willing to face the consequences of his doubts concerning the relevance of British unionism for Germany. He accepted state intervention with reluctance and abandoned it as soon as events in Germany seemed to justify a new hope for spontaneous unionism. Furthermore, he never presented his suggestions for government-initiated arbitration boards with the single-minded vigor of his earlier works on the British unions. Throughout the eighties his ideas remained unsettled, his interests uncommitted. In the remainder of this chapter we shall consider Brentano's other efforts to find a solution to the social question and thus fill the gap left by the ebbing of his faith in unions.

## 3 —

In 1888, when Brentano admitted that government action could establish arbitration boards and perhaps solve the social question, he tacitly rejected the reliance on trade unions which had been central to his thought since 1869. As we have seen, Brentano began to revise his ideas sometime in 1884, as a response to the conditions described in the first part of this chapter. He came around to supporting government action gradually, however, and the shift in his thought was first of all displayed by his interest in areas far removed from the problems of labor organizations.

[43] *Ibid.*, p. 43.

[44] Über Kartelle," published in *Mitteilungen der Gesellschaft österreichischer Volkswirte,* I (1888). My references are to the manuscript of this article in the Brentano Papers. Hereafter cited as "Kartelle."

During the Easter recess of 1884, Brentano and his wife traveled to Florence. This trip was, in his words, "epoch-making for my scholarly activity."[45] For some reason Brentano's stay in Florence inspired in him a renewed interest in history. Late into the night he would read works on Florentine history and during the day wander about the setting in which the events had taken place. He left Italy with a tremendous interest in the study of the past, no longer merely because it provided generalizations relevant to contemporary problems, but as an end in itself. In the summer of 1884, at precisely the time he wrote to Schmoller about a radical change in his views on the social question, Brentano devoted himself to a careful reworking of the historical aspects of his lectures. This project eventually developed into his course on economic history, one of the main pillars of his fame as a lecturer.[46]

Brentano's historical interests deepened throughout the eighties and were increased by the direction of his methodological writings during that period. In the 1880's the first academic reaction against the domination of German economics by the "young historical school" began. The center of this reaction was Vienna, where the Austrian economist Karl Menger was reasserting the necessity of theoretical economics and arguing for what seemed to the Kathedersozialisten to be the hated abstractions of the Manchester school.[47] When Brentano became a professor at Vienna in 1888, he indirectly attacked Menger in his opening lecture, in which he reaffirmed his distrust of what he called "abstract economics."[48]

In the light of Brentano's other writings in 1888, his closing statement in this lecture is of particular interest:

To me the most important task of scholarship is the discovery of those concrete factors such as territory, population,

---

[45] Mein Leben, p. 123.

[46] Ibid., pp. 122–23.

[47] On the so-called Methodenstreit, see Carl Brinkmann, Wirtschaftsformen und Lebensformen (Tübingen, 1950), pp. 218–31, and G. Ritzel, Schmoller versus Menger: Eine Analyse des Methodenstreits im Hinblick auf den Historismus in der Nationalökonomie (Frankfurt, 1950). A representative work by Menger is Die Irrthümer des Historismus in der deutschen Nationalökonomie (Vienna, 1884).

[48] Reprinted as Die klassische Nationalökonomie (Leipzig, 1888).

religion and government, law, social structure and cultural development which determine the economy of nations.[49]

The clear relevance of this statement for Brentano's work of that same year contrasting Germany and England, together with the fact that Brentano's increased interest in history and his reconsideration of his ideas on the social question both seem to date from 1884, surely indicates a connection between the redirection of his method and the revision of his social thought. However tantalizing it might be to construct some causal pattern in this development, we have no evidence to suggest whether the change in method led him to a realization of the gap between Germany and England or whether his disappointment with German developments prompted him to consider more carefully the historical factors conditioning economics.

In 1884, the year in which Brentano's ideas seem to have undergone their most radical change, he offered his first suggestion for a solution to social problems which did not rest on trade unions. Brentano was reacting to the same problems of unemployment and economic crisis that had prompted his writings on worker insurance in the later 1870's.[50] As has been mentioned, Brentano viewed economic slumps as the result of an overproduction of goods. During the eighties this view was supplemented by an increasing realization, rather widespread among German economists, that the problems of unemployment and overproduction had to be considered in the light of foreign, and especially American, competition.[51]

In the early 1880's Brentano was brought to a consideration of economic depression and foreign competition by the works of Alexander von Peez and Schmoller.[52] At a meeting of the

[49] *Ibid.,* p. 32.

[50] Actually, economic recovery seems to have begun sometime in 1884; see G. Bry, *Wages in Germany 1871–1945* (Princeton, 1960), pp. 474–75.

[51] It is worth noting that from 1870 to 1880 Germany maintained a steady 13 per cent of the world's industrial production, whereas the United States increased from 23 per cent in 1870 to 28 per cent in 1880. After 1880, Germany's share also increased, but at the expense of England, not the U.S.; see J. Kuczynski, *Die Geschichte der Lage der Arbeiter in Deutschland von 1789 bis in die Gegenwart* (6th ed.; Berlin, 1954), Part 2, p. 18.

[52] Brentano to Schmoller, November 30, 1884. Von Peez (1829–1912) was a friend of Brentano's family; see *Mein Leben,* p. 123. On von Peez, see his *Die amerikanische Konkurrenz* (Vienna, 1881), and Henry Cord Meyer,

*Verein*'s Executive Committee in October, 1884, he urged his colleagues to schedule a discussion on the influence of imports on food prices, wages, and production costs in Germany.[53] A month later Brentano sent a letter to Schmoller which outlined his plan for overcoming the harmful effects of foreign competition. It was impossible, he argued, to sacrifice the interests of German agriculture by totally abandoning tariff protection. On the other hand, competing nations would retaliate against a purely protectionist policy and this would be harmful to German industry, which had to export. Brentano felt the answer lay in an economic arrangement in Central Europe whereby German industry could find markets in the Habsburg Empire and the Balkans, while at the same time the agriculture of the entire area would be protected by a common tariff wall.[54]

In December, 1884, Brentano developed his ideas on a *Zollverein* for Central Europe in a lecture in Strassburg.[55] He began the lecture with a theme which was to become increasingly important to German economists over the next thirty years: the power position of Germany. The essential question, Brentano asserted, was how Germany could maintain her *Machtstellung* in the face of increasing economic competition. Although recent colonial acquisitions were to be greeted with pleasure, colonies could not solve these problems. Two things were necessary for an effective solution: protection for agriculture and markets for industry. A policy of free trade would exclude protection; tariffs would hamper industry. Only a Central European tariff union provided both markets and protection.

---

*Mitteleuropa in German Thought and Action 1815–1945* (The Hague, 1955), pp. 63–64. Schmoller, like von Peez, supported a Central European tariff union; see his article "Die amerikanische Konkurrenz und die Lage der mitteleuropäischen besonders deutschen Landschaft," *Schmollers Jahrbuch*, VI, No. 1 (1882), 274–84. Brentano had evidently been thinking about these problems since he was in Breslau in the seventies, although he studied them intensively only after his move to Vienna. See his article "Über eine zukünftige Handelspolitik des deutschen Reiches," *Schmollers Jahrbuch*, IX, No. 1 (1885), 21–22.

53 F. Boese, *Geschichte des Vereins für Sozialpolitik 1872–1932* (Berlin, 1939), p. 51.

54 Brentano to Schmoller, November 30, 1884.

55 Reprinted as "Über eine zukünftige Handelspolitik des deutschen Reiches," *Schmollers Jahrbuch*, IX, No. 1 (1885), 1–29.

As a result of this lecture Brentano was invited by Count Alexander Karolyi to address an agricultural association in Budapest in 1885.[56] The Hungarian landholders were anxious for protection from American and Russian imports, and they were therefore sympathetic to Brentano's ideas.[57] When Brentano returned from Budapest he contacted Count Berchem, an old school friend, who headed the commercial policy department in the Foreign Office.[58] Brentano gave Berchem a confidential report of the Budapest meeting and urged that his ideas be considered. Berchem at first greeted the matter with some enthusiasm, then abruptly dropped it.[59] There is every indication that Bismarck was suspicious of all economic arrangements of this kind and felt that it was dangerous to mix political and economic agreements.[60] In any case, in a short time the Hungarians' support for the project also ceased because Hungary began to suffer under competition from the Balkans.[61] Within a few months after the Budapest meeting, therefore, Brentano was again without a viable solution to Germany's social problems.

As we have seen, three years after the failure of his *Zollverein* plan, Brentano accepted the necessity of government intervention. In 1888 he also considered other methods for social progress. The fact that he was so ready to consider alternate reform proposals just a few months after he had advocated state-sponsored arbitration is indicative of Brentano's reluctance to pursue his new position further.

One of the chief advantages of the proposed Central European tariff union was that it provided security for the workers by insuring markets for German industry. In 1888 Brentano was still acutely conscious of the problems of unemployment, and he became involved in another plan for decreasing unemployment through the stabilization of demand.

Brentano spent the fall vacation of 1888 with Georg Caro, a

[56] Brentano to Schmoller, June 20, 1885.

[57] On the meeting, see *Mein Leben,* p. 124; Schmoller to Brentano, October 21, 1885; and the account in the *Berliner Tageblatt* of October 20, 1885. Meyer, *Mitteleuropa,* p. 60, incorrectly dated the Budapest meeting as 1884.

[58] On Berchem, see the *Neue deutsche Biographie* (Berlin, 1955), II, 63.

[59] Brentano to Schmoller, December 24, 1885.

[60] Meyer, *Mitteleuropa,* p. 59.

[61] *Ibid.,* p. 60.

friend of his wife's family. Caro's brother was one of the founders of a steel cartel established the year before in Silesia, and Caro could provide Brentano with information on the success of this cartel in stabilizing the Silesian labor market.[62] After this introduction, Brentano made an extensive study of cartels and spent the next two years trying to fit them into his changing views on the social question.

The interest of German economists had first been directed to cartels in 1883 when Friedrich Kleinwächter, an Austrian professor of economics, published the first scholarly treatment of the subject.[63] In an argument similar to the one Brentano was to employ in 1889, Kleinwächter proposed cartels as a compromise between the evils of unlimited competition and socialism. Kleinwächter's scholarly arguments were publicized by a journalist named Steinmann-Bucher, whose newspaper *Die Industrie* sought to influence public opinion in favor of cartels.[64]

Brentano first expressed his support for the cartel movement in a lecture given to the Austrian Economic Association in October, 1888.[65] His ideas were based largely on the information given to him by Caro and on Kleinwächter's book. In this lecture, Brentano emphasized his opinion that the main value of cartels was the security they provided for the worker. He argued that by stabilizing the domestic price of goods, cartels greatly increased an industry's ability to compete for foreign markets. The result would be greater security for the worker whose job would no longer depend on the fluctuations of supply and demand. This was particularly important, Brentano concluded, because German insurance did not properly provide for unemployment. In a

---

62 *Mein Leben*, p. 146. On Caro's brother Oscar (1852–1931) and the Silesian cartels, see *Neue deutsche Biographie* (Berlin, 1957), III, 153; O. Caro, "Der deutsche Walzwerksverband," *Schriften des Vereins für Sozialpolitik* (Leipzig, 1894), LX, 41–63.

63 Kleinwächter, *Die Kartelle* (Innsbruck, 1883). On the role of cartels in German economic thought, see W. Braeuer, *Kartell und Konjunktur: Der Meinungsstreit in fünf Jahrzehnten* (Berlin, 1934), and A. Wölfers, "Das Kartellproblem im Lichte der deutschen Kartelliteratur," *Schriften des Vereins für Sozialpolitik*, CLXXX, Part 2 (1931).

64 Braeuer, *Kartell*, pp. 7 ff. For a critical account of the role of cartels in German economics, see J. Kuczynski, *Studien zur Geschichte der zyklischen Überproduktionskrisen in Deutschland 1873 bis 1914* (Berlin, 1961).

65 Brentano, "Kartelle," as cited above, n. 44.

phrase highly reminiscent of his earlier claims for unions, Brentano called cartels the "essential fulfillment [*Ergänzung*] of the reorganization of labor relations already begun in Germany."[66]

Brentano stated his view of cartels in its final form the following spring, when he gave a public lecture at the University of Leipzig entitled "The Origins of Contemporary Social Problems."[67] Here his point of departure was the insecurity of the worker's position in the face of an unstable economy. As in most of his work in the eighties, Brentano referred to the economic crises which had gripped parts of Europe since 1873. For the first time, however, he publicly admitted the inability of even the most powerful British unions to provide support for its members during the depression.[68] Cartels, he argued, could provide security through the "planned allocation of production." Brentano was conscious of the similarities of such "planned allocation" to the socialist views he had been condemning for two decades. He hastened to point out the differences between his ideas and socialism: first, cartels preserved the creative drive of the entrepreneur and retained the profit motive; second, cartels facilitated the participation of German industry in the world market, an involvement essential for any modern nation.[69]

Taken together, Brentano's cartel articles and his acceptance of state support for arbitration boards show the extent to which his ideas changed during the 1880's. He had retreated from his liberal view of economics until only the entrepreneur and the industry's ability to compete remained. Gone was that liberal faith that prosperity and progress could emerge from the interactions of supply and demand.[70] His retreat from his union position was equally drastic. Here only arbitration remained, but it was arbitration created by the state, not gradually emerging from the voluntary organization of workers and employers. During the eighties, Brentano's increasing interest in economic history, his willingness to jettison the liberal view of economic

66 *Ibid.*

67 *Ursachen der heutigen sozialen Not,* as cited above, n. 36.

68 *Ibid.,* pp. 20–21.

69 *Ibid.,* pp. 25–26. In the light of Brentano's later free trade views, it is interesting to note that in this essay he still assumed a tariff wall for German cartels.

70 Kuczynski's critical comments on Brentano stressed this development; see *Studien zur Geschichte der zyklischen Überproduktionskrisen,* pp. 163–73.

action and to accept state direction of social reform brought him closer to the views of the other members of the "young historical school." In short, as Brentano came to doubt the relevance of England as a paradigm, he seems to have come much closer to the traditions of German economics than at any time before 1889.

In many respects, the decade from 1879 to 1889 is the most difficult period of Brentano's career to understand. The gradual shift in his ideas is almost impossible to document with any precision. Furthermore, although his position after 1900 is to some degree adumbrated during the 1880's, the impact of these years on his life is made extremely ambiguous by the fact that in 1889–90 he once again took up the cause of anti-governmental social reform based upon a belief in the spontaneous growth of unionism on the British model.

# CHAPTER VI

# The "New Course" and the Struggle Against Reaction 1889-1894

1 —

In 1889–90 the political and economic stagnation prevalent in the eighties began to disappear. Even before Bismarck's dismissal in March, 1890, it seemed apparent that the young emperor would seek to introduce some political and social innovations. At the same time, the German economy showed signs of renewed vitality. Unemployment decreased during the first half of 1889, and the labor movement, which had been rather quiescent during the eighties, again became active.[1] In May, 1889, the miners in the Ruhr region went out on strike and set off a series of labor disputes which lasted for the next eighteen months.[2] It has been estimated that from the spring of 1889 until the end of 1890 there were one thousand strikes involving one hundred thousand workers.[3]

[1] For the marked decrease in unemployment in 1889, see J. Kuczynski, *Die Geschichte der Lage der Arbeiter unter dem Kapitalismus. Vol. 1: Die Geschichte der Lage der Arbeiter in Deutschland von 1789 bis in die Gegenwart* (6th ed.; Berlin, 1954), Part 2, p. 80. For a chronology of German business cycles, see G. Bry, *Wages in Germany, 1871–1945* (Princeton, 1960), p. 474. Karl Erich Born has recently published an interesting essay on the social and economic development of Germany after 1890: "Der soziale und wirtschaftliche Strukturwandel Deutschlands am Ende des 19. Jahrhunderts," *Vierteljahrschrift für Sozial- und Wirtschaftsgeschichte*, L, No. 3 (November, 1963), 361–76.

[2] *Schulthess' Europäischer Geschichtskalender 1889*, pp. 63–64 and 66–67. Hereafter cited as *Schulthess*, with year.

[3] Kuczynski, *Geschichte der Lage der Arbeiter*, I, Part 2, p. 49.

The Ruhr miners' strike of 1889 prompted Brentano to turn his attention once again toward the German labor movement. The strike seemed to suggest that the questions of job security and unemployment which he had considered so important in the 1880's were now irrelevant. Moreover, Brentano, as well as many other social reformers, regarded the strikes of 1889–90 as a clear indication that Bismarck's approach to *Sozialpolitik* had failed and that new measures had to be found to reconcile the workers and society.[4] Brentano now forgot his disappointment with unionism and viewed with restored hope the growth of the unions after 1889.[5] He also abandoned his attempt to seek scholarly solitude. After a decade of self-restraint he returned to active participation in the search for solutions to Germany's social problems.

Brentano's renewed interest in *Sozialpolitik* in 1889–90 was part of what appeared to be a general reorientation of German politics. Gustav Mayer, who went to Berlin as a student in 1890, has thus summarized the situation:

> The solution of the social question now became the center of attention: *Sozialpolitik* was the main interest not only of the Kaiser and his advisers, but also of the political parties, the universities, the press, even the theater.[6]

Another contemporary has referred to a *"Sozialisierung* of the conscience of the educated middle class" as the hallmark of the nineties.[7] Indeed, after 1890, few politically-conscious Germans could afford to ignore the problems of the lower classes. In 1890 Protestant and Catholic groups formed organizations to promote

---

[4] For the impact of the strike on Germany, see J. Braun-Vogelstein, *Ein Menschenleben: Heinrich Braun und sein Schicksal* (Tübingen, 1932), p. 115; Brentano, *Mein Leben im Kampfe um die soziale Entwicklung Deutschlands* (Jena, 1931), pp. 151–52. Hereafter cited as *Mein Leben.* See also Brentano's remarks in *Verhandlungen von 1890, Schriften des Vereins für Sozialpolitik* (Leipzig, 1890), XLVII, 119–21. Hereafter cited as *Verhandlungen 1890.*

[5] On the development of the German unions after 1890, see below, chap. 8.

[6] G. Mayer, *Erinnerungen: Vom Journalisten zum Historiker der deutschen Arbeiterbewegung* (Munich, 1949), p. 18.

[7] Willy Hellpach, *Wirken in Wirren: Lebenserinnerungen* (Hamburg, 1948), I, 196. For Brentano's analysis, see *Die Stellung der Studenten zu den sozialpolitischen Aufgaben der Zeit* (Munich, 1897).

social harmony and reform.[8] Furthermore, whether they advocated social reform or not, the political parties almost without exception revised their organizational structures in an effort to win support from the masses.[9]

As a result of this extensive interest in *Sozialpolitik* in the 1890's, Brentano achieved more influence than at any other time in his career. During this decade, he played a central role in spreading the desire for social reform among the educated classes in Germany. In 1891 Brentano replaced his former master, Helferich, at Munich. This began the period of his greatest academic success. Now as never before his lecture hall was filled with enthusiastic listeners. Twice special quarters had to be provided to handle the increasing number of students and townspeople who wanted to hear his stirring defense of liberal social reform and his biting attacks on his reactionary opponents.[10] From his lecture hall and seminars came many of the young men whose enthusiasm sparked the new social reform organizations. For example, in the *Volksverein,* the Catholic organization for social reform, six of the leading officials came from his classes. As one of them put it, Brentano "did more than any other economist to enable the Catholic *Volksverein* to flourish in the years from 1890 to 1914."[11] Brentano's students also played a leading role in Friedrich Naumann's National Social movement, where they proved to be some of the most able and enthusiastic of Naumann's supporters.[12]

To most German social reformers in 1890, however, by far the most noteworthy aspect of the renewed interest in the social question was the action of Wilhelm II.[13] During the strikes of

---

8 See Karl Erich Born, *Staat und Sozialpolitik seit Bismarcks Sturz: Ein Beitrag zur Entwicklung des deutschen Reiches, 1890–1914* (Wiesbaden, 1957), pp. 47–62; E. Ritter, *Die katholisch-soziale Bewegung Deutschlands im neunzehnten Jahrhundert und der Volksverein* (Cologne, 1954), *passim.*

9 T. Nipperdey, *Die Organisation der deutschen Parteien vor 1918* (Düsseldorf, 1961), *passim.*

10 *Mein Leben,* pp. 167 and 256–57. For an example of Brentano's popularity with his students, see M. Freund-Hoppe, "Kleine Erinnerungen an Lujo Brentano," *Dresdener Volkszeitung,* September 15, 1931.

11 A. Pieper, "Lujo Brentano zum Gedächtnis," *Führer-Korrespondenz,* IV, No. 4 (October–December, 1931), 145; E. Ritter, *Die katholisch-soziale Bewegung,* p. 248.

12 See below, chap. 7.

13 On the Kaiser's attitude toward social reform and the general political atmosphere during the "new course," see J. A. Nichols, *Germany after*

1889 the Kaiser had shown his awareness of social problems by receiving a delegation of miners. In January, 1890, a few days after the Reichstag refused to renew the anti-Socialist law, Freiherr von Berlepsch, an experienced bureaucrat who was highly sympathetic to reform, replaced Bismarck as Prussian Minister of Commerce. On February 4, the Kaiser issued two decrees on *Sozialpolitik,* the first of which began with the words: "I have decided to act to improve the conditions of the German worker. . . ."[14] The decrees called for an international conference on labor legislation and recognized the government's responsibility for the just regulation of labor conditions.

"The world resounds with the deed of our Kaiser," Brentano wrote in late February, 1890, "and truthfully the decrees of February 4 are a unique occurrence in world history."[15] Later in the year, Brentano offered the Kaiser as a model for his students to follow in their efforts to lead the lower classes to the "blessings of civilization."[16] Brentano's enthusiasm was echoed by progressive elements throughout German society, most of whom would have agreed with Gustav Schmoller when he called the February decrees the beginning of a "new epoch of German *Sozialpolitik.*"[17]

A few weeks after the February decrees were proclaimed, Bismarck was dismissed as Chancellor and the "new course" began.[18] Despite the shock of Bismarck's dismissal, the good will

*Bismarck: The Caprivi Era, 1890–1894* (Cambridge, 1958); K. E. Born, *Staat und Sozialpolitik,* pp. 7 ff. and 84 ff.; G. A. Ritter, *Die Arbeiterbewegung im Wilhelminischen Reich: Die Sozialdemokratische Partei und die Freien Gewerkschaften 1890–1900* (Berlin, 1959), pp. 15–43. For an excellent collection of documents, see P. Rassow and K. E. Born, *Akten zur staatlichen Sozialpolitik in Deutschland 1890–1914* (Wiesbaden, 1959), pp. 1–47.

[14] *Schulthess 1890,* pp. 19–20. On the decrees, see K. E. Born, *Staat und Sozialpolitik,* pp. 7–32, and the comments on Born's interpretation in Ritter, *Die Arbeiterbewegung,* p. 19, n. 12.

[15] Brentano, "Über internationalen Arbeiterschutz," *Deutsches Wochenblatt,* III, No. 8 (February, 1890), 86.

[16] Brentano, *Die Stellung der Gebildeten zur socialen Frage* (Berlin, n.d. [1890]), p. 14.

[17] G. Schmoller, "Die kaiserlichen Erlasse vom 4. Februar 1890," reprinted in *Zur Social- und Gewerbepolitik der Gegenwart: Reden und Aufsätze* (Leipzig, 1890), p. 470.

[18] It is a tribute to Bismarck's hold on the German peoples' imagination that even Brentano, who had opposed almost all of the Chancellor's domestic policy, felt "mixed emotions" at the news of his dismissal. *Mein Leben,*

of the new Chancellor, Caprivi, and the social legislation of 1890–91 allowed many Germans to face the future with hopeful anticipation.[19]

Although in retrospect it is possible to regard the achievements of the "new course" as ephemeral, it should not be overlooked that in the early 1890's some of the crucial problems of the next quarter century were posed. In a later section of this chapter we shall examine the agrarian movement which arose as a response to the commercial policies introduced by Caprivi. Equally significant, the end of the anti-Socialist laws and the improvement of the economic situation caused a dramatic increase in the Socialist party and the union movement.[20] In February, 1891, Caprivi told the Reichstag:

> I am convinced that it is this question of [Social Democracy] which will be the dominating one for the end of this century and perhaps for decades in the next century. . . .[21]

Caprivi's remarks were indeed prophetic. The increase in the size and strength of the labor movement, together with the response this increase evoked from the conservative and liberal parties, remained a major theme of German domestic politics throughout the Wilhelmian period.

2 –

The emergence of organized labor as a force in German internal affairs after 1889 revitalized Brentano's earlier faith in unions as the answer to social problems. In September, 1889, just three months after the outbreak of the miners' strike, he succeeded in convincing the Executive Committee of the *Verein für Sozialpolitik* that a discussion of strikes and arbitration should be included in the agenda for the *Verein* meeting in 1890.[22] At

---

p. 156. For Bismarck's fall and the social question, see Born, *Staat und Sozialpolitik*, pp. 7 ff.

[19] *Ibid.*, pp. 98 ff.

[20] See the figures on union growth cited below, Chap. 8, n. 4. Between 1895 and 1913 the number of Socialists in the Landtage of the German states grew from 36 to 231 (Ritter, *Die Arbeiterbewegung*, p. 232); the Socialists' Reichstag delegation grew from 35 to 110, their total vote from 1.4 million to 4.25 million (K. Pinson, *Modern Germany* [New York, 1954], p. 573).

[21] Quoted in Nichols, *Germany After Bismarck*, p. 75.

[22] F. Boese, *Geschichte des Vereins für Sozialpolitik 1872–1932, Schriften des Vereins für Sozialpolitik* (Berlin, 1939), CLXXXVIII, 60 ff.

the same time, he was able to have two volumes of the *Verein*'s *Schriften* devoted to questions of unions and collective bargaining.[23]

When the *Verein* met in Frankfurt in 1890 there was a general feeling among the members that once again problems of domestic reform needed their attention. As Schmoller put it in his opening address: "The nation stands before the important question of whether to retain the existing *Sozialpolitik* or seek new methods. Thus our *Verein* also has new tasks."[24] The renewed sense of purpose which spread throughout the *Verein* in 1890 facilitated a resumption of the co-operation between Schmoller and Brentano.[25] Almost as soon as their correspondence began again, Brentano attempted to encourage Schmoller to lead the *Verein* toward more vigorous social action. Schmoller, however, was resolved that the *Verein* should remain a scholarly organization.[26]

The renewal of Brentano's faith in unionism, which prompted him to encourage the *Verein*'s interest in the labor movement, also caused him to revise his earlier doubts about the relevance of English developments for Germany. In the spring of 1890 he left for England, as though to refresh himself at the source of his earlier enthusiasm.[27] The statements on the differences between Germany and England which marked his writings in 1888–89 were now, if not forgotten, at least left unsaid. In 1890 he again urged his students to study England, "a nation many decades ahead of us in social and economic developments."[28]

23 *Arbeitseinstellungen und Fortbildung des Arbeitsvertrages* (ed. Brentano) and *Arbeiterausschüsse in der deutschen Industrie, Schriften des Vereins für Sozialpolitik*, XLV and XLVI (Leipzig, 1891).

24 Boese, *Geschichte des Vereins*, p. 62, and *Verhandlungen 1890*, p. 3.

25 *Mein Leben*, p. 161, and Schmoller's letter to Brentano on Brentano's seventieth birthday, December 13, 1914. Unless otherwise stated, all unpublished letters are in the Lujo Brentano Papers.

26 Brentano to Schmoller, March 24, 1892; Schmoller to Brentano, April 26, 1893. Schmoller stressed the scholarly nature of the *Verein* in each of his addresses to the general meetings; see, for example, *Verhandlungen von 1897, Schriften des Vereins für Sozialpolitik* (Leipzig, 1898), LXXVI, 2–14.

27 *Mein Leben*, p. 154, and Brentano's introduction to Vol. XLV of the *Verein*'s *Schriften*, cited above, n. 23, pp. xxxiii ff.

28 Brentano, *Die Stellung der Gebildeten zu den sozialpolitischen Aufgaben der Zeit*, p. 4. In 1890 Schmoller charged that Brentano was ignoring the differences between Germany and England which he had come to accept in

In 1890 Brentano wrote a memorandum for the Canton of Geneva on the problems of social insurance. This work indicated that he was still conscious of the differences between Germany and England which he had articulated in 1888. His preference for the English system, however, was quite clearly stated. The emphasis of German *Sozialpolitik,* Brentano argued, had been on authoritarian measures which had not yet demonstrated an ability to reconcile the workers and the nation.[29] Brentano best summarized his views on Germany and England in a letter to Schmoller written in March, 1891. The era of bureaucratic reform was over, Brentano wrote, and although the British experience would not be precisely duplicated in Germany, there could be no solution for German social problems aside from the British principle of unrestricted labor organizations.[30]

Thus, the apparent failure of Bismarck's bureaucratic *Sozialpolitik* and the renewal of the German labor movement restored Brentano's earlier faith in the necessity of a spontaneous growth of unions and arbitration. During his trip to England in 1890, Brentano again became convinced that the effectiveness of arbitration boards in handling labor disputes would have been impossible if these boards had been introduced by the state, which, as we have seen, was a possibility he had considered in the late eighties.[31] There is no alternative to the free and unhindered growth of unions and arbitration, Brentano told the *Verein* in 1890, "one must give them complete freedom to develop. . . . An organization of workers and employers decreed from above would be condemned to impotence from the start. . . ."[32]

Brentano rejected the attempts of the German government to

---

the late 1880's. Brentano answered by saying that his study trip to England and his relationship with the German Printers' Union convinced him that British labor relations were as relevant for Germany as he had thought in 1870. See *Verhandlungen 1890,* pp. 201 ff. and 268.

29 "Memorandum über die Regelung der Krankenversicherung im Kanton Genf." This typewritten manuscript is in the Brentano Papers, dated 1890. Although the author is not indicated, style and content make it almost certain that it was written by Brentano. On the title page it is noted that it was written at the request of the Canton of Geneva.

30 Brentano to Schmoller, March 19, 1891.

31 *Mein Leben,* p. 155.

32 *Verhandlungen 1890,* p. 127. See also Boese, *Geschichte des Vereins,* p. 64, and *Schriften,* XLV, lxv.

introduce arbitration legislation in the early nineties.[33] To set up arbitration boards artificially, he said, was comparable to a woman who wanted children without labor pains.[34] As in the early seventies, Brentano argued that strikes and lockouts were a necessary prelude to arbitration because they demonstrated the wastefulness of labor disputes and thus instilled in both labor and management the desire for compromise settlements. Furthermore, the decisions of the arbitration board could only be implemented by means of authentic labor organizations such as unions. In fact, whether the specifics of Brentano's diagnosis were correct or not, the optional workers' committees set up by the legislation of the early nineties had relatively little effect.[35]

One can sense a note of relief and a renewed confidence in Brentano's writings of the early 1890's, when he returned to the liberal views of his youth. He could once again unambiguously speak out against the evils of bureaucratic control and look forward to the blessings of a free economy. When Beatrice Webb defended socialism in her book on co-operatives, Brentano replied:

> . . . Germany, and especially Prussia, was to a large extent governed during the last century by state socialism. . . . If your ideal civil servant who is to take the place of the profit maker has ever been realized this has been done in Prussia. . . . The results are most deplorable. They are tyranny and the utmost absence of truthfulness, self-esteem and the power of self-help in the lower classes, at the same time the most stupid red-tapism and an utter neglect of the laws of the market. . . .[36]

Before suggesting socialism, Brentano concluded, Mrs. Webb had best study not only English capitalism, but also the German alternative. It is indeed ironic that some British social reformers seemed to be admiring the state-directed German reforms at the

---

[33] On this legislation see K. E. Born, *Staat und Sozialpolitik*, pp. 106 ff.

[34] Brentano, *Über die Fortbildung des Arbeitsvertrages* (Vienna, 1892), p. 17.

[35] H. J. Teuteberg, *Geschichte der industriellen Mitbestimmung in Deutschland* (Tübingen, 1961), pp. 386 ff.

[36] Brentano to Beatrice Webb (written in English), October 16, 1892, Passfield Papers, London School of Economics. See also Brentano's introduction to the translation of Mrs. Webb's book, *Die britische Genossenschaftsbewegung* (Leipzig, 1892), pp. i–x.

same time that Brentano was trying to convince his countrymen that spontaneity was an essential ingredient in social progress.

Brentano's renewed interest in British unionism was complicated by the fact that in 1889–90 the British union movement was undergoing a radical change. Although this transformation can be traced back to the early 1880's, it was dramatized by the London dock strike in the summer of 1889, which heralded the arrival of the so-called new unionism.[37] The new unions differed in several important respects from those organizations which had been Brentano's models in the 1870's. In the first place, the new unions were composed of unskilled workers and thus lacked many of the indirect means of collective bargaining available to a union like the Engineers. They tended, therefore, to be far more aggressive and willing to strike. Furthermore, the leaders of the new unionism were socialists who felt that it was the task of the state, not of the unions, to provide insurance benefits for the workers. These leaders also made clear that they considered unions a means for organizing the workers for political action on behalf of the socialist cause.[38]

Brentano fully realized the ferment going on in the British labor movement and made every attempt to study the new unions during his trip to England in 1890.[39] He reported his

[37] The most recent study of new unionism de-emphasizes the importance of the dock strike for the movement and argues that the new unions were significant before 1889. A. E. P. Duffy, "New Unionism in Britain, 1889–1890," *Economic History Review*, 2d series, XIV, No. 2 (December, 1961), 306–19. The most complete account of British unionism after 1889 can be found in H. A. Clegg, A. Fox, and A. F. Thompson, *A History of British Trade Unions Since 1889. Vol. I: 1889–1910* (Oxford, 1964), pp. 55 ff.

[38] On March 8, 1890, John Ludlow wrote Brentano that the new unions "marked an epoch in the history of trades unions." (Brentano Papers, cited in N. C. Masterman, *John Malcolm Ludlow* [Cambridge, 1963], p. 235.) For further information on the new unions see Beatrice and Sidney Webb, *The History of Trade Unionism* (rev. ed.; London, 1926), pp. 383 ff.; H. Pelling, *A History of British Trade Unionism* (Baltimore, 1963), pp. 93–122; E. J. Hobsbawm, "General Labour Unions in Britain, 1889–1914," *Economic History Review*, 2d Series, I, Nos. 2 and 3 (1949), 123–42. The Webbs' account should be used with caution since they tended to overestimate the novelty and radicalism of the new unions, just as they underestimated the radicalism of the union movement in the seventies.

[39] *Mein Leben*, pp. 151 ff., 157 ff. Brentano's unwillingness to condemn the new unions entirely was perhaps due to his friendship with John Burns, one of the new union leaders. Although Burns was a great deal more

findings in a letter to the economist Gustav von Schulze-Gävernitz, which the latter published as an appendix to his own study of British social developments.[40] Brentano first of all noted with pride the achievements of the older unions, their acceptance by the public and their clear opposition to socialist ideology.[41] There were, however, two changes in Britain he viewed with far less satisfaction. First was the growth of socialist sympathies among middle-class intellectuals. Brentano knew the Webbs and found their political views far less congenial than those of Ludlow and Harrison in the early seventies. Second was the growth of the new unionism. Brentano objected to the political character of these unions, their emphasis on strikes, and their disavowal of benefit funds for their members.[42]

It is a tribute to the depth of Brentano's anglophilia that he was able to retain it intact in the face of these new developments. He was never entirely sure why anyone should turn to socialism in his British liberal utopia, but he assured his readers that these bourgeois socialists had no following among the workers. Furthermore, he did not believe that the new unions had much of a future. He felt that as soon as economic conditions worsened or public sympathy waned they would be unable to strike successfully and, because they could give the workers no other benefits, their membership would decline. Besides this promise of their speedy demise, the only encouraging aspect of the new unions which Brentano observed was a certain tendency to emulate the older, more conservative organizations.[43] He hoped that the logic of events would force the new union leaders to follow the patterns set by the Amalgamated Societies in the 1870's.

English developments in the early nineties seemed to confirm the diagnosis Brentano formulated in 1890. After 1892 the strength of the new unions ebbed somewhat and the older organizations appeared to be still in control of the labor move-

---

radical than the bureaucrats of the Amalgamated Societies Brentano knew in the 1870's, he was far from being a revolutionary. See Robert Michels' remarks on Burns in *Political Parties* (New York, 1959), pp. 110, 349.

[40] G. von Schulze-Gävernitz, *Zum socialen Frieden: Eine Darstellung der socialpolitischen Erziehung des englischen Volkes im neunzehnten Jahrhundert* (Leipzig, 1890), II, 479 ff.

[41] *Ibid.*, pp. 473–74.

[42] *Ibid.*, pp. 475 ff.

[43] *Ibid.*, pp. 482–83.

ment.[44] Moreover, Brentano continued to see signs of co-operation between the old and new unions and persisted in dismissing the socialistic views of new union leaders as having no real relevance for everyday politics.[45] Throughout the rest of his career, he was prepared to defend the British union movement against critics in either Germany or England. However, after 1900 his championing of British unionism had to be modified by the pressure of events peculiar to the German situation.

3 —

In 1892 Brentano's attention was distracted from the problems of unionism by the debate over tariff policy which had begun to play an increasingly important part in German politics. In the spring of 1890, when the end of the anti-Socialist laws and the imperial decrees seemed to introduce a new era in social reform, the Caprivi government began to consider revising Bismarck's commercial policies. Since 1887, food prices in Germany had been rising steadily, causing considerable agitation for a reduction of the tariff on agricultural products. Furthermore, the new Chancellor seems to have become convinced that Germany's future strength depended on its industrial power. He felt that in the years to come Germany's increasing population could only be supported by industries capable of exporting manufactured goods. As Caprivi put it on one occasion: "We must export: either we export goods or we export people."[46] For this reason he was prepared to revise the tariff laws to encourage industrial growth. The McKinley tariff, presented to the American Congress in April, 1890, made Caprivi aware of the dangers of an all-out tariff struggle and of the necessity of reaching some commercial agreements with European nations.[47]

[44] See Hobsbawn, "General Labour Unions," p. 135, and Brentano, "Der englische Gewerkvereinskongress 1892," *Sozialpolitisches Centralblatt*, I, No. 38 (September, 1892), 471–74.

[45] Ludlow to Brentano, June 3, 1895, and Brentano, "Entwicklung und Geist der englischen Arbeiterorganisationen," *Archiv für soziale Gesetzgebung und Statistik* (1895), VIII, 75–139.

[46] Nichols, *Germany After Bismarck*, p. 148.

[47] On Caprivi's commercial policy, see Nichols, *Germany After Bismarck*, pp. 138–53; R. Stadelmann, "Der neue Kurs in Deutschland," *Geschichte in Wissenschaft und Unterricht*, IV, No. 9 (September, 1953), 548 ff.; and W. Lotz, *Die Handelspolitik des deutschen Reiches unter Graf Caprivi und Fürst Hohenlohe (1890–1900)*, Schriften des Vereins für Sozialpolitik, XCII (Leipzig, 1901).

By the end of 1891, trade treaties had been signed with Austria-Hungary, Italy, and Belgium. They were presented to the Reichstag for ratification in December, 1891, thus beginning a debate which was to be one of the central themes in German politics for the next decade. In a speech to the Reichstag on December 10, Caprivi outlined the arguments that were constantly to recur throughout the debate: the tariffs, he said, protected a single class at the expense of the nation; the national interest demanded not only a decrease in food prices but also encouragement for industry to expand and thus provide employment for an increasing population. "To continue in the previous way," he warned, "would be the ruin not only of our industry and of our laboring class, but perhaps of the state as well."[48]

Proposals to decrease the tariffs protecting their products naturally found little support from the representatives of German agriculture. In the debate of December, 1891, agrarian interests were represented by a few outspoken critics of the Chancellor's position.[49] In 1891, however, this opposition was divided and as yet unsure of itself; only forty-eight Reichstag deputies voted against Caprivi's treaties.[50] In the next three years, against increasing resistance from the agrarians, Caprivi was able to conclude commercial agreements with several countries, including Russia.[51]

Brentano's interest in tariff and trade problems seems to have arisen at the same time as the government's first reconsiderations of Bismarck's policy.[52] Although there is no evidence to link Brentano's views with those of the government, it is perhaps significant to note that Count Berchem, Brentano's friend and chief contact in the Foreign Office, was Caprivi's adviser in commercial matters.[53] In the fall of 1890 Brentano wrote to

48 Nichols, *Germany After Bismarck*, pp. 145 ff. On the treaties, see S. Tirrell, *German Agrarian Politics After Bismarck's Fall: The Formation of the Farmers' League* (New York, 1951), pp. 100–143.
49 See the speech by Kanitz in the *Stenographische Berichte über die Verhandlungen des deutschen Reichstages*, 8th Legislative Period, 1st Session, Vol. V (Berlin, 1892), pp. 3312–18.
50 Tirrell, *German Agrarian Politics*, p. 145.
51 Nichols, *Germany After Bismarck*, pp. 287–307.
52 In *Mein Leben* (pp. 148–49) Brentano recalls having been impressed by the anti-tariff position of Wilhelm Roscher while the two men were colleagues in Leipzig in 1889. However, there is no indication that Brentano took a position on the question until after 1890.
53 Stadelmann, "Der neue Kurs," p. 548. On Berchem, see above, chap. 5.

Schmoller suggesting that the *Verein* sponsor twelve monographs on trade policy. Schmoller disapproved of so extensive a study, but Brentano's protégé Walther Lotz was given the task of examining German trade policies in a single volume in the *Verein's Schriften*.[54]

In January, 1892, a few weeks after the Reichstag debate on the commercial treaties, Brentano made his first public statement on the tariff question. In a lecture devoted to the English Corn Laws, he pointed out the connection between Britain's industrial power and her policies of free trade.[55] This correlation between industrial growth and liberal tariff policies, the point stressed by Caprivi in his speech of December 10, 1891, was the foundation upon which Brentano was to construct most of his arguments for free trade. It is important to note that here, as in so much of his thought, the example of Great Britain played a decisive role.

There is little in Brentano's career before 1890 to suggest why so much of his attention would be absorbed by the tariff question during the Wilhelmian period. It will be remembered that in 1879 he was outspoken in his criticism of Bismarck's *Sozialpolitik*, but had little or nothing to say about the protective tariff. Furthermore, in his 1885 essay on trade policy, his only important statement on the subject before 1890, he advocated a customs union which would be provided with whatever tariff barriers might be necessary. In fact, because of Brentano's earlier stand on tariffs the agrarians evidently assumed that he was a potential ally.[56] Whatever expectations they may have had were quickly disappointed. His lecture of January, 1892, defending the free trade policy of Great Britain, began ten years of intensive agitation for liberal commercial policies and a passion for free trade which he retained for the rest of his life.

Brentano's enthusiasm for liberal trade policies was in part the result of a change in his assessment of the German economic situation. In 1885 he advocated tariff protection for his customs union because he felt that this would provide some degree of job

---

54 Schmoller to Brentano, November 20, 1890. Lotz's volume covered German commercial policies from 1860 to 1891; it was published as Vol. L of the *Schriften*.

55 *Mein Leben*, p. 172; "Anfang und Ende der englischen Kornzölle," *Allgemeine Zeitung* (Munich), January 15 and 16, 1892.

56 *Mein Leben*, p. 171.

security and thus alleviate the unemployment problem which weighed so heavily on his mind during the eighties. When he began to detect a renewed vigor in the German economy after 1890, his concern for unemployment gave way to a concern for the ability of the German economy to support a steadily growing population. Like many other economists in the Wilhelmian period, Brentano no longer saw social and economic problems in such static terms as security, but now perceived that only dynamic industrial expansion could benefit the German workers and at the same time enable Germany to play a leading role in the modern world.[57]

A further reason for his passionate and persistent advocacy of tariff reduction must be sought in the vehemence with which his first, essentially moderate remarks were criticized by the agrarians. As we have noted, the vigor with which Brentano expressed his view on the labor question in the 1870's was partly a result of the bitterness of the liberals' attacks on his ideas. Similarly, in the 1890's his enthusiasm for free trade was at least partly inspired by the polemics directed against his ideas by the representatives of German agriculture. In order to understand the context within which Brentano's ideas were evolved, we must consider for a moment the agrarian movement which began to gather momentum in 1892–93.

The agrarians' leadership and goals were provided by the Prussian landed nobility, and hence the movement's essential characteristics were a reflection of the unique social, economic, and political position of that group. In the course of the nineteenth century the large landholders in Prussia had turned their estates into capitalistically-organized, moneymaking institutions. Along with this reconciliation with modern economics, however, the Prussian landholder preserved a social and political outlook that was both pre- and anti-industrial. The estate owners looked with suspicion on the urbanization of their nation and regarded

---

[57] *Ibid.*, pp. 171 ff. For Brentano's mature ideas on commercial questions, see *Das Freihandelsargument* (Berlin-Schöneberg, 1901). On the population question, see his essay "Die Malthussche Lehre und die Bevölkerungs-bewegung der letzten Dezennien," *Abhandlungen der historischen Klasse der königlichen bayerischen Akademie der Wissenschaften*, XXIV, No. 3 (Munich, 1909).

city dwellers with distrust.[58] The Prussian nobility persisted in regarding itself as the only safeguard between the monarchy and the revolutionary rabble from the cities.[59]

The vigor of the agrarians' response to Caprivi's commercial treaties must be seen in the light of these characteristics. As agricultural entrepreneurs, the estate owners were hard hit by foreign competition and the steady decline in the price of their products after 1891.[60] Perhaps equally important, as representatives of a conservative social and political order they watched with growing dismay the Chancellor's desire to encourage the development of Germany as a predominantly industrialized nation; they realized that industrialism and the rapid pace of urbanization would almost certainly produce pressures for political and social change.[61]

Significantly, much of the strength of the agrarian movement was drawn from a willingness to compromise with modern life, on the one hand, and a rigid reactionary outlook, on the other. Thus, the agrarians formed the *Bund der Landwirte,* which attempted to rally the peasants behind a program of economic self-interest.[62] Furthermore, the estate owners were prepared to

[58] As early as 1852 Bismarck had remarked, "I mistrust the population of large cities, the true Prussian people are not to be found there." Quoted in W. Shanahan, *German Protestants Face the Social Question. Vol. I: The Conservative Phase 1815–1871* (Notre Dame, 1954), p. 258.

[59] This interpretation of the Prussian estate owners is based on Hans Rosenberg, "Die Demokratisierung der Rittergutsbesitzerklasse," *Zur Geschichte und Problematik der Demokratie,* ed. W. Berges and C. Hinrichs (Berlin, 1958), pp. 459–86. See also J. Croner, *Die Geschichte der agrarischen Bewegung in Deutschland* (Berlin, 1909); P. Anderson, *The Background of Anti-English Feeling in Germany 1890–1902* (Washington, 1939), pp. 132–54; and Tirrell, *German Agrarian Politics, passim.*

[60] From 1891 until 1894 the price of rye dropped from M. 208 to M. 118 (per metric ton), wheat from M. 222 to M. 135. Nichols, *Germany After Bismarck,* p. 289.

[61] It is significant to note that in the decade between 1890 and 1900 Germany's rural population for the first time dropped below 50 per cent (from 53 per cent in 1890 to 45 per cent in 1900). The pace of urbanization is also suggested by the fact that in 1871 only eight cities in Germany had a population of over 100,000; in 1910 there were 48. E. Keyser, *Bevölkerungsgeschichte Deutschlands* (Leipzig, 1938), p. 327. See also F. Lütge. *Deutsche Sozial- und Wirtschaftsgeschichte: Ein Überblick* (2d ed.; Berlin, 1960), p. 446.

[62] Tirrell, *German Agrarian Politics,* pp. 144–206; Croner, *Geschichte der agrarischen Bewegung,* pp. 133 ff.

compromise with the representatives of heavy industry in order to protect their economic position.[63] At the same time, the agrarians were able to exploit to the fullest the influence over the army, bureaucracy, and court which their social position gave them. Finally, the Prussian nobility attempted to use its firm stand against the Socialists as a banner beneath which to gather allies for the agrarian cause.

Brentano's lecture of January, 1892, on the English Corn Laws evidently passed unnoticed by the representatives of German agriculture. Throughout 1892, however, the agrarian movement gathered strength and became increasingly sensitive to attacks directed against its interests. Brentano's first clash with the agrarians came not over liberal trade policies but over the question of the inheritance of rural property (*Anerbenrecht*). In October, 1893, a pro-agrarian economist named Gustav Ruhland wrote a series of articles in the *Münchener Neueste Nachrichten,* in which he attacked the attempts of certain professors to apply doctrinaire liberal principles to the laws of rural inheritance.[64] On December 16, 1893, Brentano answered Ruhland in a lecture to the Munich Jurists' Society, in which he argued that the laws governing inheritance should apply to all forms of property. In contrast to Ruhland and the agrarians, Brentano felt that no legal efforts should be made to encourage the passing of a farm or estate to a single heir.[65] Brentano emphasized the fact that primogeniture increased the price of land and thereby made it more difficult for industrial workers to acquire property. Thus, just as an industrial Germany demanded free trade, it also required free and unrestricted division of land.[66]

---

[63] E. Kehr, *Schlachtflottenbau und Parteipolitik, 1894–1901* (Berlin, 1930), *passim,* and Anderson, *Anti-English Feeling,* pp. 214–16.

[64] On Ruhland, see F. Bülow, *Gustav Ruhland: Ein deutscher Bauerndenker im Kampf gegen Wirtschaftsliberalismus und Marxismus* (Berlin, 1936). Bülow attempts to enshrine Ruhland in the National Socialist hierarchy by showing how he prefigured Nazi agricultural policy.

[65] *Mein Leben,* p. 172, and "Über Gebundenheit und Teilbarkeit des ländlichen Grundeigentums," *Allgemeine Zeitung* (Munich), December 20, 21, 1893.

[66] For a complete statement of Brentano's position on *Anerbenrecht,* see *Verhandlungen von 1894, Schriften des Vereins für Sozialpolitik* (Leipzig, 1895), LXI, 270–300, and his *Gesammelte Aufsätze. Vol. 1: Erbrechtspolitik: Alte und neue Feudalität* (Stuttgart, 1899).

The controversy between Brentano and Ruhland dragged on for the rest of the decade. It was marked by extraordinary bitterness, personal insult, and finally, slander trials.[67] In 1894 Ruhland joined the *Bund der Landwirte* and from there led the fight against Brentano and the other advocates of free trade. Ruhland was soon joined by other publicists and politicians who kept the debate alive until the agrarians' victory in the tariff law of 1902.[68]

In 1894 the debate against the representatives of German agriculture was given new impetus by the clear association of the agrarians with the reactionary direction taken by government policy in that year. By 1894 the Emperor obviously had had enough of the policy of reconciliation with the labor movement urged by Caprivi, Berlepsch, and Lohmann. Although in 1890 Wilhelm had no doubt enjoyed posing as the workers' friend, there is no indication that even then he had had any very profound commitment to social reform.[69] In any case, strikes in 1892, Socialist gains in the elections of 1893, and finally an outbreak of anarchist terrorism in France and Italy in June, 1894, convinced the Kaiser that only repressive measures could save Germany from social revolution.[70] During the fall of 1894, Wilhelm began to get rid of those bureaucrats who had been the true bearers of the "new course," and turned instead to men like von Stumm, Eulenburg, and Miquel, who had always advocated decisive action against the Socialists.[71]

---

[67] *Mein Leben,* pp. 173 ff., 405–12.

[68] See, for example, Brentano's article "Gesamtinteresse und Sonderinteresse mit Rücksicht auf die Landwirtschaft: Eine Abwehr gegen Herrn Dr. Ratzinger," *Allgemeine Zeitung* (Munich), January 17, 1894. For Brentano's view of the *Bund der Landwirte,* see his letter to Schmoller of May 20, 1895.

[69] G. Ritter, *Die Arbeiterbewegung,* pp. 19–20; Born, *Staat und Sozialpolitik,* pp. 28 ff., 90 ff. Perhaps the depth of the Kaiser's conciliatory attitude can be gauged by his order to his generals "to use their repeating rifles at the first opportunity" against strikers. The order was given one month after the February Decrees of 1890. Nichols, *Germany After Bismarck,* p. 77.

[70] For the extreme to which Wilhelm seemed willing to carry his reactionary policies, see E. Zechlin, *Staatsstreichpläne Bismarcks und Wilhelms II, 1890–1894* (Stuttgart and Berlin, 1929), pp. 87–152.

[71] The years after 1894 are sometimes called the "Stumm Era"; see E. Eyck, *Das persönliche Regiment Wilhelms II* (Erlenbach-Zurich, 1948), pp. 104–8;

The chief result of this shift in policy was the so-called *Umsturzvorlage*, a bill directed against the labor movement which the new Chancellor, Hohenlohe, presented to the Reichstag in December, 1894.[72] Brentano spoke out against this resurgence of reaction in an article printed in Maximilian Harden's *Zukunft* in March, 1895.[73] As in the past, Brentano condemned reactionary politics because they resulted in an increase in revolutionary sentiment among the workers. The harassment of labor organizations by the police, laws against picketing, and the use of soldiers against strikers showed that although "the right to collective bargaining exists, the worker is forbidden to exercise this right."[74] The refusal to grant complete freedom to unions, the "industrial feudalism" of a man like Stumm, and repressive measures like the law proposed in December, 1894, all served to convince the worker that his aspirations could not be realized within the existing social order. On the other hand, Brentano concluded, the history of the British labor movement clearly demonstrated that "as soon as unions provide the opportunity to improve the workers' condition within the existing social order, all revolutionary desires die out."[75]

In 1894–95 the agrarians were quick to realize the significance of increased social tensions for their struggle against tariff reduction.[76] They asserted again and again that only the strength of agrarian Germany preserved the nation from democracy and social reform. As the *Kreuzzeitung* put it in 1894:

Agriculture represents the strongest and, because of its social significance, the most important force against the radical transformation of the existing social and economic order.

---

F. Hellwig, *Carl Ferdinand Freiherr von Stumm Halberg 1836–1901* (Heidelberg-Saarbrücken, 1936), pp. 506–56; Born, *Staat und Sozialpolitik,* pp. 112 ff., argued that although the government may have followed a policy to which Stumm was sympathetic, his actual influence was slight.

[72] On the *Umsturzvorlage,* see *Schulthess 1894,* pp. 183 ff., and the documents in Rassow and Born, *Akten zur staatlichen Sozialpolitik,* pp. 48–61.

[73] Brentano, "Sozialpolitik und Umsturzvorlage," *Die Zukunft,* X (March 2, 1895), 397–407.

[74] *Ibid.,* p. 403.

[75] *Ibid.,* p. 406.

[76] As early as May, 1894, Bismarck had remarked that a vigorous anti-Socialist policy was the most important part of the agrarians' fight against Caprivi; see Nichols, *Germany After Bismarck,* p. 331.

We see in Germany's development into an industrial nation a great danger which threatens our fatherland and our monarch. . . .[77]

Characteristically, the conservatives' conviction that agriculture was an irreplaceable ingredient in social order was also expressed in their argument that the army had to have an agrarian base. For them, the army was "the rock in the sea of revolution that threatens on all sides, the talisman of loyalty and the palladium of the prince."[78] In the event of the civil war which many conservatives felt was inevitable, peasant soldiers led by Junker officers would provide the king's only reliable defense.[79]

The conservatives' emphasis on the political aspects of the agrarian question merely reinforced what the liberals in Germany had long realized: any extensive reform of Germany's social and political order necessitated a curtailment of the power of the Prussian estate owners, whose economic position depended on protective tariffs.[80] The debate on commercial policy in the nineties, therefore, was enhanced by the realization of both sides that they fought not only for economic measures, but for social and political goals as well. For many of the men who took part in the tariff controversy, the issue of free trade versus protectionism was transcended by other conflicts which touched on the most basic problems of German society: industry versus agriculture, city versus country, bourgeois versus noble, Prussia versus Germany. In 1896, Max Weber gave this conflict a clear formulation

[77] Quoted in W. Steglich, "Beitrag zur Problematik des Bündnisses zwischen Junkern und Bourgeoisie in Deutschland 1870–1880," *Wissenschaftliche Zeitschrift der Humboldt Universität Berlin*, IX, No. 3 (1959–60), 330.

[78] Quoted from the *Militärwochenblatt* (1882) in G. A. Craig, *The Politics of the Prussian Army, 1640–1945* (New York and Oxford, 1956), p. 236.

[79] See the letters reprinted in *Conrad Freiherr von Wangenheim. Briefe und Reden* (Berlin, 1935), pp. 58–59. Brentano tried to combat this attitude by pointing out the impossibility of retaining an agrarian-based army in the modern world. For a typical statement of his position, see Brentano and Robert Kuczynski, *Die heutige Grundlage der deutschen Wehrkraft* (Stuttgart, 1900).

[80] The liberals' dislike of the agrarians was as deep-seated as the Junkers' distrust of the cities. In 1866 one liberal remarked that "agriculture and slavery have always gone hand in hand. . . . Freedom is only possible in industrialized nations." Quoted in L. Maenner, "Deutschlands Wirtschaft und Liberalismus in der Krise von 1879," *Archiv für Politik und Geschichte*, IX, No. 11 (1927), 357.

when he spoke of the two great alternatives facing Germany, industrialism or "feudalism." Only by breaking the strength of the landed nobility, Weber argued, could Germany's internal peace and national power be assured.[81] The growing consciousness of these alternatives lay behind the increasing harshness of the attacks on the Prussian Junker during the nineties.[82]

In 1885 one of the reasons Brentano had given for accepting protective tariffs for agriculture was his unwillingness to deprive Prussia of her ruling class and thus endanger the security of the Reich.[83] By 1895, Brentano, as well as men like Weber, Theodor Barth, Friedrich Naumann, and Hugo Preuss, realized that both the internal and external security of Germany demanded industrialism and social reform, both of which required the destruction of the power of the Prussian landholders.

The years 1889-95 had an important impact on Brentano's career. His renewed interest in *Sozialpolitik*, which coincided with a general awareness of social problems in Germany, brought him to the peak of his influence as a teacher. Equally significant, his participation in the struggle against reaction put him into contact with some of the leaders of political liberalism in Germany. For the next decade, Brentano's career was linked with the German left liberals' attempts to reorient their policies and ideals in light of the problems of Wilhelmian Germany.

[81] Wolfgang J. Mommsen, *Max Weber und die deutsche Politik 1890-1920* (Tübingen, 1959), pp. 103 ff. As late as 1893 Weber was still somewhat reluctant to condemn the Junkers; see Mommsen, pp. 27-34, and Weber's letter to Brentano of February 20, 1893, reprinted in Weber's *Jugendbriefe* (Tübingen, n.d.), p. 365. However, in 1896 Weber told Naumann's *National-sozialer Verein:* "You have one and only one choice of which of the two struggling classes you want to support: the bourgeoisie or the feudal-agrarians." Weber, *Gesammelte politische Schriften* (2d ed.; Tübingen, 1958), p. 27.

[82] On the anti-Junker sentiment in these years, see Anderson, *Anti-English Feeling,* pp. 132 ff.

[83] "Über eine zukünftige Handelspolitik des deutschen Reiches," *Schmollers Jahrbuch,* IX, No. 1 (1885), 20.

# CHAPTER VII

# Barth, Naumann, and the Evolution of Liberalism 1895-1904

## 1 —

In the last chapter we suggested two developments which became increasingly important in German politics after 1890: first, the vigorous growth of the German labor movement, and second, the mobilization of the forces of agrarian protectionism and political reaction. No sector of German society responded to these developments more strongly than the left liberals, those small parties on the far left of the bourgeois political spectrum.[1] Although these parties remained splinter groups, caught between the growing mass movements of left and right, they became the source of some of the most original social and political thinking in the Wilhelmian period.

The battle for free trade provided the initial impetus for Brentano's co-operation with the left liberals. In 1896 several of the leading members of this group asked him to join them in

---

[1] The following is a brief summary of the history of the left liberal parties: in 1861 the *Fortschrittspartei* was founded in Prussia. It split in 1867 when those in favor of Bismarck's indemnity bill formed the National Liberal party. The National Liberals split in 1880. In 1884 the "secessionists" from the National Liberal party joined with the *Fortschrittspartei* to form the *Freisinnigepartei*. This party split in 1893 over the army bill and formed the *Freisinnige Volkspartei* (Eugen Richter) and the *Freisinnige Vereinigung* (Barth and Rickert). In 1910 the left liberals were again united as the *Fortschrittliche Volkspartei,* which became the Democratic party after the war. See the brief survey of party history in O. Stillich, *Die politischen Parteien in Deutschland. Vol. II: Der Liberalismus* (Leipzig, 1911), pp. 213–334.

their campaign against the agrarians. As one of them wrote to him in March, 1896, the situation was such that the future of liberalism depended on the unity of the educated middle class. Brentano responded by making clear his own view of political liberalism: its failure, he wrote, was due in large measure to a narrow bourgeois standpoint which had alienated the workers.[2] Undaunted by his response, the liberals continued to seek his support. In June, 1896, Theodor Barth asked Brentano for an article for *Die Nation,* the chief organ of the *Freisinnige Vereinigung,* which Barth edited. Evidently Barth was aware of Brentano's reluctance to take part in political activity because he stressed the fact that writing for the *Nation* would involve no loss of intellectual independence.[3]

Brentano accepted Barth's offer and in 1896 began to publish articles in the *Nation.*[4] As the struggle over commercial policy intensified in the 1890's, his contacts with the left liberals increased. He made it clear, however, that his support of the liberals' cause would be limited to publishing under their auspices. When Barth offered to support him if he would run for the Reichstag, Brentano categorically refused.[5]

His work for *Die Nation* marked a rapprochement with many of those liberal thinkers he had once attacked as representatives of *Manchestertum.*[6] In 1897 he began to give lectures to the Economic Society, an organization composed of former members of the liberal *Kongress deutscher Volkswirte.* At the same time, some of his writings began to appear in the Society's series of publications which had previously been devoted to attacks on

---

2 Paul Nathan to Brentano, March 8 and 24, 1896. Unless otherwise stated, all unpublished letters are in the Lujo Brentano Papers. On Nathan see E. Feder, *Politik und Humanität: Paul Nathan. Ein Lebensbild* (Berlin, 1929).

3 Theodor Barth to Brentano, June 5, 1896. On Barth, see the *Neue deutsche Biographie* (Berlin, 1953), I, 606–7; E. Feder, *Theodor Barth und der demokratische Gedanke* (Gotha, 1919).

4 Barth to Brentano, December 31, 1896. During 1897 Brentano used *Die Nation* to carry on a polemic against those who argued that German military power required an agrarian basis. See his articles in *Die Nation* of October 20 and 30, 1897.

5 Barth to Brentano, August 9 and 13, 1897.

6 Brentano's co-operation with his former enemies came as a surprise to some of his associates. On August 1, 1896, his former student Moritz Bonn wrote to Brentano that "certainly the most interesting fact about the article was that it was published in the *Nation.*"

the *Verein für Sozialpolitik*.[7] Symbolic of this transformation in Brentano's relationship with these liberals was his reconciliation with Ludwig Bamberger. In March, 1897, Bamberger wrote to Barth that Brentano's latest article in the *Nation* was so "relevant and profound" it should be reprinted.[8] A year later, Bamberger and Brentano were personally reconciled and Bamberger omitted from his collected works the critique of Brentano he had written in the seventies.[9]

The most obvious reason for the co-operation between Brentano and his former opponents was their common dislike of the Prussian Junker and the tariffs which protected him. Even in 1879 the left liberals had realized the political significance of Bismarck's tariff.[10] In the 1890's this significance was still more apparent. As Barth wrote to Brentano in 1898, the influence of the Prussian estate owners had to be broken if Germany was to retain her place in the modern world.[11] One liberal manufacturer perhaps best summarized the sentiments of this entire group when he told Brentano: "Everyone must unite against the *one* enemy, the Junker."[12]

Brentano's relationship with some of the left liberals transcended their common stand on tariff policy and extended to agreement on questions of *Sozialpolitik* and political action. This agreement, mainly with members of Barth's *Freisinnige Vereinigung,* reflected a basic change in left liberalism since the 1870's. After the split in the National Liberal Party in 1881, the position of the left liberals had steadily deteriorated. In the 1880's some of them had sustained themselves on the expectation of future influence under the Crown Prince.[13] After the tragedy

[7] Max Broemel to Brentano, October 21, 1897.
[8] Ludwig Bamberger to Barth, March 31, 1897. Barth sent this letter to Brentano on April 1, 1897.
[9] Brentano, *Mein Leben im Kampfe um die soziale Entwicklung Deutschlands* (Jena, 1931), pp. 206–7. Hereafter cited as *Mein Leben.*
[10] In 1879, when Barth was asked what possible difference a few pennies of tariff would make, he answered: "These fifty pennies will cause the political collapse of the German bourgeoisie." Quoted in E. Eyck, *Bismarck: Leben und Werk* (Erlenbach-Zurich, 1944), III, 298.
[11] Barth to Brentano, August 30, 1898. See also L. Bamberger, *Erinnerungen* (Berlin, 1899), p. 541.
[12] Heinrich Flinisch to Brentano, September 7, 1897.
[13] Feder, *Barth,* p. 25; Barth, *Politische Porträts* (Berlin, 1904), pp. 84–93. See also A. Dorpalen, "Emperor Frederick III and the German Liberal Movement," *American Historical Review,* LIV, No. 1 (October, 1948), 1–31.

of his brief reign, a few had found cause for renewed hope in the "new course."[14] By the mid-nineties, however, the weakness of left liberalism was clear. As Barth wrote in 1893:

> The danger of becoming ossified is at hand. . . . The party has lost its powers of attraction, it lives from the old traditions, from its dependence on some of the great liberal principles. . . . New times create new problems . . . [and] the *Freisinnige Partei* is no longer the party of reform which liberalism was at the time of the *Reichsgründung*. . . .[15]

Conscious of their weakness, threatened by the aggressive forces of left and right, the left liberals reacted in two ways. Eugen Richter, who dominated the *Freisinnige Volkspartei* until his death in 1906, refused to compromise any of his liberal ideals and merely repeated them to a loyal but gradually diminishing audience.[16] Men like Barth, however, were prepared to reconsider "the old traditions" and were determined to restore liberalism to its former place in German life.[17] In the first place, Barth abandoned the left liberals' traditional refusal of support for military measures and, as we shall see, led the *Freisinnige Vereinigung* to a qualified co-operation with the drive for *Weltpolitik*. Furthermore, in the nineties Barth came to realize that since any alliance with parties of the right would involve a complete abdication of liberal party goals, the only hope for a renewed and powerful liberal party lay in an alliance of workers and bourgeoisie under liberal leadership.

The liberals' hope of finding allies among the workers was in part the result of the emergence of revisionism in the Social Democratic Party during the 1890's. At the beginning of the decade Barth had reprinted a pamphlet harshly critical of the Socialists which he had written in 1879. He noted in the preface that he had found it unnecessary to make any significant changes

14 Feder, *Barth*, p. 26.

15 *Die Nation*, July 22, 1893, quoted in L. Grambow, *Die deutsche Freihandelspartei zur Zeit ihrer Blüte* (Jena, 1903), pp. 381–82.

16 F. Rachfahl, "Eugen Richter und der Linksliberalismus im neuen Reiche," *Zeitschrift für Politik*, V, Nos. 2–3 (1912), 261–374; L. Krieger, *The German Idea of Freedom* (Boston, 1957), pp. 461 ff.; P. Anderson, *The Background of Anti-English Feeling in Germany 1890–1902* (Washington, D.C., 1939), pp. 106–11.

17 On the *Freisinnige Vereinigung*, see Anderson, *Anti-English Feeling*, pp. 98–106; Krieger, *German Idea of Freedom*, pp. 461 ff., T. Nipperdey, *Die Organisation der deutschen Parteien vor 1918* (Düsseldorf, 1961), pp. 176 ff.

in the pamphlet because the character of the S. P. D. had remained essentially the same.[18] However, by 1895 Barth was emphasizing the evolution of the party from a revolutionary to a "reformist treatment of politics."[19] A few years later he advocated electoral alliances with the Socialists. By the turn of the century his vision of revitalizing liberalism by means of a bourgeois-worker coalition was shared by such venerable old liberals as Bamberger and Theodor Mommsen.[20]

This hope for an alliance with the S. P. D. obviously caused Barth to revise his ideas on social reform and thus added another dimension to his relationship with Brentano. In 1897 Barth wrote Brentano to ask his advice on unions. From that point on, Brentano's views on labor organizations were an important influence on Barth and his followers.[21]

Barth's efforts to win the loyalties of the workers coincided with what Brentano had been telling the German liberals since the early seventies. Brentano had long maintained that the failure of liberalism in Germany was due to its refusal to consider the interests of the lower classes. He once again addressed himself to the condition of German liberalism in a lecture which he gave to a Munich student group in January, 1897.[22] In terms significantly similar to Barth's article quoted above, Brentano traced the way in which liberalism had lost its hold on the public imagination and was now being submerged by the forces of right and left. Liberal ideals, Brentano argued, lost their "party-forming strength" when they ceased to be concerned with the equality of all men and the common good and began to represent special interests. Brentano called upon his young listeners to revitalize liberalism, to make it once again attractive to the lower classes and the idealistic youth.[23]

Brentano had also long been aware of the potentially reformist character of the German Socialists. He regarded the S. P. D. as analogous to British chartism and was therefore convinced that

---

[18] T. Barth, *Die sozialdemokratische Gedankenwelt* (Berlin, 1890), pp. 2–3.

[19] *Stenographische Berichte über die Verhandlungen des deutschen Reichstages,* 9th Legislative Period, 3d Session, Vol. III (Berlin, 1895), p. 2142.

[20] On Bamberger, see *Mein Leben,* p. 207; on Mommsen, see A. Heuss, *Theodor Mommsen und das 19. Jahrhundert* (Kiel, 1956), p. 217.

[21] Barth to Brentano, November 26, 1897.

[22] Brentano, *Die Stellung der Studenten zu den sozialpolitischen Aufgaben der Zeit* (Munich, 1897).

[23] *Ibid.,* p. 22.

if the German government behaved as the British government had after 1848, the Social Democrats would evolve into a peaceful, conservative organization.[24] The "new course" had aroused his hopes that such an enlightened policy was at hand. In 1890 he convinced Schmoller that the S. P. D. should be invited to send representatives to the Frankfurt meeting of the *Verein für Sozialpolitik*.[25] Although the mood of hope caused by the new course quickly evaporated, and Brentano's efforts to get Socialists to attend the *Verein* meetings failed, he continued his attempts to make contacts with the Socialists throughout the nineties.[26]

Brentano's hopes for the S. P. D. in the nineties were perhaps conditioned by the character of the Social Democratic Party in Bavaria. In 1891, the year Brentano moved to Munich, the leader of the Bavarian S. P. D., Georg von Vollmar, gave his famous *Eldorado-Palast* speech, one of the first significant statements of German revisionism.[27] During the 1890's Vollmar and Brentano became friends, and this undoubtedly reinforced Brentano's view on the essentially moderate character of German socialism.[28]

Brentano's relationship with Eduard Bernstein has received

[24] *Mein Leben*, pp. 198 ff.

[25] Schmoller to Brentano, June 30, 1890; draft of Brentano's letter to Bebel, June 30, 1890. Bebel accepted in a letter to Brentano of July 5, 1890, but the Socialist representative did not arrive; see *Verhandlungen von 1890, Schriften des Vereins für Sozialpolitik* (Leipzig, 1890), XLVII, 201.

[26] For example, Brentano sought for a time to work with Heinrich Braun; see J. Braun-Vogelstein, *Ein Menschenleben: Heinrich Braun und sein Schicksal* (Tübingen, 1932), pp. 115 ff., 221 ff., 253 ff. Brentano was also active in the *Gesellschaft für Sozialreform*, led by the former Minister of Commerce von Berlepsch, which also sought contact with the Socialists. See Berlepsch to Brentano, February 28, May 1, 1899, and May 17, 1900.

[27] Vollmar was called to Brentano's attention by Brentano's former student Heinrich Herkner, who wrote him that "a trade unionist of the old school could not have written more reasonably, more calmly." Herkner to Brentano, August 3, 1891. On Vollmar, see R. Jansen, *Georg von Vollmar: Eine politische Biographie* (Düsseldorf, 1958), and G. A. Ritter, *Die Arbeiterbewegung im Wilhelminischen Reich: Die sozialdemokratische Partei und die freien Gewerkschaften 1890–1900* (Berlin, 1959), pp. 87 ff. See also Ritter's comments on the Bavarian S. P. D. (pp. 128 ff).

[28] There are a number of letters from Brentano to Vollmar in the Vollmar Papers, International Institute for Social History, Amsterdam. These letters show a mutual respect and a warm, although not intimate friendship. Naturally, because they lived in the same city, Brentano and Vollmar would have spoken about most important affairs in person. See also P. Kampffmeyer, *Georg von Vollmar* (Munich, 1930), p. 89.

more attention than his friendship with Vollmar.[29] In the opinion of radical Socialists like Rosa Luxemburg, Brentano and the *Kathedersozialisten* had enticed Bernstein into the bourgeois camp, a charge recently repeated by the East German historian, Jürgen Kuczynski.[30] In somewhat more moderate fashion, other historians have also pointed to a link between Bernstein and Brentano.[31] Their correspondence does indicate a great deal of mutual respect, and also gives evidence of their common regard for England and for the importance of unions.[32] Furthermore, in two articles written in 1899 Brentano showed his sympathy for Bernstein's views and stressed Bernstein's significance for the evolution of German socialism.[33] It would be a mistake, however, to overemphasize the connection between Brentano's and Bernstein's thought. Although Brentano may have had some impact on him, Bernstein's revision of Marxist theory is basically the ideological reflection of his own experiences in England and of the practical changes in German socialism made by party leaders like Vollmar and union leaders like Legien.[34]

[29] On Bernstein, see P. Angel, *Eduard Bernstein et l'évolution du socialisme allemand* (Paris, 1961); P. Gay, *The Dilemma of Democratic Socialism: Eduard Bernstein's Challenge to Marx* (New York, 1952); C. Gneuss, "Um den Einklang von Theorie und Praxis: Eduard Bernstein und der Revisionismus," *Marxismusstudien*, II (1957), 198–226. The best short statement of Bernstein's position is his *Evolutionary Socialism* (New York, 1961), first published in 1899.

[30] Rosa Luxemburg, *Gesammelte Werke. Vol. III: Gegen den Reformismus* (Berlin, 1925), pp. 104, 244 ff., and J. Kuczynski, *Die Geschichte der Lage der Arbeiter unter dem Kapitalismus. Vol. I: Die Geschichte der Lage der Arbeiter in Deutschland von 1789 bis in die Gegenwart* (6th ed.; Berlin, 1954), Part II, pp. 278–97.

[31] Angel, *Eduard Bernstein*, p. 131, and G. Landauer, *European Socialism* (Berkeley, 1959), II, 1611.

[32] For Bernstein's view of English thought, see his letter to Brentano, December 17, 1914; Gay, *The Dilemma of Democratic Socialism*, pp. 56–57; Angel, *Eduard Bernstein*, p. 120. Bernstein's letters to Brentano (in the Brentano Papers), and Brentano's replies (in the Bernstein Papers, Institute for Social History, Amsterdam), show the warmth and mutual admiration which marked their relationship.

[33] Brentano, "Der soziale Friede und die Wandlungen der Sozialen Demokratie," *Allgemeine Zeitung* (Munich), April 23, 1899, and "Die Wandlungen der Sozialen Demokratie und die *Berliner Korrespondenz*," *ibid.*, May 2, 1899.

[34] Gneuss, "Um den Einklang von Theorie und Praxis," *passim*. See Ritter, *Die Arbeiterbewegung*, pp. 176–217, for the general context of reformism within which Bernstein's ideas developed.

The co-operation between Brentano and the left liberals, reinforced by their common view of the future of liberalism and of the true nature of German socialism, was deepened by the events of 1897, 1898, and 1899. In 1897 the government set up the Economic Committee on the Preparation of the Commercial Treaties.[35] From this time until the agrarians' victory in 1902 the controversy over the tariffs steadily intensified. Brentano's participation in the debate and his publication in liberal journals kept pace with this intensification. Again and again he condemned the protectionists as representatives of special interests and argued that his own position was actually a defense of the common good. The welfare of the consumer and the strength of the nation depended on free trade. A return to protectionism would increase prices, hinder industrial growth, and damage Germany's position in the world; tariffs would not produce a revival of agriculture, but only stifle industry and commerce. The protectionist policy, Brentano wrote in 1901, "is a policy of hate and envy" which threatens Germany's strength. Free trade and industrial growth provide the only means for progress at home and success in foreign affairs.[36]

At the same time that the tariff issue became urgent, the government again attempted to have extraordinary legislation against the Socialists passed by the Reichstag. Early in 1897 a strike in Hamburg focused the attention of the public on labor problems.[37] General von Waldersee, a close associate of the Kaiser's who commanded the garrison at Altona, sent Wilhelm confidential reports on the strike, in which he urged prompt and vigorous action against the Socialists.[38] In the next months, agitation for repressive legislation increased and even the *Kathedersozialisten* were attacked.[39] A significant shift in the develop-

[35] Anderson, *Anti-English Feeling*, pp. 156–57.

[36] For two samples of Brentano's arguments during this period, see "Theorie contra Sonderinteresse," *Die Nation*, October 6, 1900, and *Die Schrecken des überwiegenden Industriestaats* (Berlin, 1901); see also *Das Freihandelsargument* (Berlin-Schöneberg, 1901).

[37] *Mein Leben*, pp. 200 ff.

[38] K. Born, *Staat und Sozialpolitik seit Bismarcks Sturz: Ein Beitrag zur Entwicklung des deutschen Reiches 1890–1914* (Wiesbaden, 1957), pp. 136–37.

[39] *Mein Leben*, pp. 200 ff. On Stumm's attack on the *Kathedersozialisten*, see F. Hellwig, *Carl Ferdinand Freiherr von Stumm-Halberg, 1836–1901* (Heidelberg-Saarbrücken, 1936), pp. 525–26; H. Delbrück, G. Schmoller, and A.

ment of the social question in Germany is suggested by the fact that in the 1890's the struggle against the Socialists and state social reform was no longer led by men like Bamberger and Barth, but by conservatives like Baron von Stumm, who defended not liberal principles but political reaction and economic self-interest.

The impatience with the Socialists increased in 1898, and Count Posadowsky, the new Minister of the Interior, began to prepare a law against organized labor. In September, 1898, the Kaiser prematurely and somewhat inaccurately announced:

> A law is being completed which will be presented to the Reichstag this year and which will send to the penitentiary anyone . . . who prevents or hinders a German worker from going to his labor or who encourages him to strike.[40]

The Kaiser's speech triggered a series of protests from the Socialist and liberal parties even before the so-called penitentiary bill (Zuchthausvorlage) was presented to the Reichstag in May, 1899.[41] The Kaiser's threats indicated that the government intended to act against the Socialists by curtailing the unions. Until 1899 the government had used two clauses (numbers 152 and 153) from the Reich Industrial Code to justify criminal proceedings against strikers. The new legislation was obviously aimed at expanding and concretizing these clauses in order to make collective bargaining even more difficult. The law's announced purpose was the protection of "those willing to work" during a strike; its actual purpose was to prevent picketing and facilitate the use of strike breakers.[42]

By thus inhibiting the unions' power to strike, the Zuchthausvorlage threatened unionism's existence and with it the whole basis of Brentano's social thought. He vigorously condemned the proposed law in a lecture to the Economic Society in January,

---

Wagner, Über die Stummische Herrenhausrede (Berlin, 1897). On Stumm, see A. Ascher, "Baron von Stumm. Advocate of Feudal Capitalism," Journal of Central European Affairs, XXII, No. 3 (October, 1962), 271–85.

[40] Born, Staat und Sozialpolitik, p. 146; Anderson, Anti-English Feeling, pp. 37.

[41] Born, Staat und Sozialpolitik, pp. 148 ff.

[42] On the Zuchthausvorlage, see ibid., pp. 146–65, and the documents in K. Born and P. Rassow, Akten zur staatlichen Sozialpolitik in Deutschland 1890–1914 (Wiesbaden, 1959), pp. 107–28.

1899.[43] In this lecture Brentano traced the evolution of the workers' right to organize and the means used in Germany to hinder and harass these organizations. What was needed, he argued, was not a tightening of the government's restrictions on unions but an abolition of these restrictions.

Until the final defeat of the bill in November, 1899, the debate on the *Zuchthausvorlage* continued. Brentano's lecture in January was the first of a series of lectures and pamphlets which he wrote against the law.[44] Even when it had become clear that there was not a Reichstag majority in favor of the law, certain statements by Prussian officials led him to fear similar measures might be introduced in Prussia.[45] Within this reactionary political context co-operation among parties of the left increased. Brentano, Barth, and others organized meetings and wrote articles against the bill.[46] At this time Brentano found a new ally in Friedrich Naumann, whose *Nationalsozialer Verein* was outspoken in its opposition to the *Zuchthausvorlage*.

2 —

In June, 1899, at the height of the debate on the *Zuchthausvorlage*, Brentano received a letter from Naumann asking for an article on the bill for Naumann's paper *Die Hilfe*.[47] Brentano answered promptly, criticizing the proposed law in a statement with which Naumann expressed his complete agreement.[48] A month later Brentano was asked by Naumann and by their mutual friend Rudolf Sohm to speak at the annual meeting of the *Nationalsozialer Verein*, to be held that October in Göttingen.[49] Despite his belief that politics and scholarship were irreconcilable, Brentano agreed to speak at Göttingen. His decision was based on the admiration he had come to feel for Naumann in the late nineties and on the conviction that every

43 Published as *Der Schutz der Arbeitswilligen* (Berlin, 1899).

44 Brentano, *Reaktion oder Reform: Gegen die Zuchthausvorlage* (Berlin-Schöneberg, 1899).

45 *Ibid.*, p. 8.

46 Barth to Brentano, September 13, 1899.

47 Naumann to Brentano, June 2, 1899.

48 Naumann to Brentano, June 6, 1899.

49 Sohm to Brentano and Naumann to Brentano, both letters dated July 22, 1899.

ally was needed against the government's reactionary policies.[50] Brentano's speech to the Göttingen meeting repeated his stand on labor organizations and collective bargaining. The *National-sozialen* enthusiastically accepted his ideas, which became the basis for their official policy on unions.[51]

Brentano's appearance at Göttingen began nine years of co-operation with Naumann. In the last months of 1899 they were in close contact about possible measures against the *Zuchthaus-vorlage*.[52] After the defeat of the bill Brentano collaborated with Naumann in the struggle for liberal commercial policies which ended unsuccessfully in 1902.[53] Equally important for the relations between them were the many young men who joined Naumann after studying with Brentano. Brentano's students were active in the Munich National Social group and also assumed important positions on *Die Hilfe* and in the party organization.[54]

Since the beginning of his career as a Lutheran pastor in the 1880's, Friedrich Naumann had shown an interest in social problems.[55] His gradual realization of the economic, political,

[50] Brentano, *Mein Leben,* pp. 208–9. In this account Brentano stressed that he was called in to save the National Socials from complete collapse. Although never particularly robust, there is no evidence that the party was in extraordinarily bad shape in 1899.

[51] *Mein Leben,* p. 209; Naumann to Brentano, October 13, 1899. For Brentano's influence on the National Socials see the *National-sozialer Wegweiser* (Berlin-Schöneberg, 1903), p. 22.

[52] Naumann to Brentano, October 30 and November 17, 1899.

[53] See Naumann's letters to Brentano in 1900–1902. Brentano always received unqualified support from *Die Hilfe* in his polemics against the agrarians. See, for example, *Die Hilfe,* September 1, 1901.

[54] For example, see the following: L. Curtius, *Deutsche und antike Welt: Lebenserinnerungen* (Stuttgart, 1951), pp. 125 ff.; W. Goetz, *Historiker in meiner Zeit: Gesammelte Aufsätze* (Cologne, 1957), pp. 28–29; T. Heuss, *Vorspiele des Lebens: Jugenderinnerungen* (Tübingen, 1953), p. 223. A very interesting account of Naumann's movement is to be found in some of the letters written to Brentano by his students in the *Nationalsozialer Verein;* see especially the letters of Eugen Katz and Wilhelm Cohnstaedt.

[55] The basic sources of information on Naumann and his movement come from his former associates: M. Wenck, *Geschichte der Nationalsozialen von 1895 bis 1903* (Berlin-Schöneberg, 1905); Wenck, *Friedrich Naumann: Ein Lebensbild* (Berlin-Schöneberg, 1920); and most important, T. Heuss, *Friedrich Naumann: Der Mann, das Werk, die Zeit* (2d ed.; Stuttgart and Tübingen, 1949). In recent years Heuss's interpretation of Naumann as a

and cultural dimensions of the social question is one of the most interesting examples of the general awakening of social consciousness in Germany during the 1890's. Naumann began his work for social reform as a chaplain with the "Inner Mission," a charitable organization devoted to caring for the impoverished urban masses.[56] He then joined Adolf Stoecker's Christian Social Party.[57] By the mid-nineties Naumann was disenchanted with Stoecker's attempts to win the masses by means of conservative promises of reform and immoderate anti-Semitic demagogy. At this point in his career, two men were of paramount importance for his development: Rudolf Sohm, who taught Naumann that religion and politics had to be separated; and Max Weber, who taught him the primary importance of the nation and the close interrelationship of national power and social reform.[58]

In 1895 Naumann resigned from the ministry and in the next year founded the *Nationalsozialer Verein* for the purpose of gaining mass support through a combination of nationalism and *Sozialpolitik*. As one wit put it in the nineties, the *Nationalsozialen* wanted to sing the *"Marseillaise"* to the tune of *"Die Wacht am Rhein."* Always in need of funds, never able to find a broad popular base, the National Social movement remained "a

great German liberal has been questioned. Historians have made an effort to see Naumann's ideas, particularly on foreign policy, in the context of the tensions of Wilhelmian Germany. The most important of these revisions are: R. Nürnberger, "Imperialismus, Sozialismus und Christentum bei Friedrich Naumann," *Historische Zeitschrift*, CLXX, No. 3 (October, 1950), 525–48; and W. Conze, "Friedrich Naumann. Grundlagen und Ansatz seiner Politik in der nationalsozialen Zeit (1895 bis 1903)," *Schicksalswege deutscher Vergangenheit*, ed. W. Hubatsch (Düsseldorf, 1950), pp. 355–87. For a complete bibliography of Naumann's writings and a survey of the works about him, see A. Milatz, *Friedrich Naumann Bibliographie* (Düsseldorf, 1957).

56 On the origins and character of the Inner Mission, see W. Shanahan, *German Protestants Face the Social Question. Vol. I: The Conservative Phase, 1815–1871* (Notre Dame, 1954).

57 On Stoecker, see W. Frank, *Hofprediger Adolf Stoecker und die christlichsoziale Bewegung* (Berlin, 1928), and Heuss, *Naumann*, pp. 40–45, 87–99.

58 For Sohm's views on Christianity and politics, see his speech at the National Socials' convention in 1896, *Protokoll über die Vertreterversammlung aller Nationalsozialen. Erfurt* (Berlin-Schöneberg, 1896), pp. 36 ff. For a good account of Sohm, Weber, and Naumann, see W. Shanahan, "Friedrich Naumann: A Mirror of Wilhelmian Germany," *Review of Politics*, XIII, No. 3 (July, 1951), 278–82.

general staff without an army." Nevertheless, Naumann's ideas struck a responsive chord in Germany's educated middle class. His movement attracted a significant number of university students.[59] Equally impressive is the list of German intellectuals who looked to the National Socials with hopeful expectation: Sohm, Brentano, Weber, Schulze-Gävernitz, Hans Delbrück, and Friedrich Meinecke.[60]

Because of his connection with thinkers like Sohm and Weber and because of his sensitivity to the currents of his age, one historian has called Naumann "a mirror of Wilhelmian Germany."[61] It is worthwhile to examine in some detail Brentano's relationship to Naumann, not only because it illuminates Brentano's relationship to the generation of social reformers who matured after 1890, but also because it suggests Brentano's place in the history of Germany in the quarter century before the great war.

In many respects his alliance with Naumann rested on the same foundation as his collaboration with the left liberals. Like Brentano and Barth, Naumann had come to realize that the only hope for German liberalism was an alliance of workers and bourgeoisie under the leadership of the educated middle class. As he expressed it in 1901:

> The renovation of German liberalism can only occur if the bourgeois-liberal elements recognize that the workers must form the basis of future liberal organization. . . .[62]

Furthermore, Naumann based his hopes for an alliance between the middle class and the workers on an assessment of the S. P. D. similar to that of Brentano and some of the left liberals in the

---

[59] For a representative tribute to Naumann's effect on university students, see Curtius, *Deutsche und antike Welt*, p. 160.

[60] For Naumann and Weber, see W. Mommsen, *Max Weber und die deutsche Politik 1890–1920* (Tübingen, 1959), pp. 138 ff.; on Delbrück, see A. Thimme, *Hans Delbrück als Kritiker der Wilhelminischen Epoche* (Düsseldorf, 1955), pp. 55–58. Meinecke gave Naumann what is perhaps his most impressive epitaph: "Had Naumann been successful there probably would never have been a Hitler movement" (Meinecke, *The German Catastrophe: Reflections and Recollections* [Cambridge, 1950], p. 18.)

[61] Shanahan's article cited above, n. 58.

[62] Quoted by A. Damaschke, *Aus meinem Leben* (Leipzig, 1925), II, 386.

late nineties.[63] As early as 1896, Naumann had tried to make contact with the leaders of German socialism.[64] As the revisionist wing of the party grew more articulate, the *Nationalsozialen* tried to encourage it in every way.[65] Naumann also shared Brentano's high regard for Vollmar and used Brentano as an intermediary to meet him and to seek his co-operation for a reconciliation between bourgeoisie and worker.[66] Although Naumann had long appreciated the importance of social reform as a means of winning the workers, under Brentano's influence he came to emphasize the role of the union movement. Like Brentano, Naumann advocated unified, politically-neutral unionism.[67]

In the years 1899–1902 the co-operation between Naumann and Brentano was deepened by their common opposition to protective tariffs. Like Brentano, Naumann was conscious of Germany's steadily increasing population and was convinced that her future would be determined by her industrial strength.[68] Furthermore, Naumann realized that the power of the Prussian estate owner was one of the greatest barriers to a fulfillment of his image of Germany's future: "The main responsibility for Germany's failure to develop into a free and great nation in the world rests with the agrarian Junkers."[69] For these reasons, although he was not a doctrinaire free trader, Nauman willingly supported Brentano and Barth in their struggle for liberal commercial policies.[70]

Although this community of ideals and practical goals prolonged Brentano's co-operation with Naumann until 1908, significant differences of opinion remained just beneath the surface

---

[63] Naumann, *Demokratie und Kaisertum* (3d ed.; Berlin-Schöneberg, 1904), pp. 3–8.

[64] Heuss, *Naumann*, pp. 105, 157 ff., 533.

[65] For example, see *Die Hilfe*, May 20, 1900.

[66] *Mein Leben*, p. 228; Naumann to Brentano, November 7, 1903, and Naumann to Vollmar, April 4, 1899. The latter is in the Vollmar Papers, International Institute for Social History, Amsterdam.

[67] Heuss, *Naumann*, pp. 155–56.

[68] *Ibid.*, pp. 127, 316. See Naumann, "Was heisst Industriestaat?" *Die Hilfe*, April 6, 1902.

[69] Quoted by A. Ascher, "National Solidarity and Imperial Power: The Sources and Early Development of Social Imperialist Thought in Germany, 1871–1914" (unpub. diss.), Columbia, 1959), p. 171.

[70] Heuss, *Naumann*, pp. 161–62. See also *Demokratie und Kaisertum*, pp. 88 ff.

of their friendship. First, Naumann's ideas still bore the imprint of his conservative background. In contrast to Weber and other contemporaries, as well as to Brentano, Naumann retained until 1908 his faith that Wilhelm II could be won over as the leader of a progressive, industrialized Germany. This concept was most clearly stated in Naumann's book, *Demokratie und Kaisertum,* first published in 1900. Brentano, although a monarchist, expressed serious doubts about Naumann's expectations for the Kaiser.[71] Second, Brentano and Naumann differed profoundly on the role of the nation state and the nature of foreign policy. Since Brentano's view of the nation will be the subject of a later chapter, it is sufficient here to suggest briefly his difference with Naumann. Naumann belonged to the generation which had grown up basking in the glory of the *Reichsgründung* and had matured under the banners of *Weltpolitik*. For him the nation had always been of primary importance. In the mid-nineties Max Weber taught him that although social reform was an important component of national power, the strength of the state came first. As Naumann once expressed it: "Is he [Weber] not right? Of what use is the best *Sozialpolitik* if the Cossacks come?"[72] Like Weber, Naumann felt the power of the state could not be jeopardized by allowing considerations of ethics and morality to interfere in foreign policy.[73]

The first sign of Brentano's disagreement with Naumann's view of the nation came in his review of *Demokratie und Kaisertum,* printed in the *Allgemeine Zeitung* in May, 1900.[74] Although Brentano praised Naumann as "one of those rare men who has the potential of redirecting the life of his nation," he cautioned him against an overemphasis on national power. Brentano was prepared to accept the primary importance of foreign policy, but he warned that the workers would only listen to someone who advocated justice in foreign as well as in domestic affairs. Brentano expressed his views even more candidly in a letter published anonymously in *Die Hilfe* on August 19, 1900.

[71] *Mein Leben,* p. 228.
[72] Quoted from *Die Hilfe,* July, 1895, by J. P. Mayer, *Max Weber and German Politics* (London, 1956), pp. 45–46.
[73] See Naumann's article on politics and morality in *Die Hilfe,* June 10, 1900, and Wenck, *Naumann,* p. 83; Mommsen, *Weber,* pp. 22, 39 ff., 78.
[74] Brentano's review was reprinted in *Die Hilfe,* June 3, 1900. See also Heuss, *Naumann,* pp. 128–33.

Here he warned of the danger implicit in separating morality and foreign policy: to do so, he argued, was tacitly to admit the role of power without justice in domestic affairs.[75]

Naumann's reaction to Brentano's critique illuminates the reason these disagreements did not hinder their co-operation during the first years of their friendship. A few weeks after Brentano's review of his book, Naumann wrote to thank him, "especially for the negative parts." He admitted that his ideas on ethics and foreign policy could well use more thought.[76] Naumann maintained this willingness to listen and to learn for several years. He treated Brentano as his mentor, and was prepared to accept Brentano's frequent admonitions without taking offense, particularly in questions of economics where Naumann had no formal training.[77] Even though Brentano did not always succeed in winning Naumann over to his point of view, Naumann's respectful attitude undoubtedly helped to preserve their friendship in spite of the important differences between them.

Although Naumann's willingness to learn from Brentano facilitated their co-operation, in the last analysis it was their common struggle against protective tariffs and political reaction that brought them together. Participation in this struggle also encouraged the co-operation of Naumann and Barth. During the election of 1898 the differences of opinion between the *Freisinnige Vereinigung* and the National Socials were still apparent. In the next year, however, relations between the two groups improved.[78] In 1900 Barth referred to Naumann as a man who "shows Germany the road to robust political health."[79] By this time Naumann and Barth were co-operating on the tariff ques-

75 Brentano can be identified as the author of this letter by references in a letter from Max Maurenbrecher to Brentano, August 13, 1900. See also *Mein Leben*, p. 228.
76 Naumann to Brentano, July 20, 1900.
77 Heuss, *Naumann*, pp. 174–75; see also the description of Naumann's attitude towards Brentano in E. Heuss-Knapp, *Ausblick vom Münsterturm: Erlebtes aus dem Elsass und dem Reich* (Berlin-Tempelhof, 1934), pp. 66–67.
78 Wenck, *Naumann*, p. 95.
79 From Barth's review of *Demokratie und Kaisertum*, reprinted in *Die Hilfe*, November 25, 1900. For a comparison of Naumann's and Barth's ideas, see G. Daniels, *Individuum und Gemeinschaft bei Theodor Barth und Friedrich Naumann* (diss., Hamburg, 1932).

tion, and in 1901 *Die Hilfe* endorsed Barth's candidature for the Reichstag, because, as it said, he had completed the transition from "Manchester liberalism to free trade and social reform."[80] In 1903 Barth wrote in the *Nation* that the National Socials should be considered a part of the liberal movement because of their energetic championing of free trade. "Liberalism," Barth added, "could rejoice if a man with Naumann's gifts . . . swore allegiance to its cause."[81]

Until 1903, however, the co-operation between the *National-sozialen* and the left liberals had been limited to the friendship of a few leaders like Barth, Naumann, and von Gerlach. Efforts to bring the groups into close harmony did not meet with success before 1903.[82] Many of Barth's liberal colleagues were not as willing as he to sponsor social reform and to contemplate an alliance with the Socialists. These men tended to distrust the Naumann group and were distrusted in return by the National Socials.

The decisive event in the relationship between the National Social Party and the *Freisinnige Vereinigung* was the election of 1903. Naumann regarded the election as crucial for the life of his party.[83] The outcome was disastrous: Naumann and all but one of the National Social candidates were defeated; after five years of intensive agitation the party received only a few hundred more votes than it had in the election of 1898.[84] Naumann drew the obvious conclusion from these results:

> We are not in the position to establish a party. That is the bitter truth, but true nonetheless. There is no longer any question of attempting to be a party.[85]

[80] See *Die Hilfe*, November 25, 1900, and November 10, 1901.

[81] Quoted in *ibid.*, April 5, 1903.

[82] Heuss, *Naumann*, p. 164; see also G. von Schulze-Gävernitz to Brentano, October 17, 1900.

[83] *Die Hilfe*, May 3, 1903; Naumann to Traub, August 2, 1903 (Traub Papers, Bundesarchiv, Koblenz); Eugen Katz to Brentano, May 12, 1903.

[84] In 1898 the total number of votes received was 27,208; in 1903 the total was 27,900 (*Die Hilfe*, June 28, 1903). Since these votes were only from districts where a National Social candidate ran they do not give an indication of the movement's total strength.

[85] Heuss, *Naumann*, pp. 165–66; Naumann, "Die Niederlage," *Die Hilfe*, June 28, 1903.

Naumann was determined that his party be dissolved lest it gradually and ingloriously disintegrate.[86] At first he thought about withdrawing from active politics.[87] By the end of June, however, he had begun to consider joining the *Freisinnige Vereinigung*.[88] On July 11, Naumann and von Gerlach met with the leaders of the *Vereinigung* to discuss the fusion of the two groups. Perhaps largely due to their own losses in the election, the liberals agreed to welcome any *Nationalsozialen* who chose to join them. The liberal leaders stipulated that local National Social groups might remain, but the central organization had to be dissolved.[89] At the National Socials' final meeting in August, 1903, Naumann strongly urged his followers to accompany him into the *Vereinigung*. Although there was some resistance to this request, the majority complied.[90]

A week before the last meeting of the *Nationalsozialer Verein*, Brentano wrote an article for the *Nation* recommending the fusion of the National Socials and the left liberals.[91] Two days after this meeting, he announced that he had decided to accompany Naumann into the *Vereinigung*.[92] In the light of Brentano's views on political parties, the motives for this decision require some examination.

On August 20 and 21, a few days before the National Socials' meeting, Naumann stayed at Brentano's summer home near Munich.[93] It was evidently at this time that Naumann convinced Brentano that he should join the left liberal party. Brentano had recommended that Naumann join the left liberals

---

[86] Naumann to Brentano, July 3, 1903.

[87] Heuss, *Naumann*, p. 166, and Wenck, *Naumann*, pp. 96–97.

[88] Naumann to Brentano, July 3, 1903.

[89] Heuss, *Naumann*, p. 167; Naumann to Traub, July 15, 1903 (Traub Papers); Schrader to the *Fraktion* of the *Freisinnige Vereinigung*, July 13, 1903 (G. Roesicke Papers, Bundesarchiv, Koblenz); Schrader to Naumann, July 27, 1903, reprinted in *Die Hilfe*, August 2, 1903.

[90] *Die Hilfe*, September 6, 1903; Curtius, *Deutsche und antike Welt*, pp. 242–43; A. Damaschke, *Aus meinem Leben*, II, 440–46; H. von Gerlach, "Der letzte Nationalsoziale Vertretertag," *Die Zeit*, September 3, 1903, pp. 707–10.

[91] Reprinted in *Die Hilfe*, August 16, 1903.

[92] Announcement in the *Berliner Tageblatt*, quoted in *Die Zeit*, September 3, 1903.

[93] On the timing of Naumann's visit to Brentano, see his letters of August 9 and 28, 1903. For a description of his stay, see Heuss-Knapp, *Ausblick*, p. 360.

soon after the defeat of the National Socials in 1903.[94] Perhaps he agreed to join the party in order to overcome Naumann's reluctance to take this step and to counter his desire to withdraw from party politics.[95] Perhaps he allowed Naumann to persuade him to join because it would benefit the proposed fusion in at least two important ways. First, Brentano's participation would placate those National Socials who were displeased with the prospect of giving up the independent existence of their movement.[96] Second, Brentano's prestige among the left liberals would help to ease any tension within the *Vereinigung* caused by the fusion with the National Socials.[97]

In the months immediately following his entrance into the party, Brentano devoted himself to the cause of liberal unity. Like Barth, Brentano seems to have hoped that Naumann could bring new life to German liberalism and that a powerful force might be built upon the principles of liberal reform.[98] In the fall and winter of 1903, Brentano wrote several articles advocating liberal unity and at the same time joined Naumann and Barth in their effort to win over some small liberal groups to the *Freisinnige Vereinigung*.[99]

Any hopes for liberal unity in 1903 were quickly dispelled. Eugen Richter remained completely opposed to any co-operation

[94] Naumann's letter of July 3 referred to the *Freisinnige Vereinigung* as "the way you recommended."

[95] Naumann to Brentano, August 28, 1903. See also a letter from Naumann recalling their conversations, February 26, 1907, reprinted in Heuss, *Naumann*, pp. 537–38. In *Mein Leben* (pp. 229–30) Brentano claimed that before he talked to Naumann the latter was considering joining the S. P. D. This is very doubtful. As early as July 3, 1903, Naumann wrote to Brentano that he regarded joining the S. P. D. as "completely impossible." Heuss (*Naumann*, p. 175) also questioned Brentano's account.

[96] See the opinions of the various National Social local groups reprinted in *Die Hilfe* during the summer of 1903.

[97] See M. Broemel to Brentano, November 3, 1903; H. Pachnicke, *Führende Männer im alten und im neuen Reich* (Berlin, 1930), pp. 22–23.

[98] Heuss, *Naumann*, p. 173.

[99] Barth to Brentano, September 8, 1903; Naumann to Brentano, September 7, 1903; W. Kulemann, *Politische Erinnerungen: Ein Beitrag zur neueren Zeitgeschichte* (Berlin, 1911), pp. 197 ff. Brentano wrote the following articles on liberal unity during this period: "Unsere Zukunft," *Die Hilfe*, August 9, 1903; "Zur Einigung der Liberalen," *Frankfurter Zeitung*, November 13, 1903; and "Über politische Initiative, *Die Hilfe*, November 15, 1903.

with the *Freisinnige Vereinigung*. The *Jungliberalen,* a group of young National Liberals avowedly interested in social reform, were hostile to any form of left liberal unity.[100] Perhaps most disheartening of all, it quickly became apparent that there was a significant group within the *Freisinnige Vereinigung* itself which opposed Barth's and Naumann's ideals.[101]

Naumann reacted to the problems of liberal unity by gradually trying to secure a base of power within the *Freisinnige Vereinigung.*[102] His experiences in the National Social movement had convinced him of the importance of party organization. Like his contemporaries Max Weber and Robert Michels, Naumann realized that organization was a prerequisite to political success, and he endeavored to use this knowledge to revitalize German liberalism.[103] Here was a final and significant contrast between Naumann and Brentano. It is doubtful if Brentano had ever been interested in the *Freisinnige Vereinigung* as a political party. He had been interested in Naumann and in the ideals of the National Social movement, but he had no patience for the problems of the party as a political organization.[104] Within a

---

100 See Brentano's article, "Jungliberale Krokodilstränen," *Freistatt,* V, No. 49 (December, 1903), 963–65.

101 Heuss, *Naumann,* pp. 175 ff.; Broemel to Brentano, November 3, 1903; Eugen Katz to Brentano, December 30, 1903, and March 22, 1904; Naumann to Traub, February 9, 1904 (Traub Papers).

102 See Naumann's letter to Traub, February 9, 1904 (Traub Papers). One of the central issues which divided the *Freisinnige Vereinigung* was Naumann's insistence on universal suffrage for Prussia. Many of the *Vereinigung's* members feared that if three-class suffrage was abandoned their representation in the Prussian Landtag would be significantly reduced. See W. Gagel, *Die Wahlrechtsfrage in der Geschichte der deutschen liberalen Parteien 1848–1918* (Düsseldorf, 1958), pp. 158–62.

103 Naumann's realization of the importance of organization marked an important turning point in the evolution of German liberalism. On this point, see his article "Die Organisation des Liberalismus" in *Die Erneuerung des Liberalismus* by Naumann and Barth (Berlin-Schöneberg, 1906), pp. 29–33. On Naumann's views in historical perspective, see J. Knoll, *Führungsauslese in Liberalismus und Demokratie* (Stuttgart, 1957), pp. 126–33; T. Schieder, "Das Verhältnis von politischer und gesellschaftlicher Verfassung und die Krise des bürgerlichen Liberalismus," *Staat und Gesellschaft im Wandel unserer Zeit* (Munich, 1958); and T. Nipperdey, *Die Organisation der deutschen Parteien,* pp. 187 ff.

104 In November, 1903, Brentano was elected to the left liberals' Executive Committee. He declined at first, but eventually was persuaded to accept. Judging from the very small amount of correspondence in Brentano's own

few months of joining the party Brentano again directed his attention to the more secure and scholarly activities of the *Verein für Sozialpolitik.*

As we have seen, the struggle against reaction in the 1890's provided the impetus for Brentano's alliance with Barth and Naumann. The left liberal parties were one source of resistance to the agrarian movement and to the reactionary measures against the workers. Therefore, Brentano found himself being drawn into co-operation with these parties. This co-operation, however, was always qualified by his disinterest in, indeed his aversion to, organized political action. Brentano shared most of the left liberals' principles and he was willing to defend these principles in lectures, in newspaper articles, and even in political meetings. He was reluctant, however, to take part in any political organization which sought to uphold these principles in parliamentary politics. One suspects that the left liberals' lack of influence was at least in part due to the fact that too many potential allies shared Brentano's apolitical attitudes.

---

papers and in the papers of Karl Schrader, the party chairman, Brentano took very little interest in party affairs. See the letters of the *Wahlverein der Liberalen* to Brentano, November 17 and 24, 1903. I am also indebted to the late Professor Theodor Heuss for his remarks to me on Brentano's attitude towards parties.

# CHAPTER VIII

# *"Sozialpolitik"* in the Last Decade of Peace 1904-1914

## 1 —

By 1904 the agrarians' triumph on the tariff question had removed the subject which had absorbed Brentano's attention since the late 1890's. At the same time, the quickened tempo of labor disputes after the turn of the century once again placed the problems of the worker in the center of his concern.[1]

When Brentano's faith in unionism was restored in 1889–90, the condition of the German unions was rather fluid.[2] The early nineties remained—in the words of one historian—"a period of experimentation," and Brentano could hope, as he had hoped in the early 1870's, that from the German movement would emerge unions similar to the British Amalgamated Societies. After 1890, however, there remained little on the German scene to nourish this hope. The unions' vitality of 1889–90 proved temporary and was followed by a period of decline which persisted until the middle of the decade. In 1895, aided by a significant economic upswing, the union movement began a period of tremendous growth.[3] The most striking element in this expansion was the

[1] On the number of strikes and lockouts in 1904–5, see J. Kuczynski, *Die Geschichte der Lage der Arbeiter unter dem Kapitalismus. Vol. 1: Die Geschichte der Lage der Arbeiter in Deutschland von 1789 bis in die Gegenwart* (6th ed.; Berlin, 1954), Part II, pp. 50 and 67.

[2] Theodor Cassau, *Die Gewerkschaftsbewegung: Ihre Soziologie und ihr Kampf* (Halberstadt, 1925), pp. 23 ff.

[3] Cassau, *Gewerkschaftsbewegung*, pp. 27 ff., and G. A. Ritter, *Die Arbeiterbewegung im Wilhelminischen Reich: Die sozialdemokratische Partei und die freien Gewerkschaften 1890–1900* (Berlin, 1959), pp. 150 ff.

triumph of the organizations associated with the Social Democratic Party which quickly affirmed their domination of organized labor. Under the skillful leadership of Karl Legien, these "Free Unions" combined a highly centralized organization with widespread popular support among German workers. After 1894 the Free Unions' chief competitor was the Christian Union movement which developed under the aegis of the Center Party. The Hirsch-Duncker unions maintained a steady if undramatic rate of growth, although after 1900 they were increasingly overshadowed by the Christian and Socialist organizations.[4]

Brentano implicitly recognized the direction taken by German unionism during the nineties when he was forced to admit in 1899 that Germany was still "at the beginning" of a process of social evolution similar to England's.[5] In the years immediately following the turn of the century it must have been increasingly difficult for him to overlook the fact that German labor was in the midst of its own course of development, not at the beginning of England's or anyone else's. It is hard to believe that each passing year did not make him more cognizant of the fact that German unionism had long ago opted against the course of development which he had been proposing since the 1870's. The few independent organizations of skilled workers in Germany which were comparable to the Amalgamated Society of Engineers were being swallowed up by the tide of the Socialist and Christian unions' expansion. The German unions' connection with political parties, which Brentano had always deplored as an impediment to social progress, was clearly reaffirmed during the nineties.[6] Confronted by the vigorous and well-established unions of 1900, Brentano could no longer explain the disparity between the German situation and his English models by pointing to the "immaturity" of German labor organizations as he had in the seventies.

Furthermore, by 1900 it must have been difficult for Brentano

---

4 The following figures suggest the pattern of union growth after 1890: the Free Unions had 278,000 members in 1891, 682,000 in 1900, and 2,574,000 in 1913; the Christian Unions had 77,000 members by 1900 and 343,000 by 1913; the Hirsch-Duncker went from 66,000 in 1891 to 92,000 in 1900 and 107,000 in 1913. Figures cited in G. Bry, *Wages in Germany, 1871–1914* (Princeton, 1960), p. 32.

5 Brentano, *Reaktion oder Reform: Gegen die Zuchthausvorlage* (Berlin-Schöneberg, 1899), p. 59.

6 Brentano called attention to this in *ibid.*, p. 19.

to continue to accept labor disputes as an inevitable product of union development, necessary to teach workers and employers that compromise through arbitration was the only sensible way to settle their differences. This argument for the educational value of labor conflicts seems rather less than adequate justification for the bitter and sometimes violent strikes and lockouts which occurred in Germany after 1900, and particularly from 1903 to 1906. There was, moreover, no indication that these labor troubles were producing the desired will to compromise among the participants. Not only did few arbitration boards spontaneously develop from these conflicts, but even the government's efforts to set them up proved ineffective.[7]

As the German labor movement was progressing in a fashion inconsistent with Brentano's hopes, the structure of German capitalism was undergoing some significant changes. In the late nineteenth and early twentieth centuries the economy of every industrialized nation was transformed by the development of monopolies, cartels, or trusts. Nowhere was this development more pronounced than in Germany, where economic and political conditions provided a climate particularly well suited for the growth of cartels.[8] Parallel to the spread of cartels was the tendency of German employers to form organizations to represent their common interests, particularly their common opposition to labor unions. After 1898, and especially in the years 1903–6, employers' associations grew in number and became increasingly aggressive in their relationship to the labor movement.[9]

[7] Hans Jürgen Teuteberg estimated that, with the exception of the mining industry, only about 10 per cent of the firms with over 20 employees even had committees to present the workers' grievances; see *Geschichte der industriellen Mitbestimmung in Deutschland* (Tübingen, 1961), p. 408.

[8] On cartels in Germany see the studies in *Über wirtschaftliche Kartelle in Deutschland, Schriften des Vereins für Sozialpolitik*, XL (Leipzig, 1894). For a general history of the development of monopolies in Germany, see the remarks in G. Stolper, *German Economy 1870–1940* (New York, 1940), pp. 83–88, and A. Sartorius von Waltershausen, *Deutsche Wirtschaftsgeschichte 1815–1914* (Jena, 1920), pp. 463, 472 ff. Waltershausen estimated that in 1905 there were 366 industrial cartels (p. 487). For the most recent literature on cartels, see the bibliography in L. Mayer, *Kartelle, Kartellorganisation und Kartellpolitik* (Wiesbaden, 1959), pp. 335–72.

[9] On the employers' associations see C. Schorske, *German Social Democracy, 1905–1917: The Development of the Great Schism* (Cambridge, 1955), p. 29; G. Kessler, *Die deutschen Arbeitgeberverbände, Schriften des Vereins für*

It will be recalled that Brentano had become aware of the significance of cartels during the late 1880's, when he regarded them as a "parachute" to ease the effects of an economic slump. In 1890, when he seemed to be optimistic about the chances of a union movement on the English model, Brentano encouraged the employers to organize because he felt that a parallel development of unions and employers' associations would facilitate the formation of centralized arbitration boards.[10] In 1894 he pointed out that although there were dangers in cartelization, monopolies were a necessary part of the modern economic structure. To prove this he pointed to the development of cartels in England and to the success these cartels had had in negotiating peacefully with trade unions.[11]

After 1900 Brentano became increasingly aware of the changes which cartels and employers' organizations were making in the structure of the German economy.[12] In 1902 he participated in a government commission on cartels which convinced him of their tremendous economic power and political influence. The behavior of the commission also demonstrated the government's acquiescence in the cartelization of the economy.[13] At the same time, a series of polemics with the officials of employers' associa-

---

Sozialpolitik, CXXIV (Leipzig, 1907), passim; A. Weber, Der Kampf zwischen Kapital und Arbeit (Tübingen, 1954), pp. 169–97.

[10] Die Stellung der Gebildeten zur sozialen Frage (Berlin, n.d. [1890]), p. 3; "Der Achtstundentag in England," Deutsches Wochenblatt, III, No. 48 (November 27, 1890), 573.

[11] See Brentano's remarks in the Verhandlungen von 1894, Schriften des Vereins für Sozialpolitik, XLI (Leipzig, 1895), 171–86.

[12] An interesting symptom of the awareness among German thinkers that the economy was undergoing significant changes is the interest in the origins and nature of capitalism which grew up in Germany after the turn of the century. In 1903, for example, at the time Brentano was beginning to consider the practical aspects of German capitalism's transformations, Max Weber, Werner Sombart, and Edgar Jaffe took over the Archiv für Sozialwissenschaften und Sozialpolitik, for the main purpose of the "historical and theoretical analysis of the cultural significance of capitalism."

[13] Brentano, Mein Leben im Kampfe um die soziale Entwicklung Deutschlands (Jena, 1931), pp. 231 ff. Hereafter cited as Mein Leben. See also Brentano's essay, "Die beabsichtigte Neuorganisation der deutschen Volkswirtschaft," Süddeutsche Monatshefte, I, No. 4 (April, 1904), 272. For a brief summary of the government's policy towards cartels, see Theodore F. Marburg, "Government and Business in Germany: Public Policy towards Cartels," Business History Review, XXXVIII, No. 1 (Spring, 1964), 78–101.

tions made him aware of the reactionary attitude prevalent in these groups. Furthermore, the effective co-operation of German employers during the five month lockout of the Crimmitschau textile workers in 1903 clearly displayed the power of organized capital.[14]

Brentano expressed his views on the role of cartels and employers' associations in an article entitled "The Prospective Reorganization of the German Economy," which he published early in 1904.[15] This article showed the extent to which he felt the German economy had changed:

> We still speak as though we live in an age of economic freedom [*Gewerbefreiheit*] and competition. This is an example of how our past experiences hinder our perception and judgment of the world around us. Today economic freedom and competition belong to the past. We live in an age of increasingly expanding monopoly.[16]

Brentano felt that cartelization involved significant dangers for the German economy. The first was that the cartelized producers of raw materials would exercise undue influence over those manufacturers whose modes of production made it more difficult for them to form cartels. He suggested an arbitration committee to settle whatever difficulties might arise between these groups. Brentano saw a second danger in the fact that cartels might prove detrimental to the economy as a whole by keeping in existence inefficient firms which otherwise would be destroyed by competition. This development, he argued, could be avoided by removing tariff barriers and thus subjecting the cartel to the pressures of foreign competition.

The most significant part of Brentano's 1904 article treated the implications of cartels for labor relations. Cartels, he pointed out, could "reduce the workers to bondage. . . . Unless their organizations are recognized as equal partners in the reorganization of industry, the workers' rights will be significantly reduced."[17] Brentano argued that just as the representatives of cartelized and other industries should meet to arbitrate their

14 Schorske, *German Social Democracy*, p. 30, and *Mein Leben*, p. 239.
15 "Die beabsichtigte Neuorganisation," cited above, n. 13.
16 *Ibid.*, p. 255.
17 *Ibid.*, p. 273.

differences, representatives of management and labor should also have a common organization.

In this article Brentano seemed rather uncertain as to how this organization of workers and employers would come about. There were some indications, however, that he had begun to revise his views on the role of the state in settling labor disputes. He admitted, for example, that the government should have a representative on the arbitration board, first, to prevent these organized interests from becoming too powerful, and second, to protect the interests of the consumer.[18] Perhaps more significant, Brentano seemed to be pleased that Count Posadowsky, the Minister of the Interior, was considering some legislation to set up industrial arbitration committees.[19]

On January 6, 1905, the Executive Committee of the *Verein für Sozialpolitik* met to discuss the program for their convention scheduled for that fall in Mannheim. The committee accepted Brentano's proposal that they discuss labor relations in large industries, and he was selected as the main speaker.[20]

A few days after the *Verein*'s committee met, the Ruhr miners engaged in one of the largest strikes in the prewar period.[21] Just as in 1889, the miners' strike began a year of intensive labor disputes during which almost half a million workers were involved in work stoppages.[22] Furthermore, the revolution in Russia and the tensions on the international scene added to a general feeling of anxiety and unrest throughout the year. As one observer summarized the mood of 1905: "Troubled times seem to lie ahead, war and revolution are in the air."[23] It was within this context, therefore, that Brentano prepared his speech for the *Verein*'s meeting in the first months of 1905.

[18] *Ibid.*, p. 274.

[19] *Ibid.*

[20] F. Boese, *Geschichte des Vereins für Sozialpolitik 1872–1932, Schriften des Vereins für Sozialpolitik,* CLXXXVIII (Berlin, 1939), 103.

[21] M. Koch, *Die Bergarbeiterbewegung im Ruhrgebiet zur Zeit Wilhelms II (1889–1914)* (Düsseldorf, 1954), pp. 77–108. Cf. the account in D. Fricke, *Der Ruhrbergarbeiterstreik von 1905* (Berlin, 1955).

[22] K. Born, *Staat und Sozialpolitik seit Bismarcks Sturz: Ein Beitrag zur Entwicklung des deutschen Reiches 1890–1914* (Wiesbaden, 1957), pp. 184 ff., and J. Kuczynski, *Geschichte der Lage der Arbeiter,* I, Part II, 67.

[23] The quote is from a letter from Ferdinand Tönnies to Friedrich Paulsen, November 20, 1905, printed in O. Klose, ed., *Tönnies-Paulsen Briefwechsel 1876–1908* (Kiel, 1961), p. 394.

Brentano outlined his plans in a letter to Schmoller of February 28, 1905.[24] "Things can't go on like this," he wrote, "something has to be done." Brentano wanted his speech at Mannheim to be more than "a scholarly monologue"; he wanted a "practical act." He proposed that his ideas be supported at the *Verein* meeting by those members like Schmoller and the Weber brothers who were friendly to the workers. For this reason he sent them a draft of his proposals in order to secure their agreement before the meeting. "Then," he wrote, "we must support each other in the debate following my speech, just as the members of a party support each other in parliament." Brentano's analogy clearly indicates that he wanted to disturb that delicate balance within the *Verein* between scholarship and politics in order to bridge the gap between theory and practice.

The development of cartels, the growth of employers' associations, and finally the course of the Ruhr strike had convinced Brentano that mere recognition of the unions by the government was no longer sufficient to stabilize labor relations. Besides recognizing the collective nature of labor contracts, he wrote Schmoller that the government should set up an official organization (*amtliche Organisation*) in which these contracts could be fairly and peacefully negotiated. The present unions, because of their diversity and political character, could not provide such an organization. Instead, the government should establish an organization of all the workers in an industry. The workers would then elect representatives to meet with the representatives of organized capital. The unions would continue to exist, and it would be left up to them to attempt to secure representation on the arbitration committee.

The representatives of labor and management would seek to elect a neutral person as chairman; if they failed, the state would appoint one. Although measures would be taken to enforce the decisions of the arbitration board, Brentano did not suggest what would take place if a workable solution could not be reached. Moreover, the workers' right to strike and the employers' right to lock their workers out were to remain. Brentano seems to have felt confident that the mere existence of arbitration facilities

24 Reprinted in *Mein Leben*, pp. 249–52. For a reaction to the social tensions of 1905 similar to Brentano's, see Waldemar Zimmermann, "Streikverhütung," *Preussische Jahrbücher*, CXX, No. 2 (1905), 256–95.

would make disputes much more infrequent. He concluded this letter to Schmoller by reaffirming the necessity of an organization such as he proposed:

> In the face of the increasing monopolistic character of our industry it seems to me to be unavoidable that such an organization be created. Anything else would deliver the worker over to a new serfdom and the entire German economy to labor unrest such as we are now experiencing and worse.[25]

Schmoller's response to Brentano's plan was extremely cautious.[26] Although he agreed with Brentano's assessment of the situation, he insisted that Brentano's plans be limited to a few of the largest industries like coal and iron. Schmoller tentatively agreed to support Brentano at Mannheim, but asked that, as usual, no vote be taken on the speakers' recommendations.

Throughout the spring of 1905 Brentano sent his proposals to the other members of the *Verein* whose support he hoped to gain for the Mannheim debate. Alfred Weber expressed his general agreement with Brentano's ideas, although he was worried about what would happen if the workers and the employers could find no compromise solution.[27] Max Weber was rather less enthusiastic. Weber had always shared Brentano's high regard for unions and this had not diminished after 1900. He was afraid that Brentano's proposed organization would ruin the unions. He also objected to the loss of individuality and the leveling effect which such an organization might produce. Like Schmoller, however, Weber appeared ready to support Brentano if he confined his proposals to the giant industries.[28]

---

25 *Ibid.*, p. 252. It is interesting to note that in 1892 Brentano had criticized an Austrian plan for industrial organizations quite similar to those he proposed in 1905. See *Über die Fortbildung des Arbeitsvertrages* (Vienna, 1892), pp. 11 ff.

26 Schmoller to Brentano, March 5, 1905, reprinted in *Mein Leben,* p. 252.

27 Alfred Weber to Brentano, March 6, March 20, May 27, 1905. Unless otherwise stated all unpublished letters are in the Lujo Brentano Papers.

28 Max Weber to Brentano, April 25, 1905. See W. Mommsen, *Max Weber und die deutsche Politik 1890–1920* (Tübingen, 1959), pp. 129–32. As Mommsen pointed out, Brentano took over entire phrases from Weber's letter in his speech at Mannheim. These phrases, however, expressed ideas Brentano had had for years and cannot be used as evidence for Weber's influence on Brentano.

In his talk at Mannheim, Brentano ignored Schmoller's and Weber's injunction to direct his attention to a few of the largest industries. Instead he rather ambiguously defined the industries to which his plan applied as "all private firms in which the large number of workers makes individual regulation of working conditions impossible."[29] Then, after a vigorous attack on the efforts of German industrialists to exploit their workers, Brentano presented his vision of a "corporate organization of capital and labor." His proposals at Mannheim were essentially the same as those he had written to Schmoller on February 28, although in final form he de-emphasized somewhat the official aspects of the arbitration committee. He also pointed out an added advantage to his proposal: the perpetual problem of strike breakers (*Arbeitswilligen*) would be solved by making all the workers in an industry responsible to the decisions of a single organization.

Stung by his criticisms, members of the business community at Mannheim vigorously attacked Brentano.[30] Naumann, Weber, and others defended him from these attacks, criticized the reactionary character of German entrepreneurs, and demanded equal rights for the working class.[31] There was very little support, however, for the positive proposals Brentano had made. Even before the meeting, Schmoller had expressed his disappointment with the fact that Brentano seemed to be de-emphasizing the official character of his proposed arbitration committee.[32] Schmoller did not take part in the debate after Brentano's address. Max Weber stated the same doubts that he had written to Brentano earlier in the year: Brentano's proposals, Weber felt, would be acceptable only in the rather distant future.[33]

After his address, a number of Brentano's friends expressed their surprise at the radical shift in his views.[34] In his remarks at the end of the Mannheim debate he tried to show how his

29 *Verhandlungen von 1905, Schriften des Vereins für Sozialpolitik* (Leipzig, 1906), CXVI, 135. Hereafter cited as *Verhandlungen 1905.*
30 See the speech by Dr. Leidig in *ibid.*, pp. 150–58.
31 *Ibid.*, pp. 186 ff. and 212 ff.
32 Schmoller to Brentano, May 24, 1905.
33 *Verhandlungen 1905*, pp. 212 ff.
34 Naumann, for example, regarded Brentano's address as a significant shift in his ideas; see *Die Hilfe*, October 15, 1905. See also the remarks by Otto von Zweideneck-Südenhorst, *Lujo Brentano: Grusswort und Reden bei der Feier der 110. Wiederkehr seines Geburtstages* (Berlin, 1956), p. 25.

present position was actually not inconsistent with what he had always taught about trade unionism. "It is clear," he said,

> that in political questions one does not always express one's final thoughts about the future. Fifteen years ago, when I maintained that official labor organizations should not be established, I did not think that the day might not come when the state would have to take a hand in recognizing these organizations.[35]

It is rather pointless to argue what Brentano might or might not have thought prior to 1905. It is clear, however, that his address at Mannheim marked a genuine shift away from what he had written since 1890. At Mannheim Brentano tacitly acknowledged that the nature of German unionism, the increasing cartelization of industry, and the constant danger of anti-union action by the government precluded the fulfillment of his vision of social reform on the English model.[36] Moreover, Brentano's speech suggested that he had given up not only his British model but also the liberal principles upon which this model was based. In 1868–69 the experience of British unionism had led Brentano to believe that, if the workers were allowed to organize, the free play of economic forces could produce equitable social relations. By 1905 Brentano seems to have lost faith not only in unionism but also in the benevolence and perhaps even the existence of a free market economy. His acceptance of state initiative in solving social problems reproduced in microcosm the process which transformed European liberalism as a whole in the late nineteenth and early twentieth centuries.

It is interesting to note that at Mannheim Brentano referred to the system of arbitration he proposed as a "corporate organization of industry." His plan did have some significant points in common with suggestions for reform that had been made by

---

[35] *Verhandlungen 1905,* p. 232.

[36] It is not clear to what extent Brentano realized that the British unions themselves were being radically transformed in the early twentieth century. After 1900, anti-union legislation caused the British unions to become increasingly concerned with political action. By 1905 the political neutrality which Brentano had so admired in the late sixties was almost entirely gone. See H. Pelling, *A History of British Trade Unionism* (Baltimore, 1963), p. 123.

German conservative social theorists since the 1860's.[37] Brentano's relationship with these theorists is impossible to document, but it is tempting to consider whether, after he lost his faith in the liberal vision of economics, he returned to the conservative principles of his family for inspiration.

## 2 —

It is clear that Brentano wanted to gather support for his speech at Mannheim so that it might have some practical effect in easing Germany's social tensions. His hope of bringing the *Verein* closer to practical problems coincided with the desires of some of the young men who had joined that organization after 1890.[38] Without question, the most outstanding of these young men was Max Weber. Weber was forty-one in 1905 and already a widely acclaimed sociologist. His intellect made him a formidable opponent in any debate, and like Brentano he seemed to pour into his speeches a passion which could find no other outlet in the political structure of imperial Germany. Weber was supported at Mannheim by his friend and political ally, Friedrich Naumann. Naumann's impressive appearance, his forceful personality, and his stylistic gifts made him one of the most effective political speakers of his day. If he lacked Weber's fire and genius, he possessed a smoothness and grace which he had acquired during his years as a political leader.

Against these newcomers stood a large number of older members of the *Verein*, who were determined that the conservative and scholarly character of their organization be retained. Their leader was Gustav Schmoller. In 1905 Schmoller was at the peak of his influence. A member of the *Herrenhaus*, a holder of a chair at the University of Berlin, he was one of the most powerful men in the German academic world. However, at sixty-seven Schmol-

---

[37] At Mannheim, Brentano remarked that his plan "would satisfy even the conservatives' ideal of a restored order in labor relations. . . ." *Ibid.*, p. 147. The conservative thinker whose ideas Brentano's proposals most resembled is Hermann Wagener; see H. J. Schoeps, "Hermann Wagener, ein konservativer Sozialist: Ein Beitrag zur Ideengeschichte des Sozialismus," *Zeitschrift für Religions- und Geistesgeschichte*, VIII, No. 3 (1956), 204 ff. In 1906 Brentano praised Wagener's early appreciation of the value of labor organizations, "Zum fünfundzwanzigjährigen Jubiläum der deutschen Sozialpolitik," *Münchener Neueste Nachrichten*, November 19, 1906.

[38] Schmoller to Brentano, April 26, 1892.

ler's health was beginning to fail, and he suffered from chronic headaches. Long years of overwork and heavy responsibility had taken their toll. Although he retained his calm appearance, his characteristic composure and patience occasionally gave way.

At Mannheim the conflict of generations within the *Verein* came to the surface. The tension between scholarship and politics which had marked the course of the *Verein* in the early 1870's reappeared. The occasion was the debate following an address by Schmoller on the relationship between cartels and the state. The debate was unusually long and heated. The speakers widened the scope of their discussion to include some of Germany's most important domestic issues: the condition of the workers, the attitude of German industrialists, and the government's social policies. Under the leadership of Naumann and Weber, the *Verein* seemed to have been enlivened by a new spirit which was critical of Germany's internal politics.[39] At the end of a day and a half of debate, Schmoller attacked this new spirit by attacking Naumann. I have the impression, Schmoller said, "that this is essentially a demagogue speaking . . . who repeats the old Marxist slogans without any real knowledge."[40] Schmoller's remarks were greeted with a storm of disapproval from the younger members of the *Verein*. After a bitter counterattack by Max Weber, Schmoller explained that he had not meant "demagogue" in the worst sense of the term but that he did feel that Naumann's brand of eloquence "belongs in a popular meeting rather than a scholarly discussion."[41]

Although he was obviously annoyed at the criticisms directed against his ideas during the debate, Schmoller's remarks were more a reflection of his dismay at seeing the *Verein* turned into an arena in which political issues were hotly debated. In the weeks following the Mannheim meeting the conflict between Schmoller, Naumann, and Weber continued. Brentano, whose

[39] *Verhandlungen 1905*, pp. 217–418.
[40] *Ibid.*, p. 420.
[41] *Ibid.*, p. 433; *Mein Leben*, pp. 254–55; T. Heuss, *Friedrich Naumann: Der Mann, das Werk, die Zeit* (2d ed.; Stuttgart and Tübingen, 1949), pp. 238–40. Heuss overestimated the extent to which Schmoller's remarks were motivated by his wounded vanity. Cf. Boese, *Geschichte des Vereins*, pp. 110 ff., who greatly underestimated the seriousness of the quarrel between Naumann and Schmoller.

sympathy lay with Naumann and Weber, nevertheless sought to mediate between them and Schmoller. His mediation prevented a complete break and a compromise was achieved.[42]

In the years after 1905, however, the victory of the conservative wing of the *Verein* became clear. Just as after the debate on the tariff question in 1879, after 1905 the *Verein* occupied itself with politically neutral topics. It remained what Weber had once contemptuously called it: "The *Verein für salonfähige Sozial-politik* "[43] At the same time, Schmoller was able to reaffirm the *Verein's* devotion to political conservatism. In July, 1906, he expressed the unwillingness of the majority to work for any extensive changes in the German political structure: the *Verein,* he said, had to be organized on the desire "for moderate reform, based on the present political and economic order. . . .

> I believe that it would be advisable in order to perpetuate the *Verein* in this spirit if those elements which, for example, seek a democratization of our state . . . did this as members of a political party rather than as members of the *Verein*. . . .[44]

Shortly after the conflicts between Schmoller and Naumann had died down, Brentano's own relations with Naumann began to show signs of tension. Ever since he had begun to co-operate with Naumann, Brentano had deluged *Die Hilfe* with suggestions and protests every time something was printed there of which he did not approve.[45] In 1906 there were signs that Naumann was no longer willing to listen humbly to Brentano's criticisms as in the earlier years of their friendship. In the summer of 1906 Brentano reviewed Naumann's *Neudeutsche Wirtschaftspolitik* for the *Nation*.[46] Although he made clear his admiration for Naumann, he devoted two out of the four articles

42 Naumann, "Im Verein für Sozialpolitik," *Die Hilfe,* October 8, 1905; Mommsen, *Weber,* pp. 148 ff.; Heuss, *Naumann,* pp. 238–40; *Mein Leben,* pp. 255–56; Naumann to Brentano, November 1, 1905; Weber's letters to Brentano, 1905–6, especially the letters of October 13, 23, 26, 1905; Schmoller to Brentano, October 26, 29, 1905, and Brentano to Schmoller, November 2, 27, 1905.

43 Mommsen, *Weber,* p. 148; Weber to Brentano, October 26, 1905.

44 Boese, *Geschichte des Vereins,* p. 268.

45 Heuss, *Naumann,* pp. 256–57.

46 *Die Nation,* June 30–July 21, 1906.

to exposing the errors in his book. Naumann's response to Brentano's review suggested that he was noticeably less anxious to admit his mistakes.[47]

A few months after Brentano's review of *Neudeutsche Wirtschaftspolitik,* Naumann won a Reichstag seat in the election of 1907. Although he began his career in the Reichstag by giving a speech based on Brentano's Mannheim proposals,[48] his desire for social reform was forced into the background by the position of the *Freisinnige Vereinigung* within the so-called Bülow bloc. During the electoral campaign of 1907 Bülow had succeeded in forming an alliance of liberal and conservative parties to support the government's colonial policies against the Center and the S. P. D.[49] Throughout 1907 the members of the *Freisinnige Vereinigung* de-emphasized their demands for reform in order to keep the bloc together. Naumann and others hoped to be able to use the bloc to achieve liberal unity.[50]

Throughout 1907 questions of colonial policy were the predominant national concerns. In the summer of 1907 the relationship between Naumann and Brentano was severely strained by their differences on imperialism and foreign policy.

Brentano, annoyed by Naumann's attitude toward colonial affairs, was finally alienated from the left liberals by their stand on the Reich Association Law (*Vereinsgesetz*) which was presented to the Reichstag at the end of 1907. Until 1907, laws governing associations were in the hands of the individual states, and therefore varied according to the political climate of each state. The bill proposed in 1907, actually conceived as a concession to the liberal parties in the bloc, provided uniform legislation for the entire Reich. Although the bill was less liberal than the existing laws of some states, it was more progressive than

[47] Naumann to Brentano, July 31, August 26, 1906.

[48] Naumann to Brentano, February 2, 23, 26, 1907; Teuteberg, *Geschichte der industriellen Mitbestimmung,* pp. 483 ff.; and Heuss, *Naumann,* pp. 537–38.

[49] On the election of 1907 see G. Crothers, *The German Elections of 1907* (New York, 1941), pp. 45 ff. On the politics of the Bülow bloc, see T. Eschenberg, *Das Kaiserreich am Scheideweg: Bassermann, Bülow und der Block* (Berlin, 1929).

[50] The left liberals were placated by certain minor concessions from the government. Crothers, *German Elections,* pp. 229 ff.

the regulations in a number of the most important parts of the Reich.[51]

One clause of the Association Bill, however, placed the left liberals in an uncomfortable position. As part of his anti-Polish policy, Bülow had included in the bill the requirement that the German language must be used in all public meetings.[52] Opinion within the *Freisinnige Vereinigung* was sharply divided on this question. Barth and von Gerlach, already restive in the alliance with Bülow, wanted to vote against the bill as long as it contained the language clause. Naumann, although he disapproved of the language clause, refused to sacrifice the good points in the law, the advantages of the bloc, and the chances for liberal unity. As Naumann remarked at the time: "I think that liberal unity is more valuable for Germany's future than any of the individual events of the present period."[53]

Brentano had been critical of Bülow's attitude toward the Poles since 1906.[54] He was unwilling to accept any association law that denied non-German-speaking workers the right to organize.[55] Therefore, he was harshly critical of Naumann's willingness to support the bill. On April 2, 1908, a few days before the final vote on the bill, Brentano wrote Naumann:

> I have devoted my life to the struggle for the workers' right to collective bargaining. . . . Now I see my friends acquiescing in a threat to everything that has been achieved.

Brentano concluded this letter by saying that he could not support a man or a party that would vote for such a law.[56]

---

[51] On the *Vereinsgesetz*, see Born, *Staat und Sozialpolitik*, pp. 216 ff., and the documents in P. Rassow and K. Born, *Akten zur staatlichen Sozialpolitik in Deutschland 1890–1914* (Wiesbaden, 1959), pp. 217–343.

[52] R. Tims, *Germanizing Prussian Poland* (New York, 1941), pp. 144–50.

[53] Heuss, *Naumann*, p. 254. See also Naumann, "Das Vereinsgesetz," *Die Hilfe*, April 5, 1908.

[54] Brentano, "Gedanken über die Polenfrage," *Die Hilfe*, September 23, 1906; see also "Bevölkerungsbewegung und Polenfrage," *Frankfurter Zeitung*, December 30, 1907.

[55] *Mein Leben*, pp. 277 ff. Brentano had several students among the leaders of the Polish community in Germany; see Tuzcinski to Brentano, December 30, 1907.

[56] Brentano to Naumann, April 2, 1908, reprinted in *Mein Leben*; Naumann's reply, April 4, 1908.

The Association Bill was passed by the Reichstag on April 6, 1908. The left liberals, who had the deciding votes, supported the bill. On April 5, when it was clear that the *Freisinnige Vereinigung* would vote for the bill, Brentano sent a letter of resignation to the party chairman.[57] Brentano's withdrawal was the beginning of a serious split in the party. At the annual convention held at the end of April, Barth and von Gerlach left the party because of their views on the Association Law and the position of the party in Bülow's bloc.[58] Shortly after this meeting Naumann lost patience with the sharp criticisms Brentano had continued to send him and their correspondence was broken off until 1915.[59]

After 1908 Brentano played no role in German party politics. He did, however, briefly take part in the agitation for electoral reform which gathered momentum in Germany between 1908 and 1910. In the fall of 1908, scandals in circles close to the crown, and the Kaiser's own incompetence in the *Daily Telegraph* affair, revitalized the left's demands for democratization.[60] These demands focused on the three-class voting system in Prussia, which insured that the conservative forces dominated the Prussian Landtag and, because of Prussia's position in the Reich,

[57] Brentano to Schrader, April 5, 1908, draft in Brentano Papers, original in the Karl Schrader Papers, Niedersächsisches Staatsarchiv, Wolfenbüttel. See also Brentano's attack on the left liberals, "Die Linksliberalen Anträge zum Koalitionsrecht," *Berliner Tageblatt*, April 14, 1908.

[58] *Mein Leben*, p. 281; Heuss, *Naumann*, pp. 253 ff.; E. Feder, *Theodor Barth und der demokratische Gedanke* (Gotha, 1919), p. 28; and the protocols of the meeting, *Dritter Delegiertentag des Wahlvereins der Liberalen 1908* (Berlin-Schöneberg, 1908), pp. 30 ff. For a firsthand account of the *Vereinsgesetz* and its impact on the liberal movement, see Theodor Heuss, *Erinnerungen 1905–1933* (Tübingen, 1963), pp. 65–74.

[59] Naumann to Brentano, April 28, 1908; Heuss, *Naumann*, pp. 256–57. Brentano's break with Naumann coincided with a certain disenchantment with Naumann among other German intellectuals. As one of them wrote, after 1908 Naumann ceased to be an idealistic party founder and became a Reichstag member like any other. K. A. von Müller, *Aus Gärten der Vergangenheit: Erinnerungen 1882–1914* (Stuttgart, 1958), p. 396; cf. Meinecke's remarks in *Strassburg, Freiburg, Berlin, 1901–1919: Erinnerungen* (Stuttgart, 1949), p. 125.

[60] The most recent survey of the crises of 1908 is W. Schüssler, *Die Daily Telegraph Affäre: Fürst Bülow, Kaiser Wilhelm und die Krise des zweiten Reiches 1908* (Göttingen, 1952).

exerted an inordinate amount of power in all of Germany. The left liberals managed to extract from Bülow promises for reform of the Prussian suffrage. After the collapse of the bloc and Bülow's dismissal in 1909, the parties of the left increased their demands that these promises be fulfilled.[61]

In this context Brentano publicly supported the campaign for universal manhood suffrage in Prussia. In 1909 he signed a declaration on behalf of suffrage reform which was published in the *Berliner Tageblatt*.[62] In the following year he advocated reform in two newspaper articles.[63] Brentano attacked those who condemned universal suffrage because it would ruin parliamentary life by subjecting it to the stupidity of the masses. He exposed this argument as a mask for self-interest and pointed out that stupidity was not the sole prerogative of a single class. Universal suffrage was a necessary prerequisite to the equal role of the masses in the life of the nation:

Whoever believes that the prosperity of the entire state . . . depends on a unity of culture and civilization must support suffrage reform.[64]

Brentano's agitation for universal suffrage, however, did not signify any lessening of his distrust of political parties. Even as he was advocating electoral reform, he was castigating the "bureaucratization of political life and the tyranny of political parties which alienate the best men from parliamentary life."[65] Brentano's conduct during the election of 1912 was symptomatic of his alienation from party politics. In the spring of 1911 he was asked to give an address on commercial policy to the annual meeting of the *Demokratische Vereinigung*, the political organization founded by Barth and von Gerlach after their resignation from the *Freisinnige Vereinigung*. He refused because he felt that the agitation for free trade would lose its scholarly basis if it

[61] E. Eyck, *Das persönliche Regiment Wilhelms II* (Erlenbach-Zurich, 1948), pp. 492 ff., and Schorske, *German Social Democracy*, pp. 151 ff. and 171 ff.

[62] Theodor Wolff to Brentano, November 29, December 2, 1909.

[63] "Süddeutschland und das preussische Wahlrecht," *Das Freie Volk* (Berlin), February 26, 1910; "Über die Wirkungen des allgemeinen und gleichen Wahlrechts," *Neue Freie Presse* (Vienna), May 15, 1910.

[64] *Ibid.*, p. 5.

[65] *Ibid.*, p. 4.

became associated with a political party.[66] Later that year the editor of a Berlin newspaper asked him for a statement of the principles upon which he would vote in the next election. Brentano replied that his opposition to the principles of the Center and Conservative parties was well known. Unfortunately, he added, the parties of the left had no principles to consider, and therefore there was nothing for the voter to do but base his vote on the character and beliefs of the individual candidates.[67]

In 1908 Max Weber had warned Brentano about the implications of breaking with Naumann: "If one is 'finished' with Naumann, one is 'finished' with liberalism in general."[68] After 1908 Brentano was, in fact, finished with political liberalism and with parliamentary politics. The events of 1905–8 suggest the limits of his role in German politics. In 1905 he had wanted to lead the *Verein* in a "practical act," only to find that all action was impossible within the *Verein*'s conservative atmosphere. However, his essential lack of interest in organized political action and his break with the left liberals in 1908 clearly displayed his unwillingness to seek an alternative to the *Verein* as a vehicle for fulfilling his hopes for the future of Germany. The result was that Brentano, isolated and impotent, was forced to observe the Reich's internal conflicts without a means through which he could work for their solution.

3 —

The extent to which Brentano felt isolated from German politics can be measured by his response to the social tensions which increased in Germany after 1910. In the years immediately following the intensive labor conflicts of 1905–6 there had been a decrease in the number of strikes, probably due to an economic slump.[69] In 1910, strikes in the mining industry and the lockout of 175,000 construction workers marked the beginning of a series

[66] Von Gerlach to Brentano, April 8, April 14, 1911.
[67] Editor of the *Berliner Lokal Anzeiger* and *Der Tag* to Brentano, October 31, 1911, and the draft of Brentano's reply.
[68] Weber to Brentano, June 3, 1908. See Mommsen, *Weber*, p. 150.
[69] Born, *Staat und Sozialpolitik*, p. 215.

of labor disputes that continued until the war.[70] By 1912, the year in which the S. P. D. became the largest party in the Reichstag, almost half a million workers were involved in work stoppages.[71]

As was to be expected, these labor disputes and the Social Democrats' electoral victory evoked a vigorous response from the reactionary elements in German society. As in the late 1890's, the government and the employers sought to attack the labor movement by weakening the unions through the use of strike breakers. Once again, the question of those "willing to work" became a central issue.[72]

In a number of articles and lectures Brentano defended the unions and sought to show the real motivation behind the government's concern for the rights of the so-called *Arbeitswilligen*.[73] In the reactionary climate of the years before the war, Brentano's defense of organized labor met with bitter attacks, particularly from representatives of the employers' associations. These men charged that Brentano and the other *Kathedersozialisten* had no idea of the problems of practical economics and were irresponsibly inciting the workers to violence against their employers. As one secretary of a Manufacturers' Association wrote in 1912:

For forty years the academic socialists have stirred up the German workers and encouraged them to blackmail German entrepreneurs. They have given the workers suggestions as to

[70] In 1909, there were 131,244 workers involved in labor disputes; in 1910 the number had risen to 369,011. See Kuczynski, *Die Geschichte der Lage der Arbeiter*, I, Part II, 67, and Schorske, *German Social Democracy*, p. 180.

[71] Kuczynski, *Die Geschichte der Lage der Arbeiter*, I, Part II, 67.

[72] Born, *Staat und Sozialpolitik*, pp. 242–43; D. Fricke has reprinted a very interesting memorandum on this problem, "Eine Denkschrift Krupps aus dem Jahre 1912 über den Schutz der Arbeitswilligen," *Zeitschrift für Geschichtswissenschaft*, V, No. 6 (1957), 1245–54. Unfortunately the social tensions in the years before the war have not received the attention from historians their interest merits. The only account of the subject is suggestive, but severely limited by the author's rather unenlightened Marxist approach: K. Stenkewitz, *Gegen Bajonett und Dividende: Die politische Krise in Deutschland am Vorabend des ersten Weltkrieges* (Berlin, 1960).

[73] See the report of Brentano's lecture, "Das ewige Problem der Arbeitswilligen," in the *Frankfurter Zeitung*, March 1, 1912, and his pamphlet, *Der Schutz der Arbeitswilligen* (Berlin, 1912).

how they might transform the temporary rewards of extortion into a permanent victory by means of labor contracts.[74]

Brentano's demand for a collective labor contract, he continued, was like that of a robber who wanted to extract from his victim a promise of lifetime support.[75]

Attacks like this led to further exchanges of charges and countercharges and finally to a series of slander trials.[76] After 1910, however, Brentano's willingness to engage in polemics with German industrialists was accompanied by a noticeable cooling of the ardor with which he advocated his positive reform suggestions. In 1889–90 and in 1905–6 he had greeted the outbreak of labor disputes with a vigorous program of social reform. Sometime after 1905 Brentano seems to have lost his confidence and enthusiasm; he faced the social tensions of 1910–14 in a mood very different from that of 1890 and 1905.

Symptomatic of this change in Brentano's attitude toward *Sozialpolitik* was his reaction in 1912 to Max Weber's plans for an active social reform organization. Since the 1890's, Weber, like Brentano, had wanted to instill in the *Verein für Sozialpolitik* a more vigorous spirit of social action. In the face of the increased social tensions after 1910 Weber felt that something had to be done to create an active interest in *Sozialpolitik* among the German bourgeoisie. As he wrote to Brentano in the spring of 1912: "It is necessary to create an ideological atmosphere for social action because reform doesn't seem fashionable at the moment."[77] In his answer to this letter Brentano expressed his agreement with Weber's analysis of the present situation and also agreed that something should be done about it.[78]

---

74 A. Tille, *Lujo Brentano und der akademische Klassenmoralismus* (Berlin, 1912), pp. 9–10. See also A. Kuhlo, *Kathedersozialistische Irrwege mit besonderer Berücksichtigung der Wirksamkeit und der Lehren des Universitäts-Professors Lujo Brentano* (Munich, 1913).

75 Tille, *Lujo Brentano*, p. 14.

76 G. Schmoller, "Die Hetze von Alexander Tille und Konsorten gegen Lujo Brentano," *Schmollers Jahrbuch*, XXXVII, No. 3 (1913), 1–17. See the documents which Brentano reprinted in his volume of essays, *Syndikalismus und Lohnminimum* (Munich, 1913); *Mein Leben*, pp. 292–301.

77 Weber to Brentano, September 16, 1912. The following account is based on the letters from Weber to Brentano in the Brentano Papers, and on Mommsen, *Weber*, pp. 133–37.

78 Brentano to Weber, September 1912, draft in Brentano Papers.

Because of the divisions within the *Verein* it was clear that some other means for advancing *Sozialpolitik* was necessary. In October, 1912, Weber called a meeting of reform-minded members of the *Verein* in Leipzig. He proposed that plans be made for a large public meeting to be held in Frankfurt with the purpose of establishing an organization for the active pursuit of social reform. Brentano clashed with the majority at the Leipzig meeting on two points. When he suggested that a demand for free trade be added to the agenda for the Frankfurt meeting, Weber and others insisted that this would only alienate potential allies. Secondly, Brentano wanted to include Socialists in the Frankfurt meeting. The majority at Leipzig decided that it would be better not to invite members of the S. P. D., but to wait until a reform program had been formulated before seeking the Socialists' co-operation.[79] Brentano's attitude at Leipzig suggests that he hoped for an alliance of all the anti-reactionary elements in German society, from free traders to Socialists. This vision of an all-encompassing progressive bloc was not shared by men like Weber, who realized more fully the complexity and the limitations of German politics in the years before 1914.

Two days after the gathering at Leipzig, Brentano sent a letter to the participants announcing that, because of their refusal to include Social Democrats, he would not support the Frankfurt meeting.[80] Despite assurances from several of the men at Leipzig that their decision was based on tactical rather than political considerations, Brentano persisted in his refusal of support.[81] Understandably enough, Weber was infuriated by this attitude and the affair led to a permanent rupture in their relationship.[82] In spite of Weber's attempts to salvage the project, Brentano's withdrawal doomed it to failure and the Frankfurt meeting did not take place.[83]

[79] For a description of the meeting, see Brentano's letter to the participants, October 22, 1912.

[80] *Loc. cit.*

[81] Vogelstein to Brentano, October 27, 1912; Drill to Brentano, October 25, 1912.

[82] Weber to Brentano, October 25, 1912; Brentano to Leipzig participants, October 27, 1912.

[83] Mommsen, *Weber*, pp. 136–37.

To some extent, Brentano's refusal to co-operate with Weber in 1912 reflected that inflexibility we have frequently observed in his character when he felt that his principles were involved. However, this occasionally uncompromising aspect of his personality does not seem sufficient to explain his action: the need for social reform was too obvious, the extent of his agreement with Weber too great, and the pretext for his withdrawal too slight. It is necessary, therefore, to view Brentano's reluctance to sponsor Weber's proposals as part of his general attitude toward social reform in the years before the war.

Perhaps the best expression of Brentano's attitude during this period is in a letter which he wrote to Schmoller in October, 1912, just a few weeks before the Leipzig meeting.[84] In this letter he gave the reasons for his pessimism about the German situation. He was depressed about current events, he wrote, "because after forty years of struggle, the forces of reaction remain as strong as ever." Brentano felt that he was battling these forces alone and unaided. During a recent polemic, only Schmoller had defended him from the attacks of the *Arbeitgeberverbände*. Brentano was also discouraged about the *Verein für Sozialpolitik*. It had become, he said, an organization without principles, which merely supplied unread books to others who would also not read them. Brentano's papers contain other indications of this mood of pessimism and isolation in the years before 1914.[85] Perhaps this mood contributed to his unwillingness to compromise with Weber and also to his general reluctance to take an active part in advocating social reform to meet the social problems of the years 1910–14.[86]

Although we have very little evidence to explain the depression with which Brentano viewed German developments in these years, it is not difficult to suggest some possible reasons for his dejection. In the first place, he was obviously exhausted by the polemics and legal actions which took so much of his time after

---

[84] Letter is reprinted in *Mein Leben*, pp. 300–301. Stenkewitz, *Gegen Bajonett*, p. 281, quoted from the original in Schmoller's Papers.

[85] W. J. Ashley to Brentano, March 25, 1913.

[86] There is evidence that Brentano's relationship with the *Gesellschaft für Sozialreform* also began to deteriorate at this time, Ernst Francke to Brentano, November 26, December 3, 1912.

1910. Moreover, he could certainly find reasons to be discouraged about the government's reactionary policy and lack of interest in *Sozialpolitik*.[87] Perhaps more important, he could not but have been disappointed by the obvious failure of his own reform ideas and by the *Verein für Sozialpolitik*'s lack of any real political influence. Furthermore, his optimism may never have recovered from his loss of faith in the dynamics of liberal reform in 1904–5. This loss of faith could only have been deepened by the course of English developments, because after 1912 British labor relations became increasingly tense and violent.[88] Finally, Brentano was getting old. In 1912 he was sixty-eight, still vigorous but increasingly isolated among German social reformers. Most of the friends and enemies of his youth were dead; a few, like Schmoller, had all but retired from public life. The young men whom Brentano had faced around the conference table at Leipzig represented a new generation, whose social theories and practical proposals were very different from his own liberal social reform.

Whatever the reasons for Brentano's depression in the years before 1914, his mood was very much a part of that prewar atmosphere so well described by Germany's Chancellor, Bethmann-Hollweg:

> . . . an almost inexplicable pressure weighed on the political life of Germany. . . . Malaise and dejection imparted a depressing tone to political party activity, which lacked any progressive impulse. The word *Reichsverdrossenheit* [dissatisfaction with empire] rose up out of an earlier time of troubles.[89]

[87] See Born, *Staat und Sozialpolitik*, pp. 242 ff.

[88] Pelling, *History of British Trade Unionism*, pp. 137 ff., and G. Dangerfield, *The Strange Death of Liberal England, 1910–1914* (New York, 1961), pp. 214–330.

[89] T. Bethmann-Hollweg, *Betrachtungen zum Weltkrieg* (Berlin, 1919), I, 95, quoted in Schorske, *German Social Democracy*, p. 224.

# CHAPTER IX

# Foreign Policy and War
## 1890-1918

### 1 —

Thus far we have been concerned with Brentano's relationship to German domestic problems and policies. In order to complete our portrait of his role in imperial Germany it is now necessary to turn to his view of foreign affairs and then to his activities during the World War.

After Brentano's reconciliation with a Prussian-led Germany in 1871 there is every indication that his patriotic attachment to the Reich deepened.[1] Until the 1890's, however, his writings give no indication that he was concerned with problems of foreign policy. Like so many of his contemporaries, Brentano seems to have felt confident that Germany's national security was protected by Bismarck's diplomatic genius.[2] After 1890 German diplomacy lost the confidence and finesse it seemed to have had under Bismarck's leadership. The effects of Germany's ambition for overseas expansion, aggravated by the erratic and tactless behavior of the Kaiser, contributed to an increasingly tense diplomatic climate.[3] In this context, foreign affairs began to play an important role in Brentano's thought.

[1] Brentano's feeling for the Reich is shown in his uneasiness about leaving Germany and lecturing in Vienna; see Brentano, *Mein Leben im Kampfe um die soziale Entwicklung Deutschlands* (Jena, 1931), p. 137. Hereafter cited as *Mein Leben*.

[2] As we have mentioned, Brentano referred to the importance of the *Machtstellung* of the nation for the first time in 1884; see above, chap. 5.

[3] The following works provide useful accounts of German foreign policy after 1890: George F. W. Hallgarten, *Imperialismus vor 1914* (2 vols.; Munich, 1951); E. Kehr, *Schlachtflottenbau und Parteipolitik 1894–1901* (Berlin, 1930); Pauline Anderson, *The Background of Anti-English Feeling in*

Brentano's active involvement in problems of German foreign policy dates from 1897. It was in that year that Alfred von Tirpitz was given charge of the naval ministry, an appointment that both symbolized and deepened Germany's commitment to *Weltpolitik*.[4] Tirpitz was one of the first and certainly one of the most effective modern propagandists.[5] He clearly saw that foreign policy had a domestic dimension and he conceived his task as that of winning national support for an extensive expansion of the fleet. He realized that the German universities could provide important allies for his program.[6] The connection between the naval ministry and German academicians began in the summer of 1897 when Tirpitz sent his press secretary to Gustav von Schmoller to co-ordinate scholarly support for the fleet. Schmoller recommended that Ernst von Halle, a young economist at the University of Berlin, be put in charge of a department for "scholarly agitation."[7] At the same time, Schmoller agreed to write his friend Brentano and seek his support for the fleet program.[8]

In response to Schmoller's request, Brentano agreed to write

---

*Germany, 1890–1902* (Washington, D.C., 1939); Erich Eyck, *Das persönliche Regiment Wilhelms II* (Erlenbach—Zurich, 1948). For a somewhat different interpretation see W. Frauendienst, "Deutsche Weltpolitik. Zur Problematik des Wilhelminischen Reiches," *Welt als Geschichte*, XIX, No. 1 (1959), 1–39.

[4] On the significance of 1897 in German foreign policy, see Kehr, *Schlacht-flottenbau*, p. 315; Anderson, *Anti-English Feeling*, pp. 3–4, 12, 18; F. Fischer, *Griff nach der Weltmacht: Die Kriegszielpolitik des kaiserlichen Deutschland 1914–1918* (Düsseldorf, 1961), p. 36.

[5] On Tirpitz, see the critical article by Rudolf Stadelmann, "Die Epoche der deutsch-englischen Flottenrivalität," in *Deutschland und Westeuropa: Drei Aufsätze* (Württemberg, 1948), 85–146; a more positive view of Tirpitz' achievements can be found in W. Hubatsch, *Die Ära Tirpitz: Studien zur deutschen Marinepolitik 1890–1918* (Göttingen, 1955).

[6] On the professors and the fleet, see Fischer, *Griff nach der Weltmacht*, pp. 18–19; Kehr, *Schlachtflottenbau*, pp. 360–64; the most complete account is Wolfgang Marienfeld, "Wissenschaft und Schlachtflottenbau 1897–1906," *Marine Rundschau*, Beiheft 2 (April, 1957). See also A. Ascher, "Professors as Propagandists: The Politics of the *Kathedersozialisten*," *Journal of Central European Affairs*, XXXIII, No. 3 (October, 1963), 282–302. For Tirpitz' view, see his *Erinnerungen* (Leipzig, 1920), pp. 95 ff.

[7] Marienfeld, "Wissenschaft und Schlachtflottenbau," p. 79.

[8] Schmoller to Brentano, July 23, 1897. Unless otherwise stated all unpublished letters are in the Lujo Brentano Papers.

articles for South German newspapers advocating a larger fleet.[9] His decision to support the expansion of the navy was based upon his conviction that this expansion was necessary for the protection of German commerce. As he wrote to Schmoller in July 1897: "Every policy which increases our exports can be sure of my support."[10] We have already mentioned that after 1890 Brentano became aware of the need for a dynamic economy. Thus, his free-trade ideas rested upon his belief that Germany's population growth required that the agricultural sector of the economy be sacrificed to insure industrial expansion. In the late nineties Brentano, as well as Schmoller, Barth, Naumann, and Weber, gave this argument a further dimension: a steadily growing population and increasing industrial power required that Germany have overseas markets and a fleet to protect her shipping.[11]

Brentano's support for the fleet played an important role in his publications during the period before 1914. And critical comments on German foreign policy are conspicuously absent from his work. In 1900 Tirpitz personally extended his thanks to Brentano for his role in "enlightening broad segments of the population concerning the significance of the fleet."[12] The extent of the German bourgeoisie's involvement in *Weltpolitik* is perhaps suggested by the fact that men like Brentano, Barth,

[9] Brentano to Schmoller, July 27, 1897.

[10] Brentano's concern for export is in part a reflection of the trade balance of the Reich: in 1910, Germany imported a total of 10 billion marks worth of goods and exported only 8.9 billion. Fischer, *Griff nach der Weltmacht*, p. 23.

[11] This feeling of economic dynamism reflected some important trends in Germany. For example, from 1871 to 1915 the population grew from 41 to 69 million. In the period from 1887 to 1912 German commerce grew by some 13.4 billion marks, or 214.7 per cent. Fischer, *Griff nach der Weltmacht*, pp. 22–23. For the government's view of these trends, see the statements by Bülow in Frauendienst, "Deutsche Weltpolitik," pp. 17–18. The best example of Brentano's argument for the relationship between free trade and naval expansion is in *Die Schrecken des überwiegenden Industriestaates* (Berlin, 1901), p. 31. See also "Die politische Krisis," *Die Zeit* (September, 1901), p. 8. For an analysis of Brentano's argument see Marienfeld, "Wissenschaft und Schlachtflottenbau," pp. 24, 36–37, 40.

[12] Tirpitz to Brentano, June 12, 1900. See also Tirpitz' letter of December 29, 1899.

Naumann, and Weber, even though they were acutely aware of the shortcomings of German domestic politics, not only acquiesced in, but actively supported the tragic course of Germany's foreign policy.

In the summer of 1897, when Brentano agreed to support the fleet program, he warned Schmoller that the fleet must be regarded as a means of aiding German commerce, not as a way of rivaling Great Britain.[13] Thus, as early as 1897, he seems to have realized that his acceptance of *Weltpolitik* might prove difficult to reconcile with the attachment to England which had been a constant feature of his intellectual make-up since the 1860's. Brentano's fears proved justified. Anti-English feeling was an important element in the agitation for a greater German fleet; by the turn of the century, Brentano's role in the campaign for naval expansion and his deep-seated anglophilia were clearly in conflict.[14]

The difficulty of synthesizing *Weltpolitik* and anglophilia was made increasingly apparent by the Boer War, which marked an important step in the development of anti-English feeling in Germany.[15] During the three years in which the British sought to subdue the Boers, even anglophils like Brentano and Barth lined up with the more extreme nationalists in condemning England.[16] When the British stopped a German ship from carrying material to the Boers, the arguments of those who pointed to the need for a navy to protect German commerce seemed to be greatly reinforced. In January, 1900, Barth and Brentano agreed that England's behavior necessitated an increase in German naval armaments. The imperialist forces in England, Barth wrote, must be shown that "it is not child's play to come into conflict with Germany."[17]

---

[13] Brentano to Schmoller, July 27, 1897.

[14] See Anderson, *Anti-English Feeling, passim.*

[15] See *ibid.,* pp. 285–360.

[16] *Ibid.,* pp. 308–11, 318–20. The Brentano Papers contain a number of letters showing Brentano's support for some of the pro-Boer organizations which grew up in Germany during the war. See, for example, the letter from the *Burenhilfsbund* to Brentano, January 11, 1902, thanking him for a gift of 122 marks.

[17] Barth to Brentano, January 2, 1900. See also Brentano's article "Cobdens Argument gegen Flottenvermehrungen," *Die Nation,* January 13 and 20, 1900.

During the Boer War Brentano attempted to reconcile his participation in German anti-English sentiment with his anglophilia. He argued that there were "two Englands," one liberal and peace-loving, the other reactionary and imperialistic. These two forces, personified for Brentano in Cobden and Chamberlain, were struggling for the control of British politics. Brentano felt that in recent years the forces of reaction had been gaining strength and had blackened England's name by their activities in India, in Ireland, and now in South Africa. Britain, he wrote, was at a turning point in her history. Germany had to have a strong fleet to protect herself in case the imperialist forces should win and seek to destroy German commercial competition by acting against Germany's shipping.[18]

Thus, the Boer War strengthened the alliance between Brentano and the advocates of German naval expansion. However, Brentano attempted to mitigate the ill will which had been generated between Germany and England by the Boer War and the fleet agitation. Even in January, 1900, he and Barth agreed that despite England's present behavior, a lasting friendship of Germany and England was crucial.[19] After the end of the South African war in the spring of 1902, Brentano withdrew from the *Burenhilfsbund*, a pro-Boer organization to which he had belonged during the war, because he considered "a continuation of anti-English agitation as contrary to Germany's national interest."[20]

In the fall of 1902 Brentano contacted the famous British economist Alfred Marshall in an attempt to find some way to improve relations between Germany and England.[21] In the

18 On the manuscript of his Cobden article cited in n. 17, Brentano wrote that the idea of the two Englands was suggested to him by Frederic Harrison (Brentano Papers). Brentano's student M. J. Bonn, also an anglophil, wrote to him in a very similar vein on October 26, 1898. This view was obviously an extreme oversimplification of the character of British imperialism. See, for example, B. Semmel, *Imperialism and Social Reform* (Cambridge, 1960).

19 Barth to Brentano, January 2, 1900.

20 Brentano to Graf Normann, Chairman of the *Deutscher Burenhilfsbund*, September 11, 1902. Draft in Brentano Papers. He repeated essentially the same message in a letter to the *Burenhilfe* committee in Munich, November 23, 1902.

21 Brentano to Alfred Marshall, October 10, 1902, and Marshall's reply of October 18.

spring of 1903 he joined forces with the historian Theodor Mommsen, who, like Brentano and Barth, had been critical of England during the Boer War but now wanted to reconcile the two nations.[22] At Brentano's suggestion, Mommsen wrote an open letter to the English public which was published in the liberal *Independent Review*.[23] In this letter Mommsen condemned the ultranationalist groups in Germany as "national fools." Although he sought to justify Germany's desire for colonies and a fleet, he asked for mutual understanding and friendship between Germany and Britain.[24] Mommsen's letter was greeted with a storm of protest and condemnation in England, where public opinion was still enraged by Germany's attitude during the war. Mommsen, discouraged by this reception, decided to give up plans for further action. "The storm," he wrote to Brentano, "is obviously too strong and we have underestimated it."[25]

In contrast to most of the advocates of German *Weltpolitik*, Brentano continued to hope for a reconciliation with England. Although he never questioned the justice of Germany's position, his participation in Germany's expansionist policies was always tempered by his desire for an Anglo-German rapprochement. Furthermore, Brentano continued to view *Weltpolitik* in essentially economic terms. He was convinced that a growing population made expansion necessary, but he never descended to the extremes of national ambition found in an organization like the Pan-German League.

The limitations of Brentano's support for an aggressive foreign policy clearly emerged in his relations with Friedrich Naumann,

22 On Mommsen's views, see his exchange with Max Müller reprinted in the *Deutsche Revue*, XXV (April, May, 1900), pp. 129–46, 250–62. In 1903 Mommsen wrote that "the holy alliance of nations was the goal of my youth and still the guiding star of my old age; this means that Germany and England must go their way hand in hand." Quoted in A. Heuss, *Theodor Mommsen und das 19. Jahrhundert* (Kiel, 1956), pp. 210–11.

23 Mommsen to Brentano, April 23 and August 11, 1903; Barth to Brentano, August 3, 11, 1903; Charles Trevelyan (editor of the *Independent Review*) to Brentano, August 31, September 17, 1903.

24 "A German's Appeal to the English," *Independent Review*, I, No. 1 (October, 1903), 160–65.

25 Mommsen to Brentano, October 15, 17, 1903; Trevelyan to Brentano, October 15, 1903.

who was one of the foremost advocates of German imperialism. In contrast to Brentano, Naumann did not view *Weltpolitik* solely as an economic necessity, but saw it as a part of an inevitable struggle between nations. Naumann's primary concern was not with commerce, but with conflict. For him the fleet was not only a means of protecting trade, but a necessary ingredient in national power.[26] Moreover, unlike Brentano and Barth, Naumann's hatred of England during the Boer War was not mitigated by the hope of a later reconciliation between Germany and England. "If anything in world history is certain," he wrote in 1900, "it is the future world war, that is, the war of those who seek to save themselves from England."[27] These extreme anti-English feelings were a constant source of friction during the years of Naumann's co-operation with Barth and Brentano. In 1906 Brentano was moved to write:

How pleased I would be if Naumann would take the opportunity to learn about England, indeed about all Anglo-Saxon affairs.[28]

In the summer of 1907 the conflict between Naumann and Brentano came clearly into focus. The issue was the career of Karl Peters, once an important figure in Germany's colonization in Africa.[29] Whereas Brentano condemned Peters, Naumann accepted the brutality of his career as a necessary evil in the growth of Germany's overseas empire:

If in the course of our history and also in colonizing, we have occasionally been hard and brutal, we have until now

26 For the contrast between Naumann's and Brentano's views of the nation, see above, chap. 7.

27 Quoted in Theodor Heuss, *Friedrich Naumann: Der Mann, das Werk, die Zeit* (2d ed.; Stuttgart and Tübingen, 1949), p. 160. See also Naumann's article "Der Burenkampf und die Grossmächte," *Die Hilfe*, March 11, 1900; Anderson, *Anti-English Feeling*, pp. 352–53.

28 Brentano's review of Naumann's *Neudeutsche Wirtschaftspolitik* in *Die Nation*, July 21, 1906. Commenting on this review, Barth wrote that Naumann's ignorance of Anglo-Saxon affairs "has an unfortunate effect not only on his economic but also on his political views." Barth to Brentano, May 26, 1906.

29 On the Peters trial of 1907, see *Schulthess' Europäischer Geschichtskalender 1907* (Munich, 1908), p. 128.

had the courage simply to admit it . . . and consciously take responsibility for it.[30]

This conflict between Naumann and Brentano not only indicates the limits of Brentano's role as an advocate of *Weltpolitik*, but also points up the contrast between his position and that of Naumann's generation.[31] Naumann had come to believe that the old liberalism was no longer sufficient to explain the modern world. For Naumann "the old pure theory of rational humanitarian morality" was not strong enough to prevent the intrusion of a view of foreign policy which rested upon the realization that there was an inevitable struggle for existence among nations:

> This can be suggested by saying, Rousseau must be blended [*verschnitten*] with Darwin. Only the gods know if this new wine will be better than the old, but we must drink it.[32]

Rousseau blended with Darwin made an unpalatable mixture indeed for a man like Brentano, who looked upon the writings of Cobden and John Stuart Mill as his intellectual heritage.

In the summer of 1907, while Brentano and Naumann were exchanging letters on Karl Peters, British and Russian diplomats reached an accord on the most important issues that divided their two countries. The Anglo-Russian agreement completed the polarization of Europe into two alliance systems. After 1907, and especially in the years 1910–14, the tense international situation was reflected in the steadily accelerating arms race and in the series of diplomatic crises which characterized the last years of peace.

Brentano responded to the growing tensions on the international scene by becoming increasingly concerned with the nature of national rivalries and with efforts to avoid the outbreak of

30 Naumann to Brentano, July 31, 1907, reprinted in Heuss, *Naumann*, pp. 539–40. On the conflict between Naumann and Brentano, see Heuss, p. 256, and the very incomplete account in *Mein Leben*, pp. 276–77.

31 On July 26, 1907, Naumann wrote Brentano: "I want to remain in harmony with you but there are things about which almost the entire younger generation thinks differently"; reprinted in Heuss, *Naumann*, p. 538.

32 Naumann to Brentano, August 13, 1907, reprinted in Heuss, *Naumann*, p. 540.

war.[33] During these years, he maintained the essentially moderate position on foreign policy that he had held since the nineties: qualified support for *Weltpolitik,* an unwillingness to criticize German foreign policy, and a disavowal of the extreme nationalists and imperialists.[34] Brentano's statements on the nature of foreign affairs reveal the same economic orientation we have frequently observed in his ideas on domestic policy. Just as he based his support for German *Weltpolitik* on the commercial requirements of the German economy, he analyzed international conflicts in terms of commercial rivalries.[35] Brentano argued that if the rights of private property at sea were guaranteed and tariff barriers were abolished, the chief causes for war would be removed. In a fashion analogous to his reduction of the German social problem to a question of wages and working conditions, he sought to reduce the complexities of international relations to a question of commercial competition.[36]

By 1914 the international crises of the past years had made Brentano sensitive to the dangers in the existing diplomatic system. In May, 1914, he spoke of the rising tide of irrationalism and condemned those in England, France, and Germany who "glorify primitive passions and sing the praises of war and bloodshed."[37] Earlier in the year he had warned what a war would mean for Europe: the triumph of militarism, a new

---

[33] *Mein Leben,* pp. 305 ff.

[34] For Brentano's disavowal of the extreme nationalists see his letter to Ottomar Schuchardt, December 4, 1911. His support for the main lines of German policy is clear from his letter to Frederic Harrison, January 7, 1912 (Harrison Collection, London School of Economics), and to Eduard Bernstein, March 23, 1912 (Bernstein Papers, International Institute for Social History, Amsterdam). Brentano also continued to write articles justifying the German fleet; see his "Die englische Seeherrschaft und Deutschland," *Neue Freie Presse* (Vienna), December 24, 1911, for which he received a note of thanks from the Naval Ministry (*Reichsmarineamt* [*Nachrichtenbureau*] to Brentano, January 9, 1912).

[35] "Die heutigen Hauptursachen des Krieges," *Die Friedensbewegung,* April 15, 1912, pp. 95–97; "The Right of Capture," letter to the editor of the *Nation,* XIV, No. 15 (January 10, 1914), 638–39.

[36] By 1914 Brentano seems to have been convinced that the armaments industry was a danger to peace; he advocated that it be nationalized. See "Aufrichtige Rüstungsbetrachtungen: Verstaatlichung der Rüstungsindustrie," *Neue Freie Presse* (Vienna), April 12, 1914.

[37] "Handel und Diplomatie," *ibid.,* May 31, 1914.

outbreak of barbarism, the "transfer of the center of culture to the United States and the hegemony of Russia in Europe."[38]

Despite his sensitivity to the growth of international tensions, Brentano does not seem to have realized that the crisis of the summer of 1914 would not pass. In July he confidently demonstrated to his students that modern economics made war, in any event a prolonged war, impossible.[39] Like many Europeans, Brentano feared the outbreak of hostilities, but somehow did not really believe the long-prepared conflict would come. Henri Bergson summarized the situation with the paradox: "War was probable, but impossible."[40]

## 2 –

Brentano was in a sanitarium recovering from a minor operation when the World War began in August, 1914.[41] Although he could not actively participate in the demonstration of national solidarity which occurred throughout Germany during these "August days," he viewed with pride the patriotism of the German working class. The workers' support for the war, Brentano wrote, was "the triumph of *Kathedersozialismus*."[42]

During the first weeks of the war Brentano seems to have shared the view—almost universally held in Germany—that the Germans were fighting a defensive war against the French, who wanted to recover Alsace-Lorraine, and the Russians, who were anxious to expand into eastern Europe. Although he regarded England's entry into the war with the bitterness of a disappointed admirer, he maintained that the chief enemy was Russia and saw the most pressing task in 1914 as the "defense of all civilized Europe from the Russians."[43]

[38] Quoted from the *Münchener Neuesten Nachrichten*, January 25, 1914, by A. Marchionini in *Lujo Brentano: Grusswort und Reden bei der 110. Wiederkehr seines Geburtstages* (Berlin, 1956), p. 17. See also Brentano to Miss Paget, February 11, 1914.

[39] K. A. von Müller, *Aus Gärten der Vergangenheit: Erinnerungen 1882–1914* (Stuttgart, 1958), p. 229.

[40] Quoted by G. Masur, *Prophets of Yesterday: Studies in European Culture 1890–1914* (New York, 1961), p. 8.

[41] *Mein Leben*, p. 212.

[42] *Ibid.;* see also Heinrich Herkner, "Ansprache an Lujo Brentano," *Schmollers Jahrbuch*, XXXIX, No. 1 (1915), p. 373.

[43] Brentano to Bernstein, August 22, 1914 (Bernstein Papers). On Brentano's view of England see *Mein Leben*, p. 315; Brentano to Massingham, August

Brentano had an opportunity to view the war from a neutral country when he accompanied his cousin to Italy in September, 1914, on some pressing personal business. He was shocked at the anti-German propaganda he observed south of the Alps.[44] Fresh from the idealism of the "August days," stories of German atrocities in Belgium seemed to him an allied plot to destroy the honor of the German army.[45] Brentano wrote Schmoller that steps should be taken to counteract this propaganda. Schmoller responded by seeking Brentano's support for a declaration which was being drafted in Berlin. Brentano hesitated because he could not read the declaration before signing, but finally cabled his agreement.[46]

The pronouncement Brentano signed, which came to be known as the "Declaration of Ninety-Three," was written by the Berlin professor Ulrich von Wilamowitz-Moellendorf and carried the names of some of Germany's leading intellectuals.[47] The manifesto denied charges that Germany was responsible for the war, that Belgian neutrality had been violated, or that Belgian civilians had been cruelly treated. The action of the "Ninety-Three" was taken by Germany's enemies as evidence for German scholarship's subservience to nationalism and militarism. Several of Brentano's close friends in the *Entente* nations ostentatiously severed their relations with him because he had signed the declaration.[48]

---

21, 1914. This viewpoint emerged clearly in some articles he wrote early in the war: see, for example, "Deutschland und seine Gegner, insbesondere England," *Internationale Monatsschrift*, IX, No. 3 (1914). Unlike many of his colleagues, Brentano never carried his hostility towards England into the cultural sphere; see *England und der Krieg* (Berlin, 1915). Brentano repeated his conviction that Russia was the main enemy in a letter to the *Chicago Daily News*, November 12, 1914. He absolutely rejected any suggestion that a separate peace be made with Russia; see his letter to Hoensbroech, November 28, 1914.

[44] *Mein Leben*, p. 316.

[45] On Brentano's initial reaction to the atrocity charges, see his letter to Miss Paget, October 17, 1914.

[46] *Mein Leben*, pp. 316–17.

[47] Fischer, *Griff nach der Weltmacht*, p. 180, n. 4; Hans Wehberg, *Wider den Aufruf der Dreiundneunzig!* (Berlin, 1920). Wehberg sent questionnaires to all the signers in 1920; the declaration is reprinted in R. H. Lutz, *The Fall of the German Empire* (Stanford, 1932), I, 74–78.

[48] See *Briefwechsel zwischen den Herren Guyot und Bellet und Herrn Lujo Brentano* (Munich, 1914); Frederic Harrison to Brentano, December 18,

Brentano was one of the first signers of the declaration to regret his decision. In several articles after the war he apologized for having given his signature, always emphasizing that he had signed the document without having read it.[49] It is rather point-less to argue whether or not Brentano was morally culpable for signing the declaration. Since he had never criticized the erratic course of German foreign policy, it seems rather too much to expect him to refuse his support during the height of patriotic sentiment in 1914.

The "Declaration of Ninety-Three" does, however, suggest one aspect of German politics that is worthy of our attention. The declaration was the beginning of four years of intensive political activity by the German academic community.[50] At this time of national crisis, German professors felt called upon to act as the mentors and spokesmen for their countrymen. Since, as we have frequently pointed out, the German professor had no vehicle for political action, he sought to influence events by a series of declarations, manifestos, and memoranda. At the same time, organizations of intellectuals sprang up all over Germany, pro-viding men with a chance to meet and discuss their nation's increasingly uncertain future.[51]

In the first two years of the war the main concern of these organizations of German intellectuals was the question of war

---

1917; Ernest Mahain to Brentano, October 8, 1918. See also *Mein Leben,* pp. 347–48.

[49] Brentano's defense is weakened by the fact that he did not reject the declaration after he had read it, but rather asserted his agreement. See the *Guyot-Bellet Briefwechsel* cited above, n. 48. By 1916 Brentano had realized his mistake; see Brentano to the *Kulturbund deutscher Gelehrter,* February 9, 1916; *Mein Leben,* pp. 317–18.

[50] On the behavior of the German academic community during the war, see the article by Klaus Schwabe, "Zur politischen Haltung der deutschen Professoren im ersten Weltkrieg," *Historische Zeitschrift,* CXCIII, No. 3 (December, 1961), 601–34; see also the very critical account by the East German historian Werner Basler, "Zur politischen Rolle der Berliner Universität im ersten imperialistischen Weltkrieg," *Wissenschaftliche Zeit-schrift der Humboldt Universität zu Berlin,* X, Nos. 2–3 (1961), 181–203.

[51] Brentano's papers contain many letters from these various groups. See, for example, the correspondence from the *Kulturbund deutscher Gelehrter und Künstler,* the *Bund Neues Vaterland,* and the *Vereinigung zur geistigen Anregung der deutschen Krieger im Felde.* For some interesting comments on the organizations during the war, see F. Meinecke, *Strassburg, Freiburg, Berlin 1901–1919: Erinnerungen* (Stuttgart, 1949), pp. 162 ff.

aims, a subject which came to play an important role in Brentano's thinking in the course of 1915. In the early months of the war he took no position on what should be the official goal of Germany's war effort, although he did suggest that it might be necessary to take a certain amount of enemy territory in order to secure Germany's frontiers.[52] As might be expected, Brentano viewed the war and the war aims question in predominantly economic terms. He emphasized the need for free trade and freedom of the seas in order to remove the postwar world the causes of the present conflict.[53] At the same time, he clearly disapproved of the few pacifist organizations which had grown up in Germany and Switzerland.[54] In sum, Brentano maintained a position throughout the war comparable to his view of foreign policy before 1914: advocacy of economic measures to secure the peace, disavowal of extremes of right and left, and support for the main lines of government policy.

In the first months of 1915 Brentano's views on war aims were galvanized by two factors. The first was the mobilization of pro-annexationist opinion which was expressed in the spring and summer of 1915 by declarations such as the "Petition of the Six Economic Organizations" and the "Petition of the Intellectuals."[55] Second, by March, 1915, Brentano realized that the annexationists were basing their demands on an overly-optimistic view of the military situation. "We should be happy," he wrote to a friend, "if we hold the same territory at the end of the war that we did at the beginning. There can be no more thought of a peace whose conditions we would be able to dictate."[56]

[52] Brentano to Miss Paget, October 17, 1914. See also his article "Der Kardinalfehler des Pazifismus," Berliner Tageblatt, September 1, 1915.

[53] See Brentano's articles: "Der Handel im Kriege," Kriegskultur und Heimarbeit, No. 11 (Berlin, 1915); Über den Wahnsinn der Handelsfeindseligkeit (Munich, 1916).

[54] On Brentano and pacifism, see his article "Der Kardinalfehler des Pazifismus" cited above, n. 52; Brentano to Ludwig Quidde, July 3, 1915; Brentano to Miss Paget, October 17, 1914.

[55] On the annexationists, see H. Gatzke, Germany's Drive to the West: A Study of Germany's Western War Aims during the First World War (Baltimore, 1950), pp. 44–47, 117 ff.; Fischer, Griff nach der Weltmacht, pp. 193–202; there is an excellent collection of annexationist propaganda reprinted in S. Grumbach, Das annexionistische Deutschland (Lausanne, 1917).

[56] Brentano to Leonard Nelson, March 10, 1915.

In May, 1915, Brentano attacked the extreme annexationists for what he called *Gewaltpolitik*. The article was unacceptable to the censor.[57] A month later, when Brentano received reports on the preparation of the annexationist "Petition of the Intellectuals," he wrote Hans Delbrück to encourage him to formulate a counter-declaration.[58] Throughout July, Brentano corresponded with Delbrück about the wording of the declaration, which was finally signed by 141 prominent Germans and published in the November, 1915, *Preussische Jahrbücher*. The declaration called for a renunciation of annexations which violated the principle of national sovereignty, and a limitation of German war aims to whatever might be necessary for the strategic security and economic progress of the nation.[59] The Delbrück declaration was a statement of the position of that sector of German opinion to which Brentano belonged: these men were the so-called moderates, who rejected the extreme annexationists, but at the same time did not exclude the possibility of some territorial gains for "strategic security."

About the same time that Delbrück's declaration was printed, Friedrich Naumann gave a more positive and extensive statement of the moderate position on war aims in his *Mitteleuropa*, which was published in October, 1915.[60] In this famous book

---

[57] Naumann to Brentano, May 4, 1915, with a draft of Brentano's reply.

[58] Letter of Brentano to Delbrück, June 28, 1915, cited in A. Thimme, *Hans Delbrück als Kritiker der Wilhelminischen Epoche* (Düsseldorf, 1955), p. 121. On Delbrück and the so-called moderates, see Thimme, pp. 116–46; Gatzke, *Germany's Drive to the West*, pp. 54–62; Schwabe, "Zur politischen Haltung," pp. 616–17; Basler, "Zur politischen Rolle," pp. 187 ff. and 192 ff.; W. Mommsen, *Max Weber und die deutsche Politik 1890–1920* (Tübingen, 1959), pp. 212–13.

[59] *Preussische Jahrbücher*, CLXII (November, 1915), 360. See Gatzke, *Germany's Drive to the West*, pp. 132–33. In his memoirs, *Through Two Decades* (London, 1936), p. 207, Theodor Wolff took credit for the wording of the declaration. Thimme, *Hans Delbrück*, p. 121, stated that Delbrück was the author.

[60] Naumann, *Mitteleuropa* (Berlin-Schöneberg, 1915); see Heuss, *Naumann*, pp. 333 ff.; the most complete analysis of Naumann's ideas is in Henry Cord Meyer, *Mitteleuropa in German Thought and Action 1815–1945* (The Hague, 1955), pp. 194–217; Abraham Ascher, in his "National Solidarity and Imperial Power: The Sources and Early Development of Social Imperialist Thought in Germany, 1871–1914" (unpub. diss., Columbia, 1957), pp. 184 ff., attempted to attack Meyer's approach but did not

Naumann argued that Germany's primary war aim should be the construction of a supranational organization in Central Europe. Naumann felt that just as the Reich had grown up from the *Zollverein,* so Central European unity could be achieved by close economic co-operation. He stressed that the national integrity of the states comprising *Mitteleuropa* was to be recognized, although there was little doubt that Germany would play the leading role in the union.

In January, 1915, Naumann and Brentano were reconciled.[61] When *Mitteleuropa* appeared, Brentano sent him a lengthy critique of his book,[62] in which he praised the grace and vigor of Naumann's prose and agreed with his concern for national integrity. He was opposed, however, to the tariff wall with which Naumann proposed to surround *Mitteleuropa.* It was this system of tariff barriers, Brentano wrote, which had poisoned the international atmosphere before 1914. If the relationship of nations in the postwar world did not rest on free trade, the coming peace would be only a cease-fire and Europe would be ruined by further wars.[63]

By the end of 1915 Brentano had clearly established his position between the extreme nationalists, on the one hand, and the pacifists, on the other. His goal was the security and prosperity of Germany in a peaceful world. As his correspondence with Naumann indicated, the first two years of the war had convinced him that this goal could best be achieved by liberal

---

damage it in any important way; see also J. Droz, *L'Europe centrale: Évolution historique de l'Idée de Mitteleuropa* (Paris, 1960), pp. 207–27.

61 *Mein Leben,* p. 323; Naumann to Brentano, January 23, 1915, reprinted in Heuss, *Naumann,* p. 547.

62 As early as 1901 Naumann seems to have been interested in a Central European union; in that year *Die Hilfe* favorably reviewed a book calling for a Central European *Zollverein.* At that time, Brentano registered a vigorous protest with the editor of *Die Hilfe* and evidently succeeded in convincing him that any kind of a *Zollverein* would strengthen the Junkers. See Max Maurenbrecher to Brentano, August 12 and 22, September 22, 1901. For Naumann's ideas on *Mitteleuropa* before 1914 see Meyer, *Mitteleuropa,* pp. 88–95. Brentano's critique of Naumann in 1915 is in a letter of October 29, 1915.

63 For Naumann's reply, see his letter to Brentano, October 22, 1915, reprinted in Heuss, *Naumann,* pp. 547–48. Brentano was being quite unfair when he claimed that *Mitteleuropa* reflected the pan-German ideas of Naumann's youth (*Mein Leben,* p. 325).

commercial policies, which alone could provide a firm basis for a lasting peace. This faith in free trade, when viewed in the light of the complexities of international relations, is another example of the severe limitations of the economic categories with which Brentano sought to understand both domestic and foreign affairs.

3 —

Until 1916, the debate on war aims was the main threat to the national solidarity which the Germans had displayed in August, 1914. By the end of the second year of the war, however, an increasingly tense domestic situation began to cause splits in German society which the so-called *Burgfrieden* could not contain. By 1916, therefore, Brentano's earlier absorption with foreign affairs gave way to concern for German domestic problems.

In June, 1916, Brentano was interviewed by Heinrich Kanner, a Viennese journalist. Kanner found him "deeply pessimistic" about German affairs.[64] He was concerned about the continuing annexationist agitation, particularly since he felt that the pressure of internal affairs made it necessary to end the war as soon as possible. Most of all, Brentano seemed anxious about the problem of feeding the population, a problem which Kanner felt was particularly serious in Munich and which Brentano predicted would get worse as the war continued.[65] There is every indication that Brentano's pessimism concerning German domestic affairs increased throughout 1916.[66]

[64] Heinrich Kanner was the editor of the Vienna daily, *Die Zeit*. From November, 1914, until November, 1917, he traveled to Germany every few months. His account of his travels is in manuscript form at the Hoover Library, Stanford, California. His interview with Brentano is in the first volume of this manuscript, pp. 110–15.

[65] For Kanner's view of the situation in Munich, see *ibid.*, I, 96. The following index shows the rising cost of food in Germany as a whole:

| 1914 | 100 | 1917 | 220 |
|------|-----|------|-----|
| 1915 | 138 | 1918 | 229 |
| 1916 | 207 |      |     |

J. Kuczynski, *Die Geschichte der Lage der Arbeiter unter dem Kapitalismus. Vol. 1: Die Geschichte der Lage der Arbeiter in Deutschland von 1789 bis in die Gegenwart* (6th ed.; Berlin, 1954), Part II, p. 99. On food shortages see also Lutz, *Fall of the German Empire*, II, 141–201. As early as October, 1914, Brentano advised measures to protect the food supply (*Mein Leben*, pp. 318–19).

[66] Brentano to *Neutrale Konferenz für ständige Vermittlung*, July 17, 1916. See also the letter from Brentano's cousin Irene Forbes-Mosse to Julia von

In 1917 both the military and domestic situations in Germany worsened. The failure of unrestricted submarine warfare to defeat England, and the entry of the United States into the war, were severe blows to the German war effort. At the same time, tensions at home steadily increased. For the first time since the beginning of the war, industrial disputes and political strikes occurred in significant numbers.[67]

By mid-1917, Brentano's pessimism about German affairs had deepened significantly. His own experiences in Munich, where he found talk of revolution and defeatism rampant, convinced him that something had to be done.[68] This conviction was reinforced by the pessimistic accounts of the situation in Berlin which he had been receiving from men like Maximilian Harden.[69] Brentano reacted to this situation by continuing to agitate, both privately and in print, for a reasonable formulation of Germany's war aims which would insure a just and lasting peace.[70] He urged that action be taken to counter the demands of the annexationist forces in Germany, who were not only harming Germany's image in the neutral countries but were making it impossible to negotiate with the allies, end the war, and thereby save Germany from internal chaos.[71]

---

Vollmar, November 23, 1916. The latter is in the Vollmar Papers, International Institute for Social History, Amsterdam.

[67] Kuczynski, *Die Geschichte der Lage der Arbeiter,* I, Part II, 75, 101; H. J. Varain, *Freie Gewerkschaften, Sozialdemokratie und Staat: Die Politik der Generalkommission unter der Führung Carl Legiens 1890–1920* (Düsseldorf, 1956), pp. 71–117; C. E. Schorske, *German Social Democracy, 1905–1917: The Development of the Great Schism* (Cambridge, 1955), pp. 308 ff.

[68] See Brentano's letter to Hertling, reprinted in *Mein Leben,* pp. 332–33. Brentano was moved to write to Hertling because of a report he received from a Munich businessman; see A. Fraenkel to Brentano, April 4, 1917, in the Bavarian Archives, Munich, *Akten der Bayerischen Staatskanzlei,* MA I, No. 959. See also Brentano's views on the gravity of the situation as expressed in a letter to Johannes Haller, September 21, 1917, Haller Papers, Bundesarchiv Koblenz.

[69] See Brentano to Harden, June 8, 1917 (Harden Papers, Bundesarchiv Koblenz); Harden to Brentano, May 23, June 2, June 23, 1917.

[70] See Brentano's article, "Das Friedensangebot," *Internationale Rundschau,* III (January, 1917), 20–24.

[71] Brentano to Delbrück, March 8, 1917; Brentano to G. Gothein, August 29, 1917 (Gothein Papers, Bundesarchiv Koblenz); in a letter of September 29,

At the same time, Brentano joined the agitation for democratization which became widespread among German intellectuals in the spring and summer of 1917.[72] In April, 1917, he sought to gain the support of his cousin Georg von Hertling, then Minister President of Bavaria, for a campaign to democratize the Prussian electoral system. If the Junkers' hold on the Prussian government were broken, Brentano maintained, the people's enthusiasm for the war would be greatly increased. Furthermore, the *Entente* would be far more willing to negotiate with a democratic Germany.[73] He continued to advocate universal suffrage for Prussia and parliamentary government for the Reich throughout the summer of 1917.[74]

One of the most curious aspects of Brentano's activities in wartime Germany is the fact that at the same time that internal tensions were causing him to make the most radical political protests of his career, he went to work for the *Auswärtiges Amt.* Since the early days of the war Brentano had been conscious of the necessity of winning the support of the neutral nations for Germany's cause.[75] In 1917, at the instigation of an official in the Foreign Office, he began to write articles explaining Germany's position. These articles were printed in the newspapers of neutral nations and were distributed to prisoners of war. Brentano received a monthly stipend of six hundred marks to cover his expenses.[76]

There are two points which should be made concerning Brentano's co-operation with the Foreign Office. First, his view of

1917, to *Staatssekretär* Kühlmann, Brentano called for a German declaration renouncing Belgium.

[72] See Thimme, *Delbrück*, p. 142; Schwabe, "Zur politischen Haltung," pp. 626 ff. For an excellent survey of German internal affairs during the summer of 1917, see K. Epstein, *Matthias Erzberger and the Dilemma of German Democracy* (Princeton, 1959), pp. 182–213.

[73] *Mein Leben*, pp. 332–33.

[74] *Ibid.*, p. 334; "Wahlreform und Sozialpolitik," *Die Zukunft*, XXV, No. 33 (May 19, 1917), 175–90; "Weitere Vorteile einer Parlamentarisierung," *Berliner Tageblatt*, August 10, 1917; "Die Gegner der Parlamentarisierung," *Berliner Tageblatt*, August 22, 1917.

[75] Brentano to Hoensbroech, November 28, 1914.

[76] Brentano's correspondence with the *Auswärtiges Amt* began in September, 1917, and extends until September, 1923. During the years after the war Brentano made several trips to England which he reported on to the government.

politics is illuminated by the fact that, although he felt membership in a political party would compromise his integrity, he seems to have had no qualms about clandestine work for the government. This was not hypocrisy; rather it reflected the political attitude which Brentano shared with many German professors: co-operation with the government was perfectly acceptable, but participation in party politics was suspect. Second, Brentano's active support for German foreign policy came at the time when he was most critical of German domestic affairs. This attitude is also characteristic of the German intelligentsia: like so many critics of imperial Germany, Brentano's criticism of his nation's internal affairs was always compromised by his acquiescence in matters of foreign policy.

A few weeks after he began to work for the Foreign Office, Brentano suggested that positive steps be taken to solve the labor disputes which had once again begun to disrupt the German economy. During the fall of 1917 he moved to Berlin, and in the first week of December he formulated the draft of a law for the regulation of industrial relations. Essentially this draft resembled the address he had made to the Mannheim meeting of the *Verein für Sozialpolitik* in 1905.[77] As at Mannheim, Brentano proposed that an organization of workers and employers be created to settle disputes. Each year the elected representatives of management and labor would determine wages and working conditions. If an agreement could not be reached, an arbitration board would hear evidence and offer a solution, but the right to strike and lockout remained. If either management or labor broke their contract, the guilty party would be fined.

The most important difference between Brentano's proposal of 1917 and his speech at Mannheim reflected his awareness of the central role unions had come to play during the war. In 1905 Brentano had sought to create an organization which would transcend the unions and within which they would have had to struggle for representation in accordance with their strength. In

---

[77] Brentano was convinced that the cartelization of industry had increased during the war. As has been mentioned, monopolies played an important role in Brentano's formulation of his Mannheim address. On his views of wartime cartels see "Die notwendige Forderung," *Berliner Tageblatt,* June 18, 1916; "Umwertung der Werte," *Leipziger Abendzeitung,* January 6, 1917.

1917 he proposed that the workers' representatives to his industrial organization be elected by a system of proportional representation, thus assuring the unions a decided advantage over the
unorganized workers. "The representation of the workers," Brentano wrote, "would in reality rest in the hands of the existing
unions."[78]

While Brentano was writing his proposals for a reorganization
of German industrial relations, a number of similar plans were
being considered by the government.[79] In October, 1917, the
Inter-party Committee of the Reichstag listed the creation of
some worker-employer organizations as one of the tasks for the
new Chancellor, von Hertling.[80] In November, discussions over
the draft of a law for this purpose had begun, but had quickly
become bogged down in disagreements between the unions and
the government.[81] Brentano's proposals were more extensive
than any of those being considered, none of which contained the
emphasis on arbitration which he had made the center of his
plan.

According to Brentano's account he was able to win von
Hertling's support for his ideas.[82] Brentano felt that for his plan
to have any chance of success he would need the unanimous
support of the trade unions. He began his campaign to get union

---

[78] See the typed copy of this memorandum, dated December 9, 1917, in the
Brentano Papers; *Mein Leben*, pp. 340–43; *Soziale Praxis*, XXVIII, No. 3
(May 15, 1919), 576–78.

[79] H. J. Teuteberg, *Geschichte der industriellen Mitbestimmung in Deutschland* (Tübingen, 1961), pp. 504 ff.

[80] Epstein, *Erzberger*, p. 223.

[81] Varain, *Freie Gewerkschaften*, pp. 107 ff. See also "Zum Gewerkschaftsent-
wurf eines Arbeitskammergesetzes," *Correspondenzblatt der Generalkommission der Gewerkschaften Deutschlands*, XXVII, Nos. 49, 50 (December 8
and 15, 1917), 453–57, 463–65. I am grateful to Mr. Gerald Feldman for
allowing me to use the manuscript of his dissertation, "Army, Industry and
Labor in Germany, 1914–1918" (Harvard, 1963). Chapters 8 and 9 were of
particular interest.

[82] *Mein Leben*, pp. 340–43. There is no evidence with which to check Brentano's account of Hertling's enthusiasm for Brentano's ideas. This enthusiasm does seem somewhat out of keeping with Hertling's conservative
social views and his political position in 1917. The one relevant communication from Hertling's son showed polite interest but not vigorous support,
Karl Hertling to Brentano, February 20, 1918. On Hertling's social thought,
see A. Eickhoff, *Georg von Hertling als Sozialpolitiker* (Cologne, 1932).

backing by discussing his plan with Hugo Heinemann, the attorney for the Socialist unions in Berlin.[83] He then met with the leading members of the Socialist unions, Heinemann, Legien, Umbreit, and others, who seem to have given their tentative support to the scheme.[84] On February 21, 1918, these men met and made some revisions in Brentano's ideas, which were then presented to a meeting of the leaders of all the unions on March 6.[85]

The evidence does not allow us to say with certainty what occurred in the meeting of March 6. It is clear that Adam Stegerwald, the leader of the Christian Unions, refused to support Brentano. Stegerwald was evidently annoyed that he was not consulted until after Brentano had negotiated with the Socialists. He also seems to have been concerned that the Christian Unions would be at a decided disadvantage in the proposed organizations because they controlled only a minority of the organized workers.[86] Although Brentano tended to place all of the blame for his project's failure on Stegerwald, there are indications that the Socialists' interest in his plan was also insufficient to gain their unqualified support.[87] In any case, they felt that Brentano himself should present the plan to the government, evidently without any formal statement of approval on

---

83 *Mein Leben*, p. 343.

84 See Heinemann's letter to Brentano of January 10, 1918, which contained a memorandum on Brentano's proposals.

85 Heinemann to Brentano, February 22, 1918; see also Leipart's report on Brentano's proposals, reprinted in *Beschlüsse der Konferenzen von Vertretern der Zentralverbandsvorstände* (Berlin, 1919), p. 95. This citation was pointed out to me by Dr. Henryk Skrzypczak of the Berliner Historische Kommission.

86 *Mein Leben*, p. 344; Stegerwald's attitude is made clear in his article "Tarifvereinbarungen zwischen Arbeitgebern und Arbeitern und Arbeitsgemeinschaften," *Soziale Praxis*, XXIX, No. 25 (March 17, 1920), 565–66.

87 In December, 1917, the leaders of the Socialist unions began negotiating with the representatives of big business. It is possible that the union leaders lost interest in Brentano's proposals because they hoped that they could get better results by dealing directly with the industrialists. See Werner Richter, *Gewerkschaften, Monopolkapital und Staat im ersten Weltkrieg und in der November Revolution (1914–1919)* (Berlin, 1959), pp. 156–90. Although Richter's account is distorted by his orthodox Marxist-Leninist approach, he provides invaluable information on labor relations during the war.

their part.[88] Whatever the reasons for the failure on March 6, Brentano decided to abandon his project and return to Munich.

In May, 1918, Brentano gave his last important address in imperial Germany. In a lecture to the Munich Economic Society he answered a series of attacks made on his ideas during the last years of the war. His lecture was entitled "Has the Brentano System Been Defeated?"[89] As he looked back over his role in German politics since the founding of the Reich, he argued that he could see the gradual triumph of his ideals. He recounted how the *Kathedersozialisten* had won over a hostile public to ideals of social reform until Germany possessed the most advanced social legislation in Europe. He also stressed the fact that the unions had proved themselves during the war by their patriotic behavior and noted that they had been accepted as the rightful representatives of the working class.

It is rather difficult to take seriously Brentano's claim in the spring of 1918 that his "system" had triumphed. The program of social legislation that Germany had evolved since the late 1870's was very different from the liberal measures that Brentano had once maintained were necessary for social harmony. Furthermore, the trade unions which had come to be recognized as the spokesmen for German labor were hardly similar to those British organizations from which Brentano's models had been drawn. Moreover, even if we choose to overlook the enormous disparity between Brentano's ideals and the reality of 1918, even if we accept his claim that the existing welfare measures and unions were part of his "system," the victory he claimed on the eve of revolution merely serves to reaffirm the weakness of his approach to the problems of imperial Germany. In May, 1918, when Brentano announced the triumph of his "system," he overlooked the fact that despite the welfare laws, despite the success of unions, Germany's basic political problems remained. Aggravated by long years of war and made unbearable by the shock of defeat, these were the problems that were to cast their shadow over Germany's unhappy future.

If Brentano actually felt vindicated in May, 1918, he soon saw what a hollow victory it was. Even as he spoke he was conscious

88 See *Beschlüsse der Konferenzen*, pp. 95–96.
89 *Ist das System Brentano zusammengebrochen?* (Berlin, 1918).

of the unrest in Munich and the surrounding countryside.[90] By the summer of 1918, Brentano fully realized that Germany was in a desperate situation. In September he tried to gather support for a declaration calling for an immediate end of the war on the basis of no territorial changes, democratization of the Reich, and support for a league of nations.[91] By mid-October, however, he knew that such action had been "out-distanced by the rapid course of events."[92] In the disorder and confusion of the Reich's last days, the time for declarations and memoranda was past. Germany's future was to be determined by far less resistible forces than the public statements of its professors.

[90] *Mein Leben,* p. 349.
[91] Brentano to G. Gothein, September 11, 24, 30, 1918 (Gothein Papers).
[92] Brentano to Vogelstein, October 19, 1918.

# Epilogue

During the stormy months after Germany's defeat in 1918, Brentano tried once again to render service to his nation. When Kurt Eisner's revolutionary government took over in Munich, Brentano agreed to participate because he hoped that he could exert a moderating influence on Eisner's radical economic ideas. Rarely has a man been so out of place as was this aging liberal among those youthful visionaries who sought to build a new world on the Isar. It became obvious that Brentano's position in the government was untenable, and when he realized his isolation and ineffectiveness he withdrew.[1]

Almost as soon as some measure of public order had been restored, Brentano became involved in the debate over Germay's responsibility for the war, which was beginning to play an important role in German national life. He joined the *Heidelberger Vereinigung,* one of the foremost anti-war guilt groups, and wrote a series of pamphlets and articles which sought to demonstrate that Germany was not solely responsible for the outbreak of hostilities.[2] In the winter of 1919, Brentano traveled to Britain, where he met with those members of the British left who shared his critical attitude towards the Treaty of Versailles. Throughout the early twenties, he frequently attacked the

[1] See Brentano's account of his co-operation with Eisner in *Mein Leben im Kampfe um die soziale Entwicklung Deutschlands* (Jena, 1931), pp. 349–67. Hereafter cited as *Mein Leben.* Brentano's correspondence with Eisner in 1919 is in the Brentano Papers. On the Eisner government, see A. Mitchell, *Revolution in Bavaria* (Princeton, 1965).

[2] See the correspondence between Brentano and the leaders of the *Heidelberger Vereinigung* in the Brentano Papers. The *Vereinigung* is described in W. Mommsen, *Max Weber und die deutsche Politik 1890–1920* (Tübingen, 1959), pp. 308–9.

Treaty, occasionally showing signs of the vitality that had marked his long career as a polemicist.[3]

After the war, Brentano did not abandon his commitment to the welfare of Germany's working classes. In 1920 he made a final attempt to influence the government in favor of his proposals for the reorganization of German labor relations. As in 1917–18, he was unable to gather extensive backing for his program and his plans remained without effect.[4] He also persisted in his demands for free trade and argued that the economic ills which beset Germany in the twenties might be greatly reduced by the adoption of liberal tariff policies. A conflict over the eight-hour day, the growing power of heavy industry, the ebbing interest of the *Verein für Sozialpolitik* in reform, these and other issues kept alive the passion for social justice which had spurred him on in years gone by.

Brentano's continuing involvement with public affairs is a tribute to the persistence of his spirit in the face of failing health, old age, and isolation. But his efforts to synthesize liberalism and social reform, his boundless faith in the efficacy of free trade, his desire to encourage the *Verein* to more vigorous action, all belonged to what has been called "the world of yesterday," a world which was far from the crisis-ridden course of postwar Germany. Some Germans listened to Brentano in the twenties, but one suspects they listened with an attentiveness born of respect, not of interest. By his eightieth birthday, in 1924, he had outlived two generations of German reformers. Almost all of the men whose voices had once joined his—Schmoller, Barth, Naumann, Max Weber—were now silent.

By the middle of the decade, Brentano's participation in public life noticeably declined. Shortly after his wife died in 1918 he had sold his palatial home on Munich's Mandlstrasse, and in the early twenties he moved out to a comfortable but more modest establishment at Prien on Chiemsee, a lake outside of Munich. Here he spent an increasing amount of time with his books, reworking and publishing the fruits of years of reading

3 For example, see the description of Brentano at a meeting on social reform in Prague (1924) given by Eugen Schiffer, *Ein Leben für den Liberalismus* (Berlin-Grünewald, 1951), p. 226.

4 *Mein Leben*, pp. 384 ff., and the relevant material in the Brentano Papers.

and research.[5] At last, the call of practical activity, which had again and again lured him from his study, was stilled.

The turmoil of the years after 1929 penetrated even the quiet of Chiemsee, and Brentano's life ended under the shadow of the Republic's final agonies. He died on September 9, 1931, a few weeks before his eighty-seventh birthday.

In the spring of 1932 a statue of Brentano was unveiled at the University of Munich, near the great hall where generations of students had delighted in his lectures. When representatives of the student body attempted to hold a memorial service to dedicate the statue, a band of Nazi youth disrupted the proceedings and forced their cancellation, as though to reaffirm that Brentano died an alien in a new Germany.

[5] A sympathetic description of Brentano in retirement is given in Ernst Feder, "Bei Geheimrat Brentano am Chiemsee," *Bibliographie der Rechts- und Staatswissenschaft*, XXXIX (1930/31), pp. 83–85.

# Bibliographical Notes

## I   Unpublished Materials

The most important collection of unpublished materials for this study is Lujo Brentano's *Nachlass* at the Bundesarchiv in Koblenz. These papers contain 78 folders of letters, as well as press clippings, lecture notes, and other manuscripts. When I used this collection in the winter of 1961–62 it had not been completely catalogued and was still more or less in the order which Brentano's family had given it before sending it to Koblenz.

Despite its size, the Brentano *Nachlass* has three major weaknesses as a biographical source. First, as I mentioned in the introduction, it contains almost no information on Brentano's personal life. All papers relevant to Brentano's non-professional activities were evidently removed by his daughter. It is quite likely that almost all of this material was destroyed, although some things (mainly letters from Brentano to his wife) are in the possession of Brentano's former housekeeper, Miss

Josefa Ruess, who did not feel able to allow them to be used for this study. Second, the Brentano *Nachlass* has some very unfortunate gaps. Apparently Brentano did not make a consistent effort to save his papers until after he had moved to Munich. The information on the years before 1891 is, therefore, frequently spotty and uneven. Finally, as in understandable, Brentano's letters contain mostly the letters which he received. Thus, until after the turn of the century when he began to keep copies of his most important letters, one is forced to rely on an occasional draft to get direct evidence of Brentano's point of view. This last weakness is compounded by the fact that the papers of many of Brentano's closest friends and associates have either been lost or are in East German archives and therefore inaccessible. Fortunately, Walther Goetz made copies of the correspondence between Brentano and Schmoller up to 1899 and these copies are in the *Nachlass*. Goetz published the letters from 1870 to 1878 as "Der Briefwechsel Gustav Schmollers mit Lujo Brentano," *Archiv für Kulturgeschichte,* XXVIII, No. 2 (1938), 316–54; XXIX, Nos. 1–2 and 3 (1939), 147–83, 331–47; XXX, No. 1 (1941), 142–207.

I was able to supplement the material in the Brentano papers with letters between Lujo and his brother Franz. These are in the possession of Franz Brentano's son, John C. M. Brentano. It was not possible for me to use the complete collection of these letters, but I was able to use selected copies and some microfilm of the originals.

In addition to these two collections, scattered material by or on Brentano can be found in the papers of the following individuals: Eduard Bernstein (International Institute for Social History, Amsterdam), Georg Gothein (Bundesarchiv, Koblenz), Johannes Haller (Bundesarchiv, Koblenz), Maximilian Harden (Bundesarchiv, Koblenz), Frederic Harrison (London School of Economics), Georg von Hertling (Political Correspondence, Bayerisches Hauptstaatsarchiv, Abteilung II, Geheimes Staatsarchiv, Munich), Heinrich Kanner (Hoover Library, Stanford University), Beatrice and Sidney Webb (London School of Economics), Karl Schrader (Niedersächsisches Staatsarchiv, Wolfenbüttel), Georg von Vollmar (International Institute for Social History, Amsterdam). I also used the papers of Richard Roesicke (Bundesarchiv, Koblenz) for material on the *Freisinnige Vereinigung,* and of Gottfried Traub (Bundesarchiv, Koblenz) for letters and clippings on the National Social movement.

## II    Lujo Brentano's Own Writings

The following list presents in chronological order the books and articles by Brentano which were cited in the text. For additional titles consult H. Neisser and M. Palyi, eds., *Lujo Brentano: Eine Bio-Bibliographie* (Berlin, 1924).

## 1. Books

*Über J. H. von Thünens naturgemässen Lohn- und Zinsfluss im isolierten Staate.* Dissertation. Göttingen, 1867.

*Das Industrial Partnership System: Ein Versuch zur Lösung der Arbeiterfrage* ("Katholische Studien," edited by M. Huttler.) Augsburg, 1868.

*On the History and Development of Gilds and the Origin of Trades Unions.* London, 1870.

*Die Arbeitergilden der Gegenwart.* 2 vols. Leipzig, 1871–72.

*Über Einigungsämter: Eine Polemik mit Herrn Dr. Alexander Meyer.* Leipzig, 1873.

*Die "wissenschaftliche" Leistung des Herrn Ludwig Bamberger.* Leipzig, 1873.

*Die Produktivgenossenschaft und ihre Bedeutung für die Lösung der sozialen Frage.* Breslau, 1873.

*Über das Verhältnis von Arbeitslohn und Arbeitszeit zu Arbeitsleistung.* Leipzig, 1876.

*Das Arbeitsverhältnis gemäss dem heutigen Recht.* Leipzig, 1877.

*Die Arbeiterversicherung gemäss der heutigen Wirtschaftsordnung.* Leipzig, 1879.

*Der Arbeiterversicherungszwang: Seine Voraussetzungen und seine Folgen.* Berlin, 1881.

*Die christlich-soziale Bewegung in England.* Leipzig, 1883.

*Die klassische National–Ökonomie.* Leipzig, 1888.

*Über die Ursachen der heutigen sozialen Not: Ein Beitrag zur Morphologie der Volkswirtschaft.* Leipzig, 1889.

*Meine Polemik mit Karl Marx. Zugleich ein Beitrag zur Frage des Fortschritts der Arbeiterklasse und seiner Ursachen.* Berlin, 1890.

*Die Stellung der Gebildeten zur sozialen Frage.* Berlin, n.d. (1890).

*Über die Fortbildung des Arbeitsvertrages.* Vienna, 1892.

*Über Anerbenrecht und Grundeigentum.* Berlin, 1895.

*Agrarpolitik: Ein Lehrbuch.* Stuttgart, 1897.

*Die Stellung der Studenten zu den sozialpolitischen Aufgaben der Zeit.* Munich, 1897.

*Reaktion oder Reform? Gegen die Zuchthausvorlage.* Berlin-Schöneberg, 1899.

*Der Schutz der Arbeitswilligen.* Berlin, 1899.

*Gesammelte Aufsätze. Vol. 1: Erbrechtspolitik: Alte und neue Feudalität.* Stuttgart, 1899.

*Die heutige Grundlage der deutschen Wehrkraft* (with R. Kuczynski). Stuttgart, 1900.

*Die Schrecken des überwiegenden Industriestaats.* Berlin, 1901.

*Das Freihandelsargument.* Berlin-Schöneberg, 1901.

*Die Malthussche Lehre und die Bevölkerungsbewegung der letzten Dezennien.* Munich, 1909.

*Wie studiert man Nationalökonomie?* Munich, 1911.

*Der Schutz der Arbeitswilligen: Ein unpolitischer Vortrag über ein politisches Thema.* Berlin, 1912.

*Über Syndikalismus und Lohnminimum: Zwei Vorträge nebst einem Anhang enthaltend Ausführungen und Dokumente zur Illustrierung der Kampfweise der Gegner sozialer Reform gegen deren Vertreter.* Munich, 1913.

*England und der Krieg.* Berlin, 1915.

*Über den Wahnsinn der Handelsfeindseligkeit.* Munich, 1916.

*Das ganze deutsche Volk: Unser Schlachtruf und Kriegsziel.* Munich, 1916.

*Elsässer Erinnerungen.* Berlin, 1917.

*Ist das "System Brentano" zusammengebrochen? Über Kathedersozialismus und alten und neuen Merkantilismus.* Berlin, 1918.

*Die Urheber des Weltkrieges.* Munich, 1922.

*Der wirtschaftende Mensch in der Geschichte.* Leipzig, 1923.

*Eine Geschichte der wirtschaftlichen Entwicklung Englands.* 3 vols. Jena, 1927–28.

*Mein Leben im Kampfe um die soziale Entwicklung Deutschlands.* Jena, 1931.

## 2. Articles

"Der Congress der Trades Unions zu Manchester vom 3. bis 6. Juni 1868," *Zeitschrift des königlichen preussischen statistischen Bureaus,* VIII, Nos. 4–9 (April–September, 1868), 239–43.

"Die Lehre von den Lohnsteigerungen mit besonderer Rücksicht auf die englischen Wirtschaftslehrer," *Jahrbücher für Nationalökonomie und Statistik,* XVI, No. 3 (1871), 251–81.

"Abstrakte und realistische Volkswirte," *Hamburger Correspondent,* January 11, 1871.

"Die Gewerkvereine im Verhältnis zu Arbeitsgesetzgebung," *Preussische Jahrbücher,* XXIX, No. 4 (1872), 586–600.

"Zur Reform der deutschen Fabrikgesetzgebung," *Verhandlungen der Eisenacher Versammlung zur Besprechung der sozialen Fragen am 6. und 7. Oktober 1872.* Leipzig, 1872.

"Der Ausgangspunkt und die dauernde Grundlage der sogenannten Kathedersozialisten," *Hamburger Correspondent,* November 10, 1872.

"Die Sicherung des Arbeitsvertrages," *Schriften des Vereins für Sozialpolitik,* VII (1874), 133–52.

"Die englische Chartistenbewegung," *Preussische Jahrbücher,* XXXIII, Nos. 5 and 6 (1874), 431–47, 531–50.

"Zur Lehre von den Lohnsteigerungen," *Zeitschrift für die gesamte Staatswissenschaft,* XXXII, No. 3 (1876), 466–78.

"Die liberale Partei und die Arbeiter," *Preussische Jahrbücher,* XL, No. 1 (1877), 112–22.

"Gewerbeordnung und Unterstützungswesen," *Schmollers Jahrbuch,* I, No. 3 (1877), 471–501.

"Die Arbeiter und die Produktionskrisen," *Schmollers Jahrbuch*, II, No. 3 (1878), 565–632.

"Die Hirsch-Duncker'schen Gewerkvereine: Eine Replik," *Schmollers Jahrbuch*, III, No. 2 (1879), 215–31.

"Die gewerbliche Arbeiterfrage," *Handbuch der politischen Oekonomie*. Edited by Gustav Schönberg. Tübingen, 1882.

"Über eine zukünftige Handelspolitik des deutschen Reiches," *Schmollers Jahrbuch*, IX, No. 1 (1885), 1–29.

"Die beabsichtigte Alters- und Invalidenversicherung für Arbeiter und ihre Bedeutung," *Jahrbücher für Nationalökonomie und Statistik*, XVI, No. 1 (1888), 1–46.

"Über Kartelle," *Mitteilungen der Gesellschaft österreichischer Volkswirte*, I (1888).

"Über internationalen Arbeiterschutz," *Deutsches Wochenblatt*, III, No. 8 (February, 1890), 86–89.

"Über Arbeitseinstellungen und Fortbildung des Arbeitsvertrages," *Schriften des Vereins für Sozialpolitik*, XLV (1890), ix–lxxviii.

"Arbeitseinstellungen und die Fortbildung des Arbeitsvertrages," *Verhandlungen von 1890, Schriften des Vereins für Sozialpolitik*, XLVII (1891), 119–30.

"Der Achtstundentag in England," *Deutsches Wochenblatt*, III, No. 48 (November, 1890), 571–74.

"Anfang und Ende der englischen Kornzölle," *Allgemeine Zeitung* (Munich), January 15–16, 1892.

"Der englische Gewerkvereinskongress 1892," *Sozialpolitisches Centralblatt*, I, No. 38 (September, 1892), 471–74.

"Zur Polemik über die deutschen Gewerkvereine," *Sozialpolitisches Centralblatt*, III, No. 8 (November, 1893), 93–94.

"Über Gebundenheit und Teilbarkeit des ländlichen Grundeigentums," *Allgemeine Zeitung* (Munich), December 20–21, 1893.

"Gesamtinteresse und Sonderinteresse mit Rücksicht auf die Landwirtschaft. Eine Abwehr gegen Herrn Dr. G. Ratzinger," *Allgemeine Zeitung* (Munich), January 17, 1894.

"Der Antrag Kanitz und die Getreideverteuerung," *Neue Freie Presse*, March 23, 1895.

"Entwicklung und Geist der englischen Arbeiterorganisationen," *Archiv für soziale Gesetzgebung und Statistik*, VIII, No. 1 (1895), 75–139.

"Sozialpolitik und Umsturzvorlage," *Die Zukunft*, X (March, 1895), 397–407.

"Zum Jubiläum des Vereins für Sozialpolitik," *Frankfurter Zeitung*, July 8, 9, 10, 1897.

"Der soziale Friede und die Wandlungen der sozialen Demokratie," *Allgemeine Zeitung* (Munich), April 23, 1899.

"Moderne Grosskartelle und Arbeiterkoalitionen," *Die Woche*, April 24, 1899.

"Die Wandlungen der Sozialdemokratie und die Berliner Korrespondenz," *Allgemeine Zeitung* (Munich), May 2, 1899.

"Cobdens Argument gegen Flottenvermehrungen," *Die Nation,* January 13, 20, 1900.
"*Demokratie und Kaisertum,*" *Allgemeine Zeitung* (Munich), May 25, 1900.
"Die Schwierigkeiten der Freihandelsbewegung in Deutschland," *Die Hilfe,* January 6, 1901.
"Wer nicht kauft, kann auch nicht verkaufen," *Die Hilfe,* January 13, 1901.
"Die amerikanische Gefahr," *Die Hilfe,* January 27, 1901.
"Adolf Wagner und die Getreidezölle, "*Die Hilfe,* March 17, 1901.
"Adolf Wagner über Agrarstaat und Industriestaat," *Die Zeit,* June 9, 16, 23, 30, July 7, 14, 1901.
"Unsere Zukunft," *Die Hilfe,* August 9, 1903.
"Zur Einigung der Liberalen," *Frankfurter Zeitung,* November 13, 1903.
"Über politische Initiative," *Die Hilfe,* November 15, 1903.
"Jungliberale Krokodilstränen," *Freistatt,* V, No. 49 (December, 1903), 963–65.
"Die beabsichtigte Neuorganisation der deutschen Volkswirtschaft," *Süddeutsche Monatshefte,* I, No. 4 (April, 1904), 254–82.
"Das Ziel des Liberalismus und das Programm der bayerischen Liberalen," *Freistatt,* VII, No. 2 (January, 1905), 19–21.
"Das Arbeitsverhältnis in den privaten Riesenbetrieben," *Verhandlungen von 1905, Schriften des Vereins für Sozialpolitik,* CXVI (1906), 135–48.
"Gedanken über die Polenfrage!" *Die Hilfe,* September 26, 1906.
"*Neudeutsche Wirtschaftspolitik,*" *Die Nation,* June 30, July 7, 14, 21, 1906.
"Zum fünfundzwanzigjährigen Jubiläum der deutschen Sozialpolitik," *Münchener Neueste Nachrichten,* November 19, 1906.
"Bevölkerungsbewegung und Polenfrage," *Frankfurter Zeitung,* December 25, 1907.
"Die linksliberalen Anträge zum Koalitionsrecht," *Berliner Tageblatt,* April 14, 1908.
"Am Grabe Theodor Barths," *März,* III, No. 12 (1909), 427–32.
"Süddeutschland und das preussische Wahlrecht," *Das Freie Volk,* February 26, 1910.
"Der Geist der deutschen Sozialpolitik," *Hamburger Fremdenblatt,* April 1, 1910.
"Über die Wirkungen des allgemeinen und gleichen Wahlrechts," *Neue Freie Presse,* May 15, 1910.
"Die englische Seeherrschaft und Deutschland," *Neue Freie Presse,* December 24, 1911.
"Die heutigen Hauptursachen des Krieges," *Die Friedensbewegung,* VII (April, 1912), 95–97.
"The Right of Capture," *The Nation* (London), XIV, No. 15 (January, 1914), 638–39.

"Aufrichtige Rüstungsbetrachtungen. Verstaatlichung der Rüstungs-industrie," *Neue Freie Presse,* April 12, 1914.

"Deutschland und seine Gegner, insbesondere England," *Internationale Monatsschrift für Wissenschaft, Kunst und Technik,* IX, No. 3 (November, 1914), 148–62.

"Handel und Krieg," *Deutsche Kraft.* Edited by Leo Colze. 1915.

"Über das Kriegsziel," *Blätter für zwischenstaatliche Organisation,* April, 1915.

"Allgemeine Betrachtungen über Handelspolitik," *Berliner Tageblatt,* April 22, 23, 1915.

"Der Weg zum Frieden," *Internationale Rundschau,* I, No. 2 (July, 1915), 66–72.

"Ein Kardinalfehler des Pazifismus," *Berliner Tageblatt,* September 1, 1915.

"Über den engeren wirtschaftlichen Zusammenschluss Deutschlands und Österreich-Ungarns," *März,* IX, No. 35 (September, 1915), 165–71, 185–90, 205–16.

"Die notwendige Forderung," *Berliner Tageblatt,* June 18, 1916.

"Umwertung der Werte," *Leipziger Abendzeitung,* January 6, 1917.

"Das Friedensangebot," *Internationale Rundschau,* III, No. 1 (January, 1917), 20–24.

"Wahlreform und Sozialpolitik," *Die Zukunft,* XXV, No. 33 (May, 1917), 175–90.

"Weitere Vorteile einer Parlamentarisierung," *Berliner Tageblatt,* August 10, 1917.

"Die Gegner der Parlamentarisierung," *Berliner Tageblatt,* August 22, 1917.

"Über einen Friedensbund unter den Völkern," *Münchener Neueste Nachrichten,* September 28, 1917.

"Offene Antwort an Frederic Harrison," *Berliner Tageblatt,* February 17, 1918.

"Die gesetzliche Regelung des Tarifvertrages. Ein Appell an das Gewissen des Zentrums," *Soziale Praxis,* XXIX, Nos. 23 and 24 (March, 1920), 505–10, 529–34.

## III  Secondary Literature Directly About Lujo Brentano

The only full-scale works devoted to an analysis of Brentano's career are three German doctoral dissertations. The earliest of these was published in 1936 by Werner Barich as *Lujo Brentano als Sozialpolitiker* (Frankfurt, 1936). Barich's brief account provides a helpful introduction to the most important of Brentano's works. Barich did not, however, treat his subject historically. He made no attempt to place Brentano in historical context, nor did he make clear the evolution of Brentano's position after the 1870's. The drawbacks of Barich's book appear to an even greater degree in M. A. Wehnert's unpublished dissertation, "Lujo Brentano als Sozialpolitiker" (Cologne, 1950). Georg

Römer, in his "Lujo Brentano in den geistigen Strömungen seiner Zeit" (unpub. diss., Munich, 1954), conceived his task in broader terms than either Barich or Wehnert. Römer used some of the Brentano *Nachlass* and, as his title suggests, he was interested in examining Brentano's historical position. Although frequently thoughtful and stimulating, Römer's work is weakened by his overly abstract approach. He does not show the connection between Brentano's ideas and the development of German society, nor does he substantiate many of the intellectual relationships between Brentano and his contemporaries, which he describes.

The other works directly about Brentano fall into two categories: the panegyrical and the polemical. In addition to the eulogies and memoirs cited in the introduction (see nn. 1 and 3), the following sympathetic treatments should be mentioned: Ernst Feder, "Lujo Brentano," *Berliner Tageblatt* (August 17, 1928), and Feder's "Bei Geheimrat Brentano am Chiemsee," *Bibliographie der Rechts- und Staatswissenschaften,* XXXIX (1930–31), 88–85; Charles Gide, "Der Gelehrter," *Berliner Tageblatt* (December 18, 1929); Walther Lotz, "Erinnerungen an Lujo Brentano," *Schmollers Jahrbuch,* LVI, No. 1 (1932), 1–6; August Pieper, "Lujo Brentano zum Gedächtnis," *Führer Korrespondenz,* IV, No. 4 (October–December, 1931), 145–51. A memorial service held at the University of Munich in 1954 inspired several interesting essays which are reprinted in *Lujo Brentano: Grusswort und Reden bei der Feier der 110. Wiederkehr seines Geburtstages* (Berlin, 1956). Among the most representative of the polemics directed against Brentano are: Ludwig Bamberger, *Die Arbeiterfrage unter dem Gesichtspunkte des Vereinsrechts* (Stuttgart, 1873); Alfred Kuhlo, *Kathedersozialistische Irrwege mit besonderer Berücksichtigung der Wirksamkeit und der Lehren des Universitäts-Professors Dr. Brentano* (Munich, 1913); and Alexander Tille, *Lujo Brentano und der akademische Klassenmoralismus* (Berlin, 1912).

## IV    Historical Background

In the following discussion I will mention only the most important works dealing with those aspects of the historical background which are directly related to Brentano's career. Books and articles about the more general problems of German history which are relevant to this study have been cited in the footnotes. An alphabetical listing of all the works used in an earlier version of this study can be found in the author's doctoral dissertation, "Lujo Brentano, German Intellectual, 1866–1918" (Berkeley, 1964), pp. 291–322.

### 1.   German Liberalism

One of the major themes of this monograph has been the suggestion that the branch of German liberalism to which Brentano belonged was inspired and sustained by British theory and practice. The following works provide some suggestive comments on the broader problem of German–English cultural relations: Raymond Sontag, *Germany and*

*England: Background of Conflict, 1848–1894* (New York, 1938); and the articles by Percy Ernst Schramm, "Deutschlands Verhältnis zur englischen Kultur nach der Begründung des neuen Reiches," *Schicksalswege deutscher Vergangenheit*, edited by W. Hubatsch (Düsseldorf, 1950), and "Englands Verhältnis zur deutschen Kultur zwischen der Reichsgründung und der Jahrhundertwende," *Deutschland und Europa: Festschrift für Hans Rothfels*, edited by Werner Conze (Düsseldorf, 1951). Pauline Anderson's important monograph on *The Background of Anti-English Feeling in Germany, 1890–1902* (Washington, D.C., 1939) describes the problems faced by the anglophil liberals in Germany during the time of naval rivalry and *Weltpolitik*.

Wilhelm Treue's essay on Adam Smith in Germany describes one of the first steps in the extension of the influence of British liberalism on Germany; see "Adam Smith in Deutschland. Zum Problem des politischen Professors zwischen 1776 und 1810," *Deutschland und Europa: Festschrift für Hans Rothfels* (Düsseldorf, 1951). W. O. Henderson gives a brief but informative account of one of the most important transmitters of British thought in his article "Prince Smith and Free Trade in Germany," *Economic History Review*, 2d Series, II, No. 2 (1950), 295–302. Some of the chief representatives of what can be called "classical economics" in Germany are treated in Donald Rohr's *The Origins of Social Liberalism in Germany* (Chicago and London, 1963). In his excellent study of *The German Idea of Freedom* (Boston, 1957), Leonard Krieger analyzes the German "Manchesterites" within the broader context of German liberalism. The following books should be mentioned as the most useful older works on classical liberalism in Germany: Julius Becker, *Das deutsche Manchestertum* (Karlsruhe, 1907); Ludolf Grambow, *Die deutsche Freihandelspartei zur Zeit ihrer Blüte* (Jena, 1903); and Georg Mayer, *Die Freihandelslehre in Deutschland: Ein Beitrag zur Gesellschaftslehre des wirtschaftlichen Liberalismus* (Jena, 1927).

A very old, but still indispensible survey of German liberalism is O. Stillich, *Die politischen Parteien in Deutschland, Vol. 2: Der Liberalismus* (Leipzig, 1911). Friedrich Sell's *Die Tragödie des deutschen Liberalismus* (Stuttgart, 1953) is informative in content, but unfortunately lacks coherent structure. For other works on German liberalism, see chapter 3, especially note 68. A recent and fairly complete bibliography is to be found in Thomas Nipperdey, *Die Organisation der deutschen Parteien* (Düsseldorf, 1961).

Perhaps the weakest spot in the historiography of German liberalism is the evolution of the left wing liberal parties after 1890. A lack of evidence on both the individual leaders and their organizations hampers further research. The works by Nipperdey and Krieger cited above give useful but incomplete analyses of the left liberals. Aside from these works one is forced to rely on the files of newspapers like *Die Nation* and on memoirs and eulogies of the leaders. Some of the most important of these are cited in the notes of chapter 7. In contrast to the left liberal movement as a whole, the career of Friedrich Naumann has received very careful attention from historians. An introduction to the most important literature on Naumann is given in chapter 7, note 55.

## 2.   Trade Unionism in Great Britain and Germany

The classic account of the British unions in the late 1860's is given in Beatrice and Sidney Webb, *The History of Trade Unionism* (rev. ed.; London, 1926), which was written in 1894. In the last few years it has proved necessary to revise the picture of unionism given by the Webbs. One of the first steps in this direction was taken by G. D. H. Cole in his important article "Some Notes on British Trade Unions in the Third Quarter of the Nineteenth Century," *Essays in Economic History*, edited by E. M. Carus (London, 1962). Cole suggested that the Webbs underestimated the militancy of the Amalgamated Societies and over-estimated the novelty of the "new unions" which developed after 1889. Other recent interpretations of unionism during this period can be found in Henry Pelling, *A History of British Trade Unionism* (Baltimore, 1963), and in the introductory chapter to Hugh A. Clegg, Alan Fox, and A. F. Thompson, *A History of Trade Unions since 1889. Vol. 1: 1889–1910* (Oxford, 1964).

Of particular interest for the relationship between Brentano and the unions is the article by H. W. McCready, "British Labour and the Royal Commission on Trade Unions, 1867–1869," *University of Toronto Quarterly*, XXIV, No. 4 (July, 1955), 390–409. On the Engineers, the union with which Brentano had the most contact, see the official history by James B. Jeffreys, *The Story of the Engineers 1800–1945* (Letchworth, England, n.d.). Bibliographical information on the individuals who helped to introduce Brentano to the unions in 1868–69 is given in the notes to chapter 2, section 2.

The most complete account of the so-called new union movement is given in the book by Clegg, Fox, and Thompson, cited above. See also Pelling's *History of British Trade Unionism* and the article by A. E. P. Duffy, "New Unionism in Britain, 1889–1890: A Reappraisal," *Economic History Review*, 2d Series, XIV, No. 2 (December, 1961), 306–19.

With the exception of a few outstanding studies, the literature on unionism in Germany is somewhat inferior to the works on British unions discussed above. The best survey of union development during the Empire remains Theodor Cassau's *Die Gewerkschaftsbewegung: Ihre Soziologie und ihr Kampf* (Halberstadt, 1925). Cassau provides a brief historical introduction, which is followed by a highly interesting analysis of the unions' leadership, organization, social composition, and goals. In many ways less stimulating than Cassau, but still informative, is Siegfried Nestriepke's *Die Gewerkschaftsbewegung* (3 vols.; Stuttgart, n.d.). Jacob Reindl's *Die deutsche Gewerkschaftsbewegung* (Altenburg, 1922) is another general survey, which is particularly helpful for the legal aspects of the union's role in Germany.

In addition to the works by Cassau, Nestriepke, and Reindl, one is forced to rely almost entirely on older works for information on unionism in the late 1860's, 1870's, and 1880's. The most helpful of these are Eduard Bernstein's *Die Geschichte der Berliner Arbeiter-bewegung* (Vol. I, Berlin, 1907); W. Gleichauf, *Geschichte des Verbandes der deutschen Gewerkvereine* (Berlin, 1907); and Gustav Mayer, *Johann Baptist von Schweitzer* (Jena, 1909). In contrast to the earlier period, the development of the unions, especially the Socialist unions, after 1890 has received a good deal of scholarly attention. Gerhard A. Ritter discusses the relationship between the unions and the Social Democratic Party, as well as the role of the unions in German society, in his thoughtful account of *Die Arbeiterbewegung im Wilhelminischen Reich: Die sozialdemokratische Partei und die freien Gewerkschaften 1890–1900* (Berlin-Dahlem, 1959). For the period after 1900, the best work on the Socialist unions is Carl Schorske's fine study of *German Social Democracy, 1905–1917: The Development of the Great Schism* (Cambridge, 1955). Also very helpful on the unions during the Wilhelmian period are Heinz Josef Varain's work on *Freie Gewerkschaften, Sozialdemokratie und Staat: Die Politik der Generalkommission unter der Führung Carl Legiens (1890–1920)* (Düsseldorf, 1956), and Max Koch, *Die Bergarbeiterbewegung im Ruhrgebiet zur Zeit Wilhelms II (1889–1914)* (Düsseldorf, 1954). There is a great deal of information on the wartime history of unions in Werner Richter, *Gewerkschaften, Monopolkapital und Staat im ersten Weltkrieg und in der November Revolution (1914–1919)* (Berlin, 1959). Gerald Feldman's dissertation, "Army, Industry and Labor in Germany, 1914–1918" (unpub. diss., Harvard, 1963), will soon be published and will add greatly to our knowledge of the labor movement during the war. In conclusion, mention should be made of Hans Jürgen Teuteberg's rather narrowly conceived but impressively researched monograph on the problem of "co-determination," *Geschichte der industriellen Mitbestimmung in Deutschland: Ursprung und Entwicklung ihrer Vorläufer im Denken und in der Wirklichkeit des 19. Jahrhunderts* (Tübingen, 1961).

3. German Academic Life

Despite the importance of the professor in German culture and society, the literature on the imperial German academic community is extremely limited. The standard work by Friedrich Paulsen, *The German Universities and University Study* (New York, 1906), contains valuable information, but it is outdated, narrow in focus, and totally uncritical in approach. Two brief but suggestive essays provide worthwhile supplements to Paulsen: Golo Mann, "The Intellectuals: Germany," *Encounter*, IV, No. 6 (June, 1955), 42–49, and Friedrich Meinecke, "Drei Generationen deutscher Gelehrtenpolitik," *Staat und Persönlichkeit* (Berlin, 1933). R. H. Thomas and R. H. Samuel devoted a chapter to the universities in their *Education and Society in Modern Germany* (London, 1949); like the rest of the book, this chapter is filled with provocative formulations but weakened by flimsy research. The most important sociological study of the professors is C. von Ferber, *Die Entwicklung des Lehrkörpers der deutschen Universitäten und Hochschulen, 1864–1954*, which is Volume III of *Untersuchungen zur*

*Lage der deutschen Hochschullehrer,* edited by H. Plessner (Göttingen, 1956). Kurt Rossmann has collected a great deal of interesting evidence on the Spahn case, which gives some valuable insights into the problem of intellectual freedom in Germany; see his *Wissenschaft, Ethik und Politik: Erörterung des Grundsatzes der Voraussetzungslosigkeit in der Forschung* (Heidelberg, 1949). Friedrich Lilge's *Abuse of Learning: The Failure of the German University* (New York, 1948) is a stimulating, if rather impressionistic interpretation which focuses on the relationship of the universities to the origins of National Socialism. Dieter Fricke has delivered a scathing denunciation of imperial academia in his article on the Aron case: "Zur Militarisierung des deutschen Geistesleben im Wilhelminischen Kaiserreich: Der Fall Leo Arons," *Zeitschrift für die Geschichtswissenschaft,* VII, No. 5 (1960), 1069–1107.

The only aspect of the professors' political views which has received considerable attention is their attitude toward foreign policy. A competent survey of the relationship between the academic community and the fleet can be found in Wolfgang Marienfeld, "Wissenschaft und Schlachtflottenbau, 1897–1906," *Marine Rundschau, Beiheft II* (April, 1957). Abraham Ascher has recently documented the relationship between imperialism and social reform, and in the process he discusses the ideas of several important university professors on foreign policy. See Ascher's dissertation, "National Solidarity and Imperial Power: The Sources and Early Development of Social Imperialist Thought in Germany, 1871–1914" (unpub. diss., Columbia, 1957), and his article "Professors as Propagandists: The Politics of the *Kathedersozialisten,"* *Journal of Central European Affairs,* XXIII, No. 3 (October, 1963), 282–302. Klaus Schwabe's article, "Zur politischen Haltung der deutschen Professoren im ersten Weltkrieg," *Historische Zeitschrift,* CXCIII, No. 3 (December, 1961), 601–34, is a summary of a more extensive study of intellectuals during World War I which should appear in the near future.

Because of the very uneven quality of the literature on German academic life, one must rely heavily on the biographies and autobiographies of German professors. I found these recent studies of Brentano's contemporaries particularly helpful for my work: Andreas Dorpalen, *Heinrich von Treitschke* (New Haven, 1957); Alfred Heuss, *Theodor Mommsen und das 19. Jahrhundert* (Kiel, 1956); Wolfgang J. Mommsen, *Max Weber und die deutsche Politik, 1890–1920* (Tübingen, 1959); Annelise Thimme, *Hans Delbrück als Kritiker der Wilhelminischen Epoche* (Düsseldorf, 1955); and Marianne Weber, *Max Weber: Ein Lebensbild* (Heidelberg, 1950). The following are among the most informative of the recent memoirs about German academia: Ludwig Curtius, *Deutsche und antike Welt: Lebenserinnerungen* (Stuttgart, 1951); Walter Goetz, *Historiker in meiner Zeit: Gesammelte Aufsätze* (Cologne, 1957); Elly Heuss-Knapp, *Ausblick vom Münsterturm: Erlebtes aus dem Elsass und dem Reich* (Berlin, 1934); Friedrich Meinecke, *Strassburg, Freiburg, Berlin, 1901–1919: Erinnerungen* (Stuttgart, 1949);

and Karl Alexander von Müller, *Aus Gärten der Vergangenheit: Erinnerungen, 1882–1914* (Stuttgart, 1958).

## 4.  German *Sozialpolitik* and the "Academic Socialists"

I have already had occasion to discuss the problems of translating the German term *Sozialpolitik*. For this discussion and the most important literature on *Sozialpolitik* as a concept, see chapter 3, note 1. A useful introduction to the variety of programs for social reform in nineteenth-century Germany can be found in the collection edited by Ernst Schraepler, *Quellen zur Geschichte der sozialen Frage in Deutschland* (2 vols.; Frankfurt, 1955–57). Gerhard Erdmann gives a brief survey of social legislation in his *Die Entwicklung der deutschen Sozialgesetzgebung* (Göttingen, 1957). The most complete account of Bismarck's social program is in Walther Vogel, *Bismarcks Arbeiterversicherung: Ihre Entstehung im Kräftespiel der Zeit* (Braunschweig, 1951). See also the literature on Bismarck cited in chapter 4, note 34. Governmental social policy after 1890 is treated by Karl Erich Born in *Staat und Sozialpolitik seit Bismarcks Sturz: Ein Beitrag zur Entwicklung des deutschen Reiches, 1890–1914* (Wiesbaden, 1957). A valuable supplement to Born's book is the collection of documents edited by Born and Peter Rassow, *Akten zur staatlichen Sozialpolitik in Deutschland 1890–1914* (Wiesbaden, 1959). This work also has an extensive bibliography on the theory and practice of *Sozialpolitik*.

As we have seen, the intellectual origins of the *Kathedersozialisten* are to be found in the historical view of economics which evolved in Germany during the first half of the nineteenth century. A good introduction to historical economics can be found in W. J. Fischel's article "Der Historismus in der Wirtschaftswissenschaft dargestellt an der Entwicklung von Adam Müller bis Bruno Hildebrand," *Vierteljahrschrift für Sozial- und Wirtschaftsgeschichte*, XLVII, No. 1 (March, 1960), 1–31. A more detailed treatment of the methodological problems involved in historical economics is given in W. B. Cherin's unpublished doctoral dissertation, "The German Historical School of Economics: A Study in the Methodology of the Social Sciences" (Berkeley, 1933). Anyone interested in the "older historical school" should consult the basic works of Roscher, Hildebrand, and Knies, which are cited in chapter 3, note 19.

The development of the "young historical school" can be followed in Hans Gehrig's outdated but still useful monograph *Die Begründung des Prinzips der Sozialreform* (Jena, 1914) and in the article by Eugen Philippovich, "Das Eindringen der sozialpolitischen Ideen in die Literatur," in Salomon Altman, et al., *Die Entwicklung der deutschen Volkswirtschaftslehre im neunzehnten Jahrhundert* (2 vols.; Leipzig, 1908). Because neither Gehrig nor Philippovich has written a completely satisfactory account of the "young historical school," an adequate understanding of its development requires a study of the works on and by individual members of this group. Numerous references to these works are given in the notes for chapters 3 and 4.

The most important work on the "academic socialists" before 1872 is Gerhard Wittrock, *Die Kathedersozialisten bis zur Eisenacher Versammlung 1872* (Berlin, 1939). Wittrock's interpretations are often highly questionable, and his work reflects to an unfortunate degree the ideological climate of Germany during the late 1930's. However, because he had access to documents no longer available, his book is of great value. There are two standard accounts of the *Verein für Sozialpolitik:* Else Conrad, *Der Verein für Sozialpolitik und seine Wirksamkeit auf dem Gebiet der gewerblichen Arbeiterfrage* (Zurich, 1906), and Franz Boese, *Geschichte des Vereins für Sozialpolitik 1872–1932, Schriften des Vereins,* CLXXXVIII (Berlin, 1939). Conrad's book, although obviously outdated, is a sympathetic, informative, and fairly well balanced account of the *Verein's* activities. Franz Boese was the last General Secretary of the *Verein* and had the use of the *Verein's* files to write his history. Unfortunately, however, his work is often inaccurate and persistently shallow. Nevertheless, as in the case of Wittrock, Boese's work is valuable because it is based on evidence no longer available. (Some of the *Verein's* records were lost during the war; the rest are at the *Deutsches Zentralarchiv,* Merseberg.) Because of the inaccessibility of the unpublished records, further work on the *Verein* must be based on the 188 volumes of the *Verein's Schriften* (1873–1939), especially those which contain the minutes of the general meetings. Boese's book contains a helpful guide to these *Schriften.*

# Index

Academic community in Germany, 55–58; during World War I, 188–89; and fleet agitation, 179; and Friedrich Naumann, 146; political attitudes of, 2, 56–58, 66 (n. 75), 70–71, 87, 89, 93, 196; and social reform, 49–50, 70–71 (*see also Kathedersozialisten*)

Acton, Lord, 9

Agrarian movement in Germany, 125, 127–33, 135–36, 147

Allan, William, 31–32, 36, 39–40, 104

Amalgamated Society of Engineers, 31–32, 40, 43, 104

Anti-Socialist Law (1878), 83, 85, 95, 103, 124

Applegarth, Robert, 32, 36

Arbitration of industrial disputes, 41–42, 44, 105–6, 121, 157, 159, 160–64, 196–97, 202

Arnim, Achim von, 15

Arnim, Claudine von, 15

Aschaffenburg, 7–9, 11–12, 102

Augsburg, Benedictine school in, 9

Austro-Prussian War, 11–12, 14

Baader, Franz von, 23

Bamberger, Ludwig, 73–74, 142; and German liberalism, 63–64; polemic against Brentano, 60–65, 91; shift in views during the 1890's, 136, 138

Barth, Theodor, 133, 169–70, 202; and Brentano, 135–38, 143, 147, 152–53, 180–84; and German foreign policy, 180–84; and Naumann, 143, 147, 149–50, 152–53; and tariff issue, 135–38

Bebel, August, 47–48, 59

Berchem, Maximilian Count von, 110, 125

Bergson, Henri, 187

Berlepsch, Hans von, 117, 130, 139 (n. 26)

Berlin, 15–16; University of, 53

Bernstein, Eduard, 139

Bethmann-Hollweg, Theobald von, 177

Bismarck, Otto von, 15, 25, 64, 114, 117, 124, 136, 178; program of social reform, 74–79, 83, 86, 95, 115, 120, 126

Boer War, impact on Germany of the, 181–82, 184

Bonn, Moritz J., 182

Boretius, Alfred, 100

Braun, Heinrich, 139 (n. 26)

Brentano (family), 6, 8, 11

Brentano, Bettina (von Arnim), 6, 8, 9 (n. 9), 15

Brentano, Christian, 6–8

Brentano, Clemens, 6, 8–9 (n. 9)

Brentano, Emily, 7–9, 11, 53

Brentano, Franz, 9, 53 (n. 28), 98

Brentano, Lujo: appearance, 3, 4; and Bismarck's social reform program, 74–78, 94; and cartels, 110–12, 158–61, 164; childhood, 8–9; and co-operative movement, 17–20, 26–28, 30–31; economics, view of, 12–15, 17, 20–21, 33–39, 53–55, 76, 80–82, 99–100, 107–8, 112–13, 164, 192–93; and England, 2, 10, 17, 22–45, 82, 100, 104–6, 113, 119–24, 126, 156, 164, 177, 181–85, 187, 201;

219